Growing Up
WRIGHT

Building a dream by hand with the
World's Greatest Architect

For Bill and Irene,

Enjoy the story!

Lonnie Loness

ISBN 978-0-9631726-1-7

Library of Congress Control Number: 2020936773

Printed and bound in the United States of America.

Edited by Gordon Maltby

The text of this book is typeset in Caslon 540, based on the work of Englishman William Caslon in the 18th century.

Headlines and captions are set in Futura, designed by German Paul Brenner in 1927.

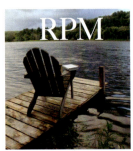

Published by
River Place Media, Inc.
P.O. Box 91
Stillwater, MN 55082

Please visit us at www.riverplacemedia.com

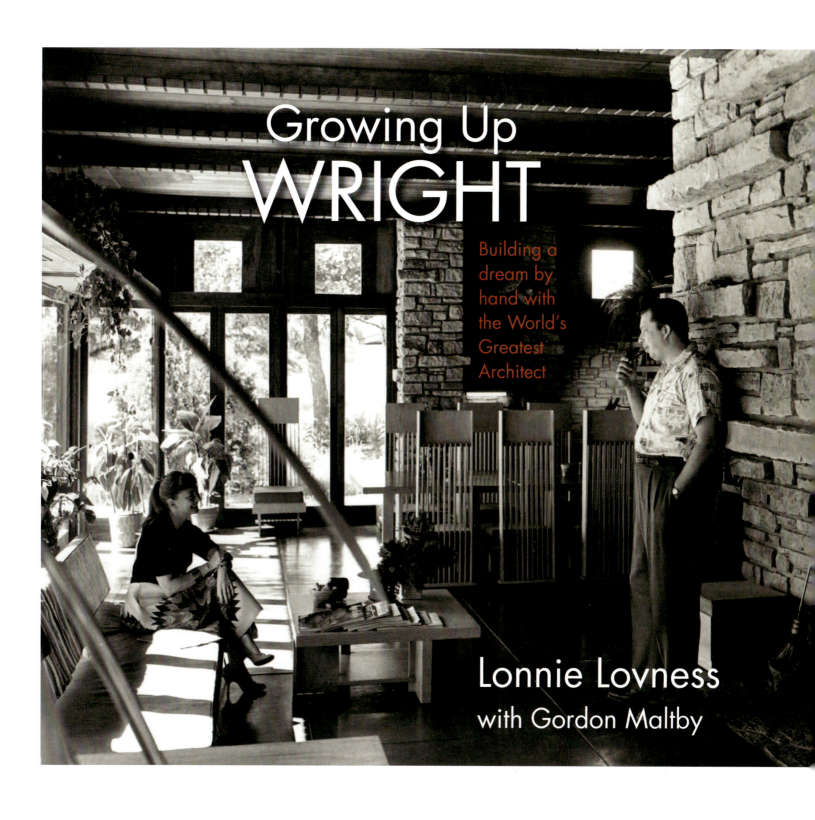

Growing Up
WRIGHT

Building a dream by hand with the World's Greatest Architect

Lonnie Lovness
with Gordon Maltby

"The human race built most nobly when limitations were greatest and therefore, when most was required of imagination in order to build at all. Limitations seem to have always been the best friends of architecture."

- Frank Lloyd Wright, 1892

For my parents, and their devotion to a dream
— L. L.

Contents

Kelly Davis

Opposite, Frank Lloyd Wright in the drafting room at Taliesin West about the time plans were being drawn for the Lovness studio.

It was summer, 1966. I was sixteen years old, armed with the freedom of a new driver's license and my mom's red Volkswagen Beetle. Windows were down and the sunroof wide open as I combed the back roads west of my hometown of Stillwater, Minnesota searching for "The Wright House". Finally, I found it. Without batting an eye, up the long curving drive I barreled, through the open gate and into the forecourt where I was rewarded with my first glimpse of the Lovness studio. But it was to be a quick one. Before I could blink, a black Doberman was halfway inside the car, a hellish vision of froth, bulging eyes and big teeth. Only then did the audacity of my unannounced visit dawn on me. After what seemed an eternity, out calmly strode Virginia Lovness, and the devilish canine instantly went docile as a puppy. With great embarrassment, I introduced myself, apologized profusely, and somehow managed to convince Virginia of my passion for Mr. Wright's work and my sincere hope of seeing the house. To this day I remember her kindness, spending the next hour showing this brazen teenager what she and her husband Don together had built. So began a fifty-year relationship with the Lovnesses and this remarkable property, that would manifest itself in ways far beyond my young imagination.

My interest in Wright had begun in earnest a year or so earlier, perhaps sparked by a childhood memory of the broad, looming roofs of the Darwin Martin house in Buffalo, New York, seen from the back seat of a car on a dark, drizzly November day as a child of five. This had been my first perceived experience of Architecture. Now years later, I was reading everything about the famous architect I could place my hands on. But until the day I drove up the Lovness driveway, I had never experienced the power of a Wright house firsthand. Photographs proved woefully inadequate at capturing the intimacy of scale, the fluidity of space, the continuity of line and materials, and the seamless melding with nature. Walking through the Lovness studio was a revelation, and cemented the notion that I, too, wanted to be an architect.

Five years in the School of Architecture at the University of Minnesota proved pure torture; the notion of a student wanting to pursue Prairie-inspired residential design in the early 1970s was considered passé, and the ordeal was like fitting a square peg into a round hole. But perseverance rewarded me with a degree, and life immediately got better. Upon graduation in 1973, I had the great good fortune of being hired and mentored by Michael McGuire, a truly fine architect and no stranger to the philosophies of Wright. Years later, I became a partner in his office. Mike wisely told me early on to study the Wright books, learn from them, and then put them aside and begin to chart my own path. I was proud to be a member of his firm.

One of the unanticipated benefits of working with Mike was that he was a friend and contemporary of the Lovnesses, and this allowed me to tag along on a number of visits to Woodpile Lake over the years. All remain memorable. I was in my mid-twenties when we first toured the cottage, the second Wright-designed building on the property, and still under construction. Here for the first time I met Don, cigar in hand; a man larger than life, with a personality and a booming laugh to match. A year or so later, now completed and furnished, there was an

Growing Up Wright **7**

evening gathering at the cottage attended by legendary figures from Taliesin I had only read about in books. John and Lu Howe were there, and Aaron Green had flown in from San Francisco. Heady company for a young architect, and I soaked it up like a sponge.

In the mid-1990s, I hosted a busload of somber, gray-suited architects on a tour of the Lovness estate. Virginia, always uniquely stylish and an impeccable master of timing, was to meet us at the studio. As we stood waiting in the forecourt, I noticed the gravel had been carefully raked; a thoughtful welcome. But where was Virginia? Just as the group began to show signs of unease, out she came. Now in her later sixties, sporting a ponytail, crimson lips, and adorned with turquoise and silver rings on every finger, Virginia arrived dressed from head to toe in black leather. I watched as eyes widened and jaws collectively dropped; she was magnificent! And as she began to speak, slowly and in a quiet voice, I witnessed her audience gather closely around her; now with smiles on their faces. Within moments, this diminutive, charming, soft-spoken woman held us all in the palm of her hand. It was a memorable performance.

Not all the gatherings were happy, however. Don died at the beginning of summer, 2001 and late that fall, Mike McGuire organized an evening soirée of friends at the studio in an attempt to bring a smile to Virginia's face. All tried valiantly, but considering her loss, it was a futile attempt. My lasting memory of the evening, in addition to the bitter cold, was that I had never seen the house appear so dark and somber. There was a palpable aura of sadness and Don's laugh was sorely missed. Virginia carried on at Woodpile Lake, but in 2007 the decision was made to sell the property.

On Valentine's Day, 2014, and now a Principal at SALA Architects, I received a call from Ted Muntz, whom I had never met. Ted explained that he and his wife, Debi, had recently bought the Lovness estate and asked for our professional help in assisting with renovations. The project would consume our collective time and energy for the next four years. My colleague and decades-long collaborator Tim Old and I couldn't believe our good fortune. Ted and Debi's vision for the property was rigorous and multi-phased. They iterated that this was to be their home, not a museum. They wanted it to be functional, comfortable, meet 21st century energy standards, and they wanted to ensure the studio would stand strong for its second sixty years of existence. Lofty goals, and welcome news; it was obvious Virginia had found good stewards.

And so we began, working in a kind of ballet of musical houses around Woodpile Lake. Our first charge was to design a new structure for the property, an office/ garage/ shop that would also serve as overflow guest quarters. While Virginia stayed on in the cottage for a year, allowing her time to organize and prepare for an eventual move, Ted and Debi made the full-time move to Woodpile Lake in the summer of 2014 and a serendipitous result of this arrangement began to evolve.

There were frequent get-togethers, often over late-afternoon glasses of Champagne, and Virginia would share the history of building the two houses, the wealth of stories about Mr. and Mrs. Wright and the lore of the Taliesin Fellowship with Ted and Debi. A lasting bond of friendship was formed; one that would continue until Virginia's death in early 2018.

Kelly Davis

For quite some time, I've been aware Lonnie was writing a book about growing up in this significant Wright house, and I was honored and flattered when she and her husband, Gordon Maltby, asked me to write the book's Foreword. But when I finished my initial reading, it became obvious her efforts reach far beyond her and her sister Ty's childhood memories. The book is a labor of love honoring her parents and their remarkable accomplishments. Not only does it document in detail the construction of the studio and cottage, it also provides depth and clarity as to who her parents were; their backgrounds and the innate and inherited aspects of their personalities. Reading the stories makes it seem perfectly natural this young couple would approach the greatest architect of the times and ask him to design a home for them, and then go out and build it. "Growing Up Wright" is a memoir about the partnership between Don and Virginia, told with warmth and humor. Certainly, the book adds yet more tales for Wright historians to savor, including insights into the close relationship that developed between Wright and the Lovnesses and their decades-long connection with Taliesin. But Lonnie also addresses a wider audience. More than anything, this is a book about the indomitable human spirit; of setting out to do the seemingly unachievable, of persevering, and succeeding against great odds.

Kelly Davis, Principal Emeritus, SALA Architects

Debi and Ted Muntz with Virginia at the restored studio in November, 2017.

Lonnie Lovness

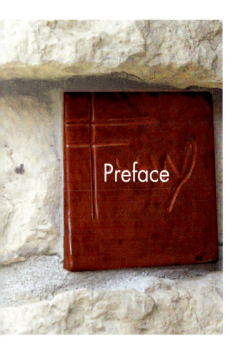

My mother, Virginia Lovness, passed away in 2018, just a few weeks past her 93rd birthday. Even at that advanced age she was active, cognizant and as always, ready with a smile and a mischievous laugh. A downside was that she had outlived so many of her friends, including her contemporaries at Taliesin, who had been a big part of her extraordinary life. She and my father were both dreamers and doers, more than anyone would expect from their humble beginnings.

My father Don was in some senses the polar opposite of petite Virginia; a big bear of a man, outspoken and gruff but with a scientist's mind and hands that could build almost anything. In another sense they were complementary; the ying and yang that together brought their dreams full circle. He passed away suddenly in 2001 and for several years the fate of the houses they had built was up in the air. But that tale has a happy ending. With new, dedicated owners my parents' physical legacy in stone, glass and wood is secure. With this book I hope that the rest of their legacy—the story behind the stone and glass, of a young couple who literally built a dream by hand—can be shared with everyone.

A complete appreciation of everything they accomplished has taken some time for me. As a girl I accepted what my parents had created as matter-of-fact. Living in a Wright house was just the way it was. But somehow I always knew we were different. Even as a young girl I could see that the other kids lived in "normal" houses with doors on the bedrooms, carpeting on the floors, light fixtures on the ceilings and many separate rooms. They didn't have concrete floors that radiated warmth in the winter, soaring ceilings and grand living spaces, or walls made of rock! Nor did they listen to Duke Ellington on a built-in hi-fi, or talk about art and architecture at the dinner table.

The book

This book has been on my mind and in my thoughts for decades; my first notes to prepare for this were written in high school. Then as an adult, I wanted to discover who my parents were and what motivated them to take on such a Herculean project as building a Frank Lloyd Wright house by themselves with no experience, no money and with two young daughters. The discoveries I have made on this quest have given me a better idea of their young hopes, and the passion and tenacity it took to complete their projects. I feel I have put the puzzle pieces together and can tell their tale.

A book like this was on my mother's mind as well. She left several sets of longhand notes, with her ideas for a book about their 'adventure' that she hoped someone would write one day. There are also interviews conducted at Taliesin, newspaper and magazine articles in which they were featured, and of course, our own conversations over the years. She also left a trove of photos, documents, letters and memorabilia. Unfortunately, much of these came to light only in the last few years of her life, when memory was fading. Others who knew my parents, however, have helped to fill in the blanks about these two exceptional, complicated, inspiring and fun people.

This is the story of growing up not just in a Wright house, but with parents completely immersed in the Wright philosophy. It is Don and Virginia's story, with a host of interesting characters intersecting their lives. Many 'stories within the story' are sometimes crazy, often humorous and occasionally far-fetched. I believe that taken together, they paint an accurate portrait of the dynamic couple they were.

The photographs and letters

This project is not meant to be a Frank Lloyd Wright coffee table book. Over the years some of the best architectural photographers in the world have documented the studio and the cottage; the buildings are featured in dozens of books, calendars and magazines. It's easy to find beauty shots in print and online, but what you will find in these pages are hundreds of images that are personal, insightful and I hope, interesting to both Wright fans and the casual reader. In other books you can see photos of the beautiful Hollyhock House design chairs in the Lovness cottage; here you can see how they were built. My father documented much of the studio and cottage construction, and took photos at Taliesin and other places; snapshots of moments in time. It was clearly his intention that the building process be captured for posterity, and I am pleased that we can do so in this book.

I am not an architectural historian and this is not a scholarly analysis of Wright or his work, nor of the Taliesin Fellowship. There are enough of those already. It is, rather, a personal memoir, a collection of my family's stories - some already well documented and some that will surprise. There may be some information that historians don't agree with, but this book is my family's story, told from my point of view.

Acknowledgments

When I left home for college I never really looked back. I was connected to my family, of course, but my sister Tracy and her husband Pat Kluempke lived for ten years in the studio, close by my parents who had moved to the cottage. Her memories of our youth together and her close involvement with our parents later on have added substantially to this work. I value her assistance and I treasure her as a sister.

My husband Gordon Maltby has been my collaborator, researcher and advisor, helping to connect the dots between all that was spoken, written and printed in the extensive archives my parents left. His writing skills have added much to this book.

Indira Berndtson at Taliesin is a longtime friend of my parents and has been instrumental in providing documents and advice. Aron Meudt-Thering and the staff at Taliesin North hosted us during a lovely tour in 2017, and Claire Barnett introduced us to the Peterson cottage. Old friend Kelly Davis was very kind to write a heartfelt Foreword. David Uppgren spent more time with my parents than I did at times and his recollections are an important addition. Ted and Debi Muntz have happily shared their part of this long journey, and Al Drap, Gus Ljungkull, Tim Old and Jim Seidl all shared their memories. We are extremely grateful to all of them.

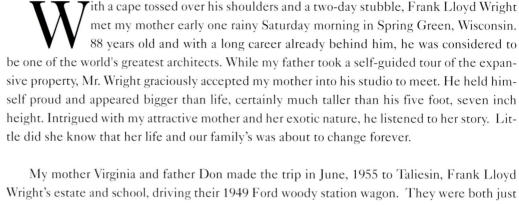

With a cape tossed over his shoulders and a two-day stubble, Frank Lloyd Wright met my mother early one rainy Saturday morning in Spring Green, Wisconsin. 88 years old and with a long career already behind him, he was considered to be one of the world's greatest architects. While my father took a self-guided tour of the expansive property, Mr. Wright graciously accepted my mother into his studio to meet. He held himself proud and appeared bigger than life, certainly much taller than his five foot, seven inch height. Intrigued with my attractive mother and her exotic nature, he listened to her story. Little did she know that her life and our family's was about to change forever.

1

A meeting with the Master

My mother Virginia and father Don made the trip in June, 1955 to Taliesin, Frank Lloyd Wright's estate and school, driving their 1949 Ford woody station wagon. They were both just thirty years old. With an early morning meeting arranged with Mr. Wright, it wasn't possible to make the 250-mile trip from their home in Minnesota without an overnight stay. Having little money for a hotel, they had slept a few hours in the car. With naive, youthful confidence my mother hoped Mr. Wright could look over her house plans and possibly make suggestions for improvements. Franz Aust, a distant relative of my father's and a friend of Mr. Wright's, had provided an introduction for the young couple. Mr. Aust had recently visited their home overlooking White Bear Lake, north of St. Paul. At the time, the house was little more than a walkout basement, a common sight in the postwar period, where young couples bought or built what they could afford and made plans to add on as circumstances allowed.

My mother was finishing plans for the expansion of the family home including her artist's studio that would be oriented over the existing flat-roof. Franz told her, "This looks great, but why don't you have Frank check it over?" She was well aware of Wright's work and had read several of the books about him, but didn't realize Franz and "Frank" were on first-name terms. He explained that they had worked together years before in his practice as a landscape architect, city planner and professor at the University of Wisconsin. Decades earlier Franz had helped plant many of the trees at Taliesin. He and his wife Mabel had known Wright's previous wives, and Mabel had helped the current Mrs. Wright, Olgivanna, polish her English.

As she waited in the Taliesin foyer, Gene Masselink, Mr. Wright's secretary approached and told her, "Mr. Wright will see you now, please come this way," and my mother walked down a corridor at Taliesin to meet the architect for the first time. She had a moment of hesitation, embarrassed to be barging in on him at 8 a.m. with her "feeble" plan. But she and Don had made the long car journey; they were there, so she sat down and showed the drawings to him.

A few years after the meeting, she documented her thoughts of that first encounter in a notepad that survives today. Her recollections:

We had been up all night driving. The rain kept pounding down in pellets and I waited with clammy cold hands. It was dark. Finally someone called my name. The walk down the corridor seemed terribly

This letter, written by Virginia to Mr. Wright long before she met him is a little presumptuous, but certainly not out of character. After Franz Aust later arranged a meeting, there followed a long and cordial series of letters, notes and phone calls between the young couple and the Taliesin group.

Bellaire is a small enclave of homes on the south shore of White Bear Lake, an unincorporated community within White Bear Lake Township. To locals it is a recognizable neighborhood but to outsiders it is not so much a town as a pleasant-sounding name that implies exclusivity.

While my mother met with Mr. Wright, Don wandered around the property with his camera. Unfortunately, he took no photos of Mr. Wright and Virginia that day. One of his shots in the lower court shows the Lovness family car next to Mr. Wright's Jaguar Mark V sedan, one of the many luxury cars the architect owned over the years.

Franz Aust, landscape
architect.

In a 1979 letter to Alden Aust,
Franz' son, Virginia and Don
wrote, "Believe me, if it had not
been for Mr. Aust, our houses
would not have been built. He was
the only person besides Mr. Wright
who not only encouraged us, but
also taught us philosophy and even
more importantly, opened the doors
and created a rapport with both
Mr. and Mrs. Wright that still
exists."

long. *Mr. Wright was seated at his desk; he stood up and came forward to meet me. I felt awed and afraid I would be unable to speak. He was all one would expect, and more. There seemed to be a aura about him - a truly majestic person with the well-known white mane. As he motioned me to a chair next to his desk, my first impulse was to give him a big grandfather kiss as I would on my favorite long-lost friends, but since this was our first visit I refrained.*

The moment had come! Mr. Wright, the most democratic person I have ever met, was about to help me and go over my designs to add a small living room onto our basement house at White Bear Lake! I, a struggling young artist had asked him to help. Of all the gall. I was mortified as he shuffled through my squared papers of our sad little basement plans and then on to my proposed living room, up through steps so that water wouldn't run in - with a fireplace at the end, and tall windows to give the sad house some semblance of ethereal quality. But Mr. Wright, the true gentleman, gave each aspect of the living room his undivided attention and made the comment that I was somewhat of an architect myself. And I said, "'No, I paint a little," and felt insignificant and unworthy. He asked reasons why on everything, and I told him. I answered each question with what I thought were perfectly valid reasons, but he seemed to have a better solution in each case. And he crossed out one thing after another; an entryway on the south would bar the sunlight, etc., until finally there was nothing left of my six months of drawing plans to scale and of my 10 years research into every article I could put my hands on of Mr. Wright's. All other architects left me unenthused by comparison.

Dismay and humiliation tore at me. "But Mr. Wright, there is nothing left," I told him.

He brushed the papers away. "That's about it. You'll never be satisfied. Just sell it."

And so I explained how we—my husband Don and I—had fallen in love with our lot and our low block house. How the lot contained the largest old willows around White Bear Lake, and the best beach and what with the hill next to us and the swamp behind, was really quite private. I felt I now had two problems. We didn't want to give up our lake property, and what it would bring would not be enough to even remotely consider Mr. Wright's suggestion.

"Go on out and buy yourself some land," he told me. "Ten acres. Sell the house!" All this with many gestures - emphatically. I was stunned. He continued, "How much can you get for this mess?"

A house by Mr. Wright... what a dream! This was perhaps the greatest moment of my life but of course, impossible. We had bought our little concrete block house on White Bear four years before with only $200 down on a contract for deed, borrowing the remainder of the down payment. Our car was old and we didn't have a cent in the bank. How much could we get for the house? Good heavens, I couldn't tell Mr. Wright it was only worth $7,000 or $8,000. Would a little white lie hurt? I couldn't tell the truth. "Maybe $10,000, Mr. Wright," was my answer.

"$10,000! I never build houses for $10,000," he said, pounding his fist on the table. "$60,000, $80,000, half a million!"

I said, "I know, I didn't ask for you to design one. I know we could never afford one of your houses." And with that the matter was dismissed.

It's easy to understand the awe Virginia must have felt when she sat down with Mr. Wright at his desk in the studio. Many clients had sat here while he sold them an idea, presented plans or consoled them over cost overruns.

My mother's plan was small potatoes in the whole scheme of things but Mr. Wright gave it serious consideration. She was clearly not well versed in architectural drawing but in the end, it wasn't what was on paper but where the house was sited that forced a difficult decision. He kept the plan for reference after the meeting.

When Virginia's plan was finally returned in 1956, the 9x12 envelope cost 4 cents to mail and notably, the return address was hand-lettered.

THE FRANK LLOYD WRIGHT FOUNDATION
T A L I E S I N
SPRING GREEN, WISCONSIN

AIR MAIL

The architect then showed Mother around the residence at Taliesin, a Welsh word that means 'shining brow'. Out on the long cantilevered "Birdwalk' balcony that overlooked the rolling hills and lake below she could see how perfectly this home blended into the landscape. This was her first realization that you need to own your own view and that the house would have to be in harmony with the land; an object lesson in choosing property. When she asked Mr. Wright how he could bear to leave this beautiful place he replied, "We manage to build something as beautiful, and make our life beautiful wherever we go." It was a piece of advice that would shape my parents attitude toward art, music and living itself. Her notes continue:

Mr. Wright showed me through his private quarters in Taliesin North at Spring Green. His lovely living room, the secluded corners, the little efficient aesthetic kitchen and work area, the rows of French doors overlooking the valley and the magnificent view from the balcony. Again overwhelmed, I asked questions and Mr. Wright answered.

"You see the creek and then in the distance the Wisconsin River? And then far out, the hills? We bought all that, so that nobody could ever mar our view with ugly billboards or factories."

"But how can you bear to leave such a utopia when you must travel so often?"

"We manage to build ourselves something just as beautiful wherever we go."

And so we moved on to talk of the rain which was still pouring down around us. How lovely it was to me, because the transition from indoors to out, rain to warmth, was imperceptible. The shadows, the well-worn Oriental rugs, the Japanese sculptures inside and out, water fountains and foliage all over. It all seemed magical, but he said how he would like to see the sun; a suggestion of weariness, I felt.

Virginia was an artist with a number of shows already in her resume, and she was no stranger to criticism, or comments on artistic matters. The trip had been undertaken ostensibly to get advice for design improvements, while the distant hope was that Mr. Wright would actually create a house plan for them. Her initial disappointment was overwhelming, even though the dream of an architect-designed house was only minutes old. This great man had offered to design a house for them but it appeared they couldn't make it happen. Recollections of the encounter told years later by people at Taliesin describe Mother breaking down in tears at that moment, but she has denied it. Most likely she shifted into charm overdrive. She may not have fully realized it at the time, but this dream was worth pursuing and she would expend whatever efforts it took to make it a reality.

Mr. Wright—whose projects underway at the time included the Guggenheim Museum in New York and the Price office tower in Oklahoma—was used to operating on a grand scale. However, the concept of housing for the masses had also been a long-standing interest and his "Usonian" houses focused on efficiency and simplicity. He must have had the latter in mind as he spoke to her. I also have to think that a less attractive woman with less charisma would have left disappointed. That day, she did not. Her notes of the encounter continue:

My mother was a dreamer but also a do-er. Behind her contemplative expression was pure determination. A friend, University of Minnesota Photography and Film professor Allen Downs took this photo at their White Bear Lake home around the time Don and Virginia met Mr. Wright.

At the time my parents visited Taliesin, Wright was involved in several major projects, two of which were in New York City. The Guggenheim Museum was beginning construction and he had begun plans for a European car showroom on Fifth Avenue for Max Hoffman. As a New York base of operations, Mr. and Mrs. Wright had taken up long-term residence at the Plaza Hotel, near Central Park. Alternating between the two Taliesins and the Plaza, he conducted business, entertained clients and friends and held court for the press. In the five years they spent there Wright remodeled their suite of rooms to his own taste, somewhat to the chagrin of management. It was the embodiment of what Wright had told my mother: "We manage to build ourselves something just as beautiful wherever we go."

The first visit to Taliesin was followed by phone calls, letters and more visits during construction of their new house. During one of these trips to Spring Green, Don's camera captured Virginia on a Taliesin terrace with a chinese Foo dog (lion). Both Wright's architecture and his taste in art would shape my parents' life.

Frank Lloyd Wright was 88 when he met my mother in 1955. The following year he visited Minneapolis where he toured the new Southdale enclosed mall (pronouncing it a monstrosity) and stopped at the Henry Neils home which he designed in 1952. A Minneapolis Star news photographer caught a pose there with his trademark huge hearth in the background.

No matter the weather, being on the Birdwalk at Taliesin is a heady experience. Over fifty years before this 2017 photo was taken, my sister Ty and I spent summer evenings on the shore of the lake below. As young girls we were entertained by apprentices dressed as pirates or Arabian nights characters, complete with elaborate props as our parents and Mrs. Wright looked on.

Then from nowhere Mr. Wright pounded his hand on a table dramatically. "We'll do it! We'll build you a house for $10,000! It will be a little studio. You'll have a large living room like this! And a little place to paint off at one end. It needn't be large. We'll do it for $10,000!"

Again, my first thought - it isn't possible. It can't be done. I know Mr. Wright as well as I know myself and I'm well aware of the financial difficulties that have always been associated with him and his clients. But there was nothing stopping him. We sat down to go over my needs.

"One bedroom enough? You're not married, are you?"

"Yes, my husband's waiting for me in the loggia."

"Oh. No children, though."

"Yes, I have two little girls." Surprised again, but undaunted, Mr. Wright made a mental provision for 2 bedrooms. And with that he took my arm and went out for his next surprise, that of meeting my husband who is a husky 6'-4" as compared to my 100 pounds and 5'-2". Beaming, they shook hands, Mr. Wright walked around Don like he was sizing up a side of beef. He felt his muscles and said, "Well, you look like you're big enough to build a studio for your spunky little spouse!"

The Birdwalk, extending from the living room at Taliesin, is an impressive appendage when seen from a distance, but even more impressive when experienced as a portal, taking you from the earthy stone of the building to a feeling of floating in air. Here Mr. Wright extolled the virtues of an uninterrupted vista to my mother, making an indelible and lasting impression on her.

There was almost no view of Taliesin that wasn't dramatic, and my mother sketched and painted it many times over the years, as she and my father became regular visitors to both Taliesins.

Rebuilt twice (most recently in 1992) but never blown down, the windmill named Romeo and Juliet has withstood the test of time and early skeptics.

After a morning of excitement talking about our plans and a lunch with Mr. Wright we left, never as thrilled or as high in our life. There was never any talk of contracts or fees (we learned later that was not Mr. Wright's strong suit), just a handshake and an enthusiastic parting. We knew nothing of costs and we didn't know at the time that there would be no one to supervise the construction.

After discussing her plans and parameters for both a studio and living quarters for the young family, with assurances he would design a new home for her, the couple left with emotions running the gamut from exhilaration to apprehension, not quite knowing what the next steps would be.

During my mother's meeting, my father had been wandering around Taliesin by himself, soaking in the feel of the place and admiring Wright's extensive collection of Asian art. Mr. Wright was fond of Japanese prints, clothing, Chinese statuary and Oriental pieces from many eras. He wrote in his autobiography, "...I found that Japanese art and architecture really did have organic character. Their art was nearer to the earth and a more indigenous product of native conditions of life and work..." This would later become another great influence on my parents.

On his walks that day I have to wonder if Don took note of the windmill Wright built and named "Romeo and Juliet" in 1897. The windmill was two parts, a tall turbine blade atop a tower that put its face to the west wind, and a smaller structure attached to give it support, literally to hold it up; something like the couple my parents would become. The windmill had already stood for five decades after Wright's uncles predicted it would "...blow over in the first big storm." Likewise, few people would have guessed this young pair could create a home with their bare hands - and that six decades later it would still stand as a testament to their dedication to a dream.

Apparently amid all the excitement and enthusiasm it never dawned on the young couple that in reality, they couldn't build their "studio" for $10,000. (My mother's original notes contain the figure $15,000 but for as long as I can remember the story she told used a $10,000 number.) There was no question that the White Bear Lake lot, with neighbors close by and South Shore Boulevard just feet from the front door, was unsuitable for a Wright structure. It had been done, of course; there were many Wright homes that were either built in existing neighborhoods or sited on open land but development encroached later. But Mr. Wright's first edict to the young couple, setting the stage for all that came later, was to "Own your view," and that would take at least ten acres. First order of business, then, was to find a buyer and sell their Bellaire property. They let their friends know the house was for sale, and when Don went to work on Monday he related his experience at Taliesin to several colleagues, most of whom were PhDs. He was surprised that only one had ever heard of Frank Lloyd Wright, but he told his co-workers at "The Mining" (as 3M was known to locals at the time) that the White Bear Lake home was on the market. The effort quickly paid off when a co-worker offered to buy the property for $15,000. The first hurdle was over!

In 1955 the lot on White Bear Lake had wonderful old trees and a nice shoreline. The one-story house had potential but Wright's advice was to relocate where there would be nothing to impinge their view.

In 2015, seen from the street side, the red house has indeed been expanded, but in the most uninspired way. A completely new building replaced it in 2019. Even had the building been updated with taste, the viewshed and privacy would never have been enough for my parents.

Mr. Wright was right.

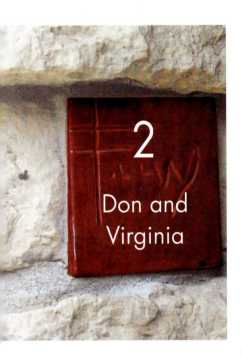

2
Don and Virginia

Asbury Street in Saint Paul is a quiet and modest part of the city that in the 1920s was on the edge of town, bordered by fields to the north, the State University Agricultural College and Experimental Farm to the west and few blocks to the east, Como Park. There, the City of St. Paul had developed recreational amenities for its citizens including sports fields, floral display gardens, picnic areas, a zoo, a huge glass conservatory with exotic plants and later, amusement rides. Lake Como had been named after that lovely body of water at the foot of Italy's Dolomite mountains, and while the Saint Paul version lacked the scale and mountain vistas of its namesake, it was beloved by locals. The lake gave its name not only to the adjacent park but to the surrounding neighborhood.

The houses on Asbury were notable to passersby only during ten days before Labor Day when the Minnesota State Fair was open. Just a block from the fairgrounds entrance, Asbury and nearby streets became congested from early morning to midnight as fairgoers jockeyed for parking or walked to and from the gate. For the other 51 weeks of the year it was a sedate, solidly middle-class enclave.

On the corner of Asbury and Fair Place, Al Lovness built a modest home for his wife Gladys and young son Donald in 1928. Donald, my father, grew up there sharing a bedroom with his younger sister Donna Mae. Al was a house painter and had much of the winter off. Gladys was large-boned, a strong-willed woman. She was always kind and loving, but had ideas of her own. She had been a nurse during the first world war and tending to the wounded gave her resiliency to put up with two men in the family as strong-willed as she. As husband and wife they had separate bedrooms - something I thought strange even as a young girl. I remember Al always sitting in the same green horsehair chair at the end of the room and not really doing much except being grumpy. Growing older, his personality became more crabby as he developed Parkinson's disease and dementia. In the last few years of his life he became an invalid and Gladys cared for him tirelessly until his death in 1962.

Gladys and Al had a comfortable life and although they were a long way from wealthy neither Donna or my father lacked for anything. They provided the necessities, giving love to their two children and instilling in them a work ethic that continued throughout their lives. Gladys (whom my father referred to as "Happy Butt", a play on her name) was an accomplished seamstress who had a lively business sewing dresses for neighborhood ladies and who later lavished her attention and skills on her granddaughters, making matching outfits and cute coats for my sister Ty and me.

My father always liked toy trucks and trains and had an inventive streak even as a child. I think his imagination was a lot closer to the surface of reality than in most people. He had sometimes outrageous ideas but even as a kid, he never seemed to be daunted by difficulties in bringing a concept to life. Supremely confident, he was one of those individuals who "didn't know that it couldn't be done."

The new Lovness home on Asbury Street was a quiet haven for the family in a nice neighborhood. Just four blocks south was Tilden Elementary School where Don started his education.

Elliot (Al) and Gladys Lovness in 1922, before their children were born.

A trip to the Como Park Conservatory and the Sunken Garden has always been a special occasion. Don, Donna and a cousin are shown during one of many visits in about 1935. Eighty years later it is still a marvelous place to spend a Sunday winter afternoon when cold and snow outside make me appreciate the warmth, humidity and lovely scents of the rotating flower displays. I love it.

He always liked pets, and later in his life with my mother they continued to fuel that love of animals with many exotic species, from snakes to birds. During the summers in the late 1930s my father would spend time on a relative's farm in Sturgeon Lake, Minnesota where he worked as a farm hand. It was hard manual labor but one benefit was being able to take a turn at driving an old car around the fields - quite a thrill for a boy just barely into his teens.

During these summer weeks spent on the farm he developed a keen interest in local Indians and their history. Nearby were burial mounds where he would dig for arrowheads and other items like pottery shards. Bones were probably easy to find and he may have also come across flint knives or other tools. "I'd ride my bicycle off the farm and find Indian mounds, and just dig and dig," he recalled. He confessed being almost obsessed with the excavations and it must have set the stage for the later effort he put into finding pre-Columbian objects in Mexico and ancient Chinese art in Asia.

Don had a typical young man's interests: cars, girls, socializing. A cousin remembers that at one time he had a "Zoot Suit". Originally favored by black musicians in the 1930s, the long coats with wide lapels and shoulders padded "like a lunatic's cell" were matched to high-waisted, wide-legged pants with tight cuffs. The outfit was often topped with a color-matching hat with a large feather, plus a long gold watch chain. Thankfully, no photos remain of Don in this outfit but he must have made an imposing impression. He was a fan of big band music and although he didn't play an instrument he appreciated sophisticated arrangements and enjoyed hearing bands perform live. Duke Ellington was one of his favorites and "Take the A Train" and other Duke tunes would echo regularly through our house as I was growing up.

A bible I have is inscribed with "Donald Lovness, January 1936, Lake Park Baptist Church". As he tells it, "My mother arranged for a neighbor to take me to church but it didn't catch on." The fact that the book today is in pristine condition verifies that with my father it never did "catch on". Instead, our family Sunday worship was jazz on the hi-fi built into a corner of the living room.

Navy Days

Just after high school he began work at Minnesota Mining and Manufacturing but the war had been underway for a few years and of course, at that time any able-bodied man was expected to join up. He chose the Navy—he always said because they had good food—and went into training as a pilot. The Navy gave him a good education at St. Olaf College in Minnesota, the University of North Carolina and later at MIT, with stints at training bases like Jacksonville, Florida. His flying career had an auspicious beginning when he made headlines across several states as a 19-year-old cadet. He was on a December training flight out of Yankton, South Dakota, alone in his Stearman biplane trainer when it caught fire over the Missouri River.

"I was flying along and all of a sudden things started burning around me," he stated in an interview years later. He was on a typical training flight out of Yankton, which is near both the Minnesota and Iowa borders, and just across the Missouri river from Nebraska. "My flight suit

Still in his teens, Don began work at 3M and was issued an I.D. badge that looked a lot like a miniature wanted poster.

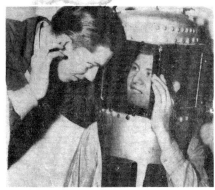

Ingenuity is one of the things about the students in the Murray high school machine shop that makes the current exhibit work there a success. They even make diving helmets. In the picture Donald Lovness, who made the helmet, has put it on Oscar Ecklund, a willing subject.

Don behind the wheel at Sturgeon Lake. Working summers on the farm brought responsiblities but also freedom to explore, to hang out with cousins and friends and to learn how to drive. By high school his inventive nature was coming to the fore; he made a diving helmet in shop class but I doubt it was ever actually used as such. As a teen he was becoming a snappy dresser, at least in this photo with Donna and a cousin.

Below, after joining the Navy he wore an officer's dress uniform proudly on a visit home in the summer of 1944, with Gladys, Al and Donna.

was on fire and I used the fire extinguisher but couldn't put it out. I never got any instructions on how to use the parachute. I looked out the side of the thing and I was over the Missouri River."

There was only one option left: parachute out! He had the presence of mind to set the controls for level flight (jumping out of an open cockpit must be traumatic enough without the plane twisting and turning as you try to make an exit). After jumping, he saw that the plane was making a circle. "I was sure as hell it was going to hit me. Then I thought I was going to land in the river, where big chunks of ice were floating down," he said (laughing at the thought after many years). As it turned out he landed 20 yards in from the river bank, but in a tree! And there he hung for several hours while the airfield sent out search planes. Finally getting those last few feet to the ground, he walked to a farmhouse, where a call was made to his training base. He spent a week in the hospital with burns but went on to spend almost four years in the Navy, serving on the island of Guam in the Pacific Theater where U.S. B-29 bombers launched raids on Japan in the closing months of WWII.

He wasn't the only pilot that day to join what was called among airmen the "Caterpillar Club" (those whose lives were saved by the silk of a parachute) but some unusual circumstances caused him to make the news. The eventual crash ended up involving three states; he took off from South Dakota, parachuted out and landed in Nebraska and the plane crashed in Iowa. In the end, his actions not only saved his own skin, but the plane also, which traveled some 70 miles before landing in a field, with minimal damage to the body, landing gear and propeller. The event made headlines over consecutive days in many newspapers, first as a curious event and again when the mystery pilot was revealed to be a 19-year-old naval cadet from St. Paul. This "News of the Weird" event captured the imagination of at least one Twin Cities radio reporter - and newscasters around the region also shared the story on the air. A young co-ed at Hamline University in St. Paul heard a radio broadcast that evening about the pilot who leapt from his flaming craft, then watched it fly away by itself across the wide Missouri. The report must have made some impression on the pretty art student, because a few years later she would remember that radio story when her new boyfriend told the same tale about himself.

Inside the Squared Circle

First at college and then at the Naval Air Station in Pensacola, Don was among the throngs of young men who trained for war. Among many traditions of that service branch was a boxing program, originally a casual recreation activity but which just after World War I became an intercollegiate program where Navy was a powerhouse. When Don went to Florida he took up the gloves, as he later said, "Because I was big and they just expected me to." With some Golden Gloves experience back home, he did well but only ever considered himself an amateur, although a few years later he would have an intersection with the highest levels of the boxing world.

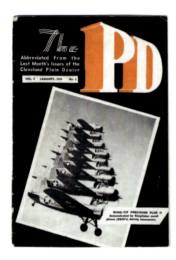

Midwest newspapers picked up the Associated Press story and even the monthly news magazine of the Cleveland Plain Dealer ran it the following month. A "Runaway Plane" captured the imagination of a wartime news audience used to battle reports and politics.

Pilotless Plane Flies 70 Miles, Lands Safely

ODEBOLT, IOWA — (P) — A Yankton, S. D., college training plane, from which the pilot parachuted 20 miles southeast of there Monday afternoon, traveled over 70 miles by itself and landed on a farm two and one-half miles northeast of here about 6:30 p.m. Monday, Deputy Sheriff J. W. Cafferty of Sac City reported today.

The pilot, attached to the naval air training detachment at Yankton, bailed out when the cockpit of the plane caught fire as he was flying at about 3,000 feet.

He made a safe landing on the bank of the Missouri river.

Residents in the Odebolt area said the plane circled twice, as if controlled by a pilot, cleared buildings on the George Mattes farm and came in for a landing in a field.

St. Paulite Piloted 'Wild' Plane

A St. Paul cadet was the pilot of a training plane which flew more than 70 miles by itself Monday after the flier bailed out near Yankton, S. D., the Navy announced Tuesday.

The pilot is Donald Elliott Lovness, 19 years old, member of the Naval air training detachment at Yankton college, the Associated Press reported. He is the son of Mr. and Mrs. Elliott Lovness, 1387 Asbury ave.

Lovness, setting the controls for level flying, bailed out after extinguishing a fire in the plane. The ship continued for 70 miles, landing in a field near Odebolt, Iowa, Monday night.

Officials who examined the plane said it apparently glided most of the distance, aided by a breeze, because most of the wiring was burned out and the motor evidently stopped at the time of the fire. Lovness landed uninjured on the bank of the Missouri river.

Runaway Plane's Pilot Is Identified

Yankton, S. D. (P) — Donald Elliott Loveness of St. Paul, Minn., navy aviation cadet, was the pilot of the Yankton college training plane which flew more than 70 miles by itself Monday, the navy announced Tuesday.

Loveness bailed out after extinguishing a fire in the plane. He had set the controls for level flying. The plane continued, landed in a field near Odebolt, Ia.

Loveness landed uninjured on the bank of the Missouri river. At Odebolt, Deputy Sheriff J. W. Cafferty, who examined the plane, said it apparently glided most of the 70 miles in a breeze because most of the wiring was burned out and the motor likely stopped at the time of the fire.

Smelter H——

St. Paul Flier Leaps, Plane Lands Self

Donald Elliott Lovness, 19, of 1387 Asbury Av., St. Paul, to-day was revealed as the pilot who yesterday bailed out of a navy training plane that then continued 70 miles before it landed by itself near Odebolt, Iowa, damaging only the propeller and landing gear. Lovness, aviation cadet at Yankton college, Yankton, S. D., abandoned the ship when fire stopped the engine. ■————

Cadets trained in all kinds of weather and dressed for the cold. The heavy leather outfit would have been a liability had he landed in the water, however. Both Don and his instructor were strapped into parachutes in this photo, although instruction in their use was apparently not a priority. Newspapers around the Midwest reported about his freak mishap.

Elmer "Kid Violent" Ray was a Florida fighter who began a ring career in his teens by taking part in "Battle Royales" where six to ten men would be inside the ropes when the bell rang, and after pummeling each other, the last man standing won. These were generally groups of black men and the contest was a warm-up for standard boxing matches. It is said that he won some sixty of these matches by dropping to the mat, crawling to a corner and with his back against the turnbuckle, punching his way to victory as the others hammered each other from all directions. The winner's reward was coins thrown into the ring by spectators.

Ray started his professional career in about 1935 as a heavyweight and during the next thirteen years amassed a record of 86 wins, 13 losses and 1 draw. He was acknowledged as one of the hardest punchers in boxing and came close to earning a title match. He moved to Minneapolis in 1945 and having met Don during the war, enlisted him to be one of his sparring partners. Their friendship extended beyond the ring; Don was godfather to one of Ray's children. In 1948, the last year of Ray's boxing career, a *St. Paul Pioneer Press* article documented their unusual relationship, with photos:

Researcher Uses Day Off To Help Train Violent

People who work in glass houses can throw things and get away with it. At least some can.

Donald Lovness, who lives at 1387 Asbury St., spends his regular days surrounded by glass tubes and bottles while doing experiments in the roofing granule laboratory of the Minnesota Mining and Manufacturing Co. Then, he spends his days off throwing punches at Elmer (Violent) Ray, leading heavyweight boxing contender, who meets Ezzard Charles April 7 in Chicago.

"And when you're mixing it up with Violent," says Don, "an off-day can turn out to be a week off if you're not careful."

Ray, who is rated as one of the half dozen top heavies, is now looking forward to a chance at the title after the current Louis-Walcott dispute is settled by a return bout in June for Walcott.

Ray won a decision from Jersey Joe in Madison Square Garden in 1946, but was voted down in their second contest at Miami last June. Coming to prominence during the war, Violent won 48 of 51 fights by knockouts on his first big tour.

But Lovness, the technical man who punches for play, does it to "help out." He was asked to box professionally a couple of times before the war, but he thinks that was just because he's big (225 pounds, six feet, three inches). Anyway, he won both bouts by decision and when he entered the Navy he began to take it more seriously.

As the ranking heavyweight at the naval air station at Jacksonville, Fla., Don was matched against Violent Ray for an exhibition there. That was the start of their friendship, and Don's been "helping out" Elmer ever since. Now he climbs into the ring with Ray three or four times a week.

Lovness is modest. When reminded that he must be pretty good to be a suitable partner for one of the nation's top ring men, he denies it flatly. "I'm just helping out," he repeats. "Elmer never really cuts loose on me."

3M's in-house news magazine did a pre-war piece on Don:

"Showing Bill Coglin how he won the decision in a four-round bout against a 192-lb opponent, when he was called in at the last minute to substitute in a National Association boxing match in the Minneapolis arena, is 186-lb Don Lovness from Color Quartz lab. Don, who fought some Golden Gloves bouts in Chicago, is retiring on his laurels after this recent battle."

Don shows Elmer Ray around the lab at 3M. The article was professionally photographed showing Elmer in Don's world and vice-versa. A few years later Don and the newly completed Lovness home would be featured in both the Minneapolis Star Tribune and the 3M house organ.

Elmer was baffled during a recent visit to the laboratory where Don does his scientific work. Remarking that most fighters try to find heavy physical jobs when they're not actually in the ring, Elmer shook his head. "I don't see how Don can stay in shape here. Why, one quick move and he might smash a thousand glass tubes."

Don just grins and says he likes variety.

Postwar, Don was able to re-claim his job at 3M and resume the life he had left behind where the main focus was cars and girls. Before long he had a new car, something that was not easy to get in those days, and soon enough he would meet a certain young lady - somewhat easier, although there were many initial obstacles.

We can only guess what's going on in this high school era photo, but it's clear that Virginia was well adjusted and happy living with Aunt Helen and Uncle Mag.

Virginia Mae Prall was born in Coldwater, Michigan. Her father was, as she describes him, an itinerant salesman who peddled all kinds of wares. "He sold hair straightener to the Blacks and Singer sewing machines," she recalls, and some early but fond memories were of accompanying him to bars. "He would take me along to the back rooms of bars where he gambled and drank. It was great fun as a little kid." A little girl on her father's knee, she was a center of attention and enjoyed it much more than returning to her mother and the "tar paper shack" they called home.

She has few other recollections of her father, since he left by the time she was five. Her mother wouldn't talk about him and burned all the pictures she had. Her mother, Rose LePage was a school teacher but in the early 1930s took up cosmetology. Rose was religious and took her daughter to "Holy Roller" meetings and tried to make Virginia find religion but like Don, it just didn't stick. It must have been difficult for a single mother at the time, and Rose didn't sugarcoat their situation. My mother reflected many times on how special it was one year when a neighbor brought her an orange at Christmas time. That was all she had in the way of presents.

"There is no Santa Claus, so don't think you're going to get anything," Rose told her. This cruel bit of wisdom was conveyed to her six-year old daughter, perhaps with good intentions, but I have to think she was not exactly overflowing with maternal love. At some point Rose decided it would be best if little Virginia went to live with an aunt and uncle in St. Paul. Younger than Rose by a year, Helen and her husband Mag were a childless couple and their financial situation was not as desperate as the young mother, but certainly not beyond middle class status. They acquiesced to having Virginia come to live with them, initially on a temporary basis. The little girl boarded a bus with a note pinned to her dress saying, "St. Paul". In a paper bag she carried her only possession, another dress. Arriving in Minnesota she had a room of her own but she didn't like the color of the walls. Helen let her choose a new color to paint them. She was already showing a trait that would be life-long: distinct preferences in what surrounded her and a willingness to go to great lengths to make those surroundings beautiful. "Everywhere I

Helen Magnuson and Virginia pose on a beach not long after she had arrived in St. Paul to live with the couple. Some eight years later they are seen on a walk, two fashionable ladies out shopping.

Mag and Helen are shown here at a banquet of the American Public Works Association. Mag was the City Engineer for several Minnesota municipalities and over his career won awards for his work in flood control and municipal services.

went I had such a compulsion to change everything in my surrounding," she said. Whether it was the clothes she wore or the place she lived, it had to be aesthetically pleasing. Helen and Mag gave her the name "Queenie" because this little girl only wanted the best. "From the time I was little," she said, " I was painting, drawing and sewing. I think you're born with it."

As months, then years passed, they took on the role of parents and gave the young girl all the support and love they could. Helen taught Virginia to sew on a foot treadle machine and she began to make her own clothes - another early skill that would continue life-long. Like Rose before her, who had taken little Virginia to "Holy Roller" meetings, Helen encouraged the girl to attend an Episcopal church, even seeing that she was baptized at twelve. But like my father's encounters with religious institutions, it never "took" and churches were never a part of her life.

Cyrus Magnuson, or "Mag" as he was known, had been a soldier in the Great War and while in France in a map making regiment wrote letters home in beautiful fine-point script. The elegant and careful writing on onionskin paper belied its message, which was pointed and blunt: "War is hell". He was an educated and accomplished man and worked as a city administrator in St. Paul. When he took a job in another small city, Virginia was just finishing high school and she began college dorm life, once again finding herself more or less on her own.

Growing up in the Midway area of St. Paul (ironically just blocks from where my father was raised) Virginia went to Hancock grade school, and Wilson high school, each just walking distance from her home. Also nearby was Hamline University, where she enrolled in 1942 and became an arts major, with a scholarship she earned in an art competition. She had won scholarships to art classes since the eighth grade and was a seasoned veteran in that arena. Hamline had a long tradition of educating females; it is the state's oldest university and its first female grads were two sisters, who in 1859 became the first graduates of any college or university in Minnesota.

My mother was a prolific painter, printmaker and graphic art designer. As she entered college she was doing portraiture and fashion drawings of smart models in the latest outfits - combining her interests of art and fashion. I'm sure she had some dreams of being a fashion designer, but she was also a realist and probably saw the handwriting on that wall. Later she took an interest in landscapes but also began working on large canvasses with non-objective themes. At Hamline she created posters for the sports teams and school events. The student body was swelling with post-war students under the GI Bill and there were constant activities that needed promotion. Virginia rose to the occasion and thrived in college. Unfortunately, upon leaving school she quickly found that making a living in the arts was not an easy thing to do, especially for a woman. After college she had a number of gallery shows but making her own way in the world—something she was determined to do—required her to tread that familiar path of other starving artists: get a job, any job.

One of her first jobs was with Henry Neils who owned a company called Flour City Ornamental Ironworks. For decades it had produced large and intricate gates, grilles, doors, fountains

Graduating from college,
Virginia's smile was well deserved.

and other elaborate beaux arts frosting for buildings, the kind of thing you would see in a Louis Sullivan design. During the war it shifted gears for the war effort, like so many other manufacturers, and began to make aluminum pontoon bridges for the army, used to cross rivers in Europe where permanent bridges had been destroyed by retreating German forces. Postwar, in 1946 the company used this new expertise and produced its first aluminum boat under the name Alumacraft. Neils was also involved in a marble and building materials distributorship and approached Wright in 1949 to design a home on his lakeside lot in Minneapolis. At first reticent, Wright agreed after a year and the house was built with "left over" marble, stone and custom-built aluminum window frames from Neils' business, making it unique among Wright homes. My mother states that she worked for one day at his company designing marble tombstones. Apparently the work did not suit her but the connection with Mr. Neils may have been influential - perhaps mutually.

Montgomery Ward's flagship Twin Cities store was a nine-story distribution warehouse building, along with five stories of administration offices in the Midway area, just a few blocks from Hamline. The lower floors were retail and like other department stores, offered everything from auto parts to ladies' corsets. The huge complex required an army of workers and being close to home, Virginia took a job there in the men's shirt department, and later was promoted

Virginia's portrait upon graduation from Hamline.

Fashion drawings helped win a scholarship, but there was little future in that area. A stylized skyline view of her town, St. Paul, from across the Mississippi.

How many young women have their own logo? Her high school senior photo shows a confident and lovely young woman, who also had talent and determination. She produced fashion drawings for a scholarship application, one of many ways she made her way through college.

To bolster her chances of success after college, she took classes in business and secretarial work, becoming proficient at shorthand.

to the ladies' hats department. She must have been good at it, and judging from the stylish headgear she wore through her later adult life, she enjoyed the work. At some point, however, she decided she needed a real career and some of the few opportunities for women at the time were as office workers. Rasmussen School of Business was a St. Paul trade school that trained young men and (mostly) women to be secretaries, stenographers, typists, accountants, bookkeepers and clerks. It's interesting to look through her sketch books from that time, where shorthand homework shares space with street scenes and quick portraits. Taking night classes, she worked hard, did well and upon completing courses in bookkeeping, shorthand and business management she was offered a chance to stay on as a teacher, which she did for a year. One of her first experiences in that line was as a teaching assistant. When the instructor was wrapping up a class composed of young men, mostly ex-G.I.s, he told them, "If you have any questions or need assistance, Miss Prall here will be happy to help." Every hand in the room went up.

Armed with a year of experience teaching and her fresh credentials in business, she was determined to put her new office skills to work. Her boyfriend at the time had a car, and he had just landed a job at Minnesota Mining and Manufacturing on St. Paul's East Side. 3M had a diversified line of products even then, and when Virginia's application to the company was accepted she was assigned as a secretary to the roofing granule department.

The pebbles that constitute the top of a shingle are not as high-tech as some other 3M products, but like the sandpaper that gave the company its start, adhering hard granules to a substrate is something that must be done well to have a successful product. A classic story in 3M's history relates how in 1914 customers complained that tiny garnet stone granules were falling off the sandpaper. They discovered the Italian stones had been shipped alongside olive oil, which had permeated the garnet. Roasting the stone over a fire removed the oil; it was 3M's first research and development attempt and led to the company later employing many engineers and researchers. By the late 1940s almost 5,000 employees worked at the 46-acre East Side manufacturing and research campus in St. Paul. One of them was a young chemical engineer named Donald Lovness. She remembers going into his office for the first time, seeing Don with his feet up on the desk smoking a pipe with an arrogant attitude. She thought he was the most obnoxious, cocky man she had ever met. Later she would relate that his mother had spoiled him and it may be true, as his baby books survive, along with scrap books filled with notes and memorabilia that only a proud and doting mother would have kept.

Long odds, short romance

Don was a snappy dresser, had a new car (quite an accomplishment in the immediate postwar years) and loved to hear bands and socialize. His boisterous personality must have rubbed off on her, despite her inital assessment and they soon began to go out together. On their first date they discussed architecture and the idea of having a large aquarium as a room divider.

Some of their outings involved digging for Indian artifacts, just as Don had done as a boy. Those quests would continue decades later in Mexico and the Far East as they pursued pre-Columbian and Chinese art together. Some of these dates were camping trips with friends, where they caught fish and enjoyed being outdoors. Her nickname "Queenie" was well earned; she liked her comforts, but in roughing it with Don she proved to be a good sport and it gave her some practice for the two years they would "camp out" while building a Wright home.

Virginia lived in an apartment on Summit Avenue in St. Paul, a tree-lined boulevard with stately homes (among them is the Governor's Residence). She shared rooms in a mansion with two other young lady teachers, and Don's first impression was that she must have money. For her part, his flashy wheels indicated he must be pretty well-off. "We were both badly mistaken," she would say years later. In spite of these misapprehensions and what would appear to be some incompatibilities, they were married within nine months.

My parents had a small wedding in a church with his sister Donna as part of the wedding party. Those invited included both sets of parents (although not Virginia's mother) as well as some relatives in attendance. My mother wore a simple gray suit nipped in at the waist with a white ruffle blouse and a large shoulder corsage. She wore a hat with a veil and black pumps but it still didn't make her appear very tall since their height different was over a foot! Don wore a double breasted dark gray suit with a white shirt and striped tie with a simple carnation above the pocket.

Virginia embraced her fiancé's interests—like fishing and camping—with good humor, and even tried out his pistol.

Several patents were issued to Don Lovness, assigned to 3M Company, for important improvements to shingle sealing and construction during the time he was with the company.

Avoiding the white dress and tux routine was typical for this couple, who would go on to spend their five decades of marriage eschewing convention, defying critics and creating, as Frank Lloyd Wright would tell them a few years later, "Something beautiful wherever we are".

The newlyweds took a honeymoon automobile trip to Mexico, with a stop in New Orleans where Virginia soaked in the ambiance of the French Quarter and put it on paper in several watercolors. My mother had been to Mexico with Helen and Mag, and for my father it was his first visit, which he must have enjoyed. Although neither of them spoke Spanish, they would return several times, and in those early years of marriage even considered moving there to open a hotel. The bright and bold colors of Mexico appealed to Virginia and reinforced her ideas about making a statement in clothing, decorating and even upholstery.

Finding a first home was Virginia's job. Some of the least expensive places to live were on the north edge of downtown St. Paul, the "Red Light District", as she called it later. The buildings were old but one had a more recent addition, an annex with high ceilings and not much more in the way of amenities. No fireplace or fancy woodwork but the $27.50 a month included water, heat and electricity. It was what today we would call subsidized housing and the City had a list of welfare families waiting for just such a place. Virginia, however, made the case to the landlord that she would turn it into a showplace. Afterwards she freely described it as a "con"—not her first and not her last—but getting her way using whatever means possible was a skill she honed all her life. In the end, the apartment outlasted much of the building and the entire area.

Settling into the apartment in St. Paul, like so many other young couples they scrounged to make it a home that reflected their personalities. Each was independent and motivated; traits that on an individual basis were an asset, but as a couple offered real possibilities for friction. Over the years these two strong-willed people would clash from time to time, but from the outset, they mostly complemented and strengthened each other.

Photos from these first years of marriage show them with a definite hipster attitude and the apartment was a perfect reflection of that. Spare and simple, it comes across in one carefully staged image as modern yet bohemian. She said the paintings she produced at the time were done in a Lazlo Moholy-Nagy style and there were direct influences from his Institute of Design in Chicago, where designer Florence Forst was active in the late 1940s. Forst, my mother said, "Took me under her wing and insisted that I be there every day at her home," adding, "She had me do weird things." Florence Forst's pottery was described in a 1946 Museum of Modern Art exhibit as "...combin(ing) fresh ideas of design and sensible housekeeping with understanding of industrial techniques." That pragmatic combo was probably a beneficial thing for a young woman who would, in a few years, take on an "art project" of monumental scale.

Being a true artist requires dedication and a commitment to your craft. Through years of school and then continuous employment, Virginia made sure she painted on a regular basis. Like a chameleon, her subjects became whatever her surroundings were. From their apartment window, from street corners and from perches above the Mississippi river bluffs she painted St.

Walking down the aisle in 1948, even as their life together began, it was clear that this was no normal couple. Fourteen inches of height difference was only one of many contrasts between them, but somehow, as a team, they would accomplish things they could not have done individually. Over the decades, the whole of their life became much greater than the sum of their respective parts.

A print of their downtown neighborhood gives it a sense of liveliness in spite of being a little seedy.

In their downtown St. Paul apartment the bride and groom began a creative partnership in making their own environment. Virginia painted the walls a bold red. Don framed one of her abstract paintings and built the minimalist couch, which she upholstered. The couch moved to the new Wright house where it served for a year or two until custom-made furniture was finished.

Restaurants and movie theaters were great places to display her work, and Virginia had many shows at these venues while they lived in St. Paul and later, White Bear Lake.

Paul. There was only one "Skyscraper" - the First National Bank building at 32 floors - but there were other structures that made interesting subjects for her watercolors, and in 1950, downtown was in a state of flux. Homes in their neighborhood were targeted for demolition and she used these broken buildings as subjects. The removal of an entire neighborhood, including some 75 structures—two churches, several apartment buildings, and many sub-standard private homes—was the culmination of plans that had been in the works for decades, ever since architect Cass Gilbert finished the State Capitol in 1907 and began to lobby for a grand boulevard and gardens to complement it. The area went downhill during the depression, and it took a war and postwar calls for a soldier's memorial to finally get something done. Even as my parents moved into their place, wrecking crews were at work a few streets away. By 1953 the new Capitol Approach had swallowed up the north edge of downtown and a few years later, a new "National Defense Highway" would remove even more neighborhoods to the west, cutting through the heart of St. Paul's African-American community.

In their apartment, however, improvements were taking shape and true to her word, it became a "smashing" place. The walls were an orange-red and the ceiling umber. Inside, Don and Virginia were building furniture and crafting jewelry. Outside, however, the streets were mean enough that they didn't even go out on New Year's eve, with fights and drunks stumbling around at all hours.

Owning a guard dog was out of the question in the small apartment (Great Danes and Dobermans would come later) but they did have two cats and a Boa Constrictor. It can be argued the snake would be a deterrent to any burglar, but that's not why Leda was kept around. Don had always liked snakes and collected them as a boy. It made perfect sense to him that a five foot long reptile would share their home. Virginia was willing to accomodate her husband's quirky taste in pets, and during their marriage many more unusual creatures would find a home with them - and their daughters.

Every day was an adventure for the young newlyweds but soon enough the handwriting was on the wall, as they say. It was their first venture at "making wherever you are a beautiful place" and even after they had moved out, one wall of their apartment—painted that vivid red—remained defiantly standing for months after the wreckers took part of the building down. My mother always laughed when she told the story of how her handiwork was on display amid the wreckage, a bright, happy spot of color in a dull world. Listening to her, I always thought maybe she was describing herself.

In spite of the flop houses, the drunks and the general seediness of the area, the apartment was a cool spot for the two of them, but not for a family. After less than three years there came along a strong motivation to find a better place. That was me.

As a young couple with no children Don and Virginia made the most of their free time with travel. A trip to New Orleans soon after their marriage was an opportunity to take in the sounds, sights and tastes of the French Quarter. Here they are finishing dinner with a dessert bombe at the Court of Two Sisters, a restaurant that still continues as a legendary spot in the heart of the city.

Virginia reveled in the color and gaiety of the Quarter, putting her notebook observations on paper in watercolor. Lower left, her sketches carried detailed notes about color for later finished paintings.

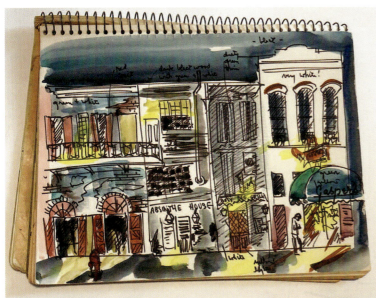

Introduced by the Herman Miller Co. in 1947, the Isamu Noguchi-designed glass top table was popular and Don did his own take on the idea.

To the most
beautiful wife
in th world
Donney

Hurry home to me baby
I love you with every-
thing I got. I hope you
like these better than
the flowers I picked
this a. m. all my love
Don & the skunk

For a big guy Don had beautiful handwriting and a romantic side to boot. These flower cards are sweet and the second one made reference to another pet, a skunk that Don sometimes kept in his desk drawer at work.

By DORIS BOCK

A few guppies, or a canary, might be all right in some homes as pets, but they're not for Mr. and Mrs. Donald Lovness, who live a stone's throw from the state Capitol. They claim to have a pet just as gentle and far more interesting—an Imperial Boa Constrictor—a honey when it comes to snakes. Besides being gentle when she's out of her cage for an airing she has other attributes in her favor—such as sleeping most of the time and not kicking up a row when the pantry goes bare.

Leda, of course, is a lady. She has been in the Lovness family three years, arriving in a burlap bag inside a cigar-like wooden box from Guatemala. About 14 inches long when she first saw St. Paul, she has grown to be about 5-1/2 feet long and Mr. Lovness says that in another two years she will grow another three feet.

Some of the Lovness' friends have long forgotten the old superstition that all snakes are harmful and insist on fondling her when they go to call. Others stay their distance, and no coaxing can make them pet her. Their snake is a very rare specimen, they tell me, and already the very fine Lincoln Park Zoo in Chicago is counting on having her as a part of their snake family. Mr. Lovness isn't so sure when that will be, certainly not while there is cold weather. At no time has Mr. Lovness been in awe of a snake. Even as a small child, his wife said, he always was in possession of one or two.

In addition to Leda, they have two beautiful cats, one Siamese and one solid black, who have become pals of Leda. They are such good pals that Mrs. Lovness says, when Leda is out of the cage they can't wait to take a little nip or two, or sit directly in front of her, watching. The nips bring a slight hiss but not enough to scare Sinbad, the Siamese. In fact, the two cats sit on top of the glass cage much of the time, coaxing to get a little closer to Leda, who seems to understand that they can take care of themselves and never will she get the chance to have them for supper.

Natural food for snakes is living food. Therefore, Mr. Lovness has a standing order at one of the pet shops for three rats, mice or hamsters, which must always be pure white. He tells me that they must be white to be sure they are healthy or Leda might become sick. And to this day she has not known one day of sickness since she was sent to them. Snakes are known to eat prey three times the size of their heads, their heads being constructed that they can "unhinge" their jaws.

Nothing is more interesting and astonishing about a snake than the way it sheds its skin several times a year. "We can always tell when Leda is going to shed her skin because her eyes get milky," said Mrs. Lovness, an amateur sculptor. "Then we place a pan of water in her cage, which she curls up in, and after a good soak she pulls out of the skin and waits for the next molting season.

"They get their new skins when their old ones are too small for them," Mrs. Lovness informed me. She said they have had no luck in keeping the old skin because they are too thin and dry up.

"Most persons don't know snakes. They think they are cold and slimy, which isn't true at all. A healthy snake is never slimy and always takes on the warmth of its surroundings. Our snake is considered a very fine one and has aroused considerable attention among those who know about it. The University of Minnesota has asked us to loan it for exhibition purposes.

"Leda has very beautiful coloring and a perfect design on her back. Her belly is coral and the back design is in black and different shades of brown."

Leda's home is all glass. If it were wire, Mrs. Lovness explains, she could be caught in the mesh.

On March 11, 1951 the St. Paul Sunday Pioneer Press ran a leading page story in the second-section about this downtown duo with an unusual pet. My mother's look of slight apprehension may have to do with the fact she was pregnant with me at the time.

A year or so after this article appeared, Leda went to join other snakes at the Lincoln Park Zoo in Chicago, where director Marlin Perkins enthusiastically accepted her. In this photo from April 1952, Perkins (left) handles some non-poisonous snakes with a hand still bandaged from a Timber Rattlesnake bite he suffered while preparing for a broadcast of the TV series Zoo Parade. He and his co-host Jim Hurlbut did the weekly show live from Lincoln Park Zoo.

A Snake in The House

MARCH 11, 1951

By DORIS BOCK

A few guppies, or a canary, might be all right in some homes as pets, but they're not for Mr. and Mrs. Donald Lovness, who live a stone's throw from the state Capitol.

They claim to have a pet just as gentle and far more interesting—an Imperial boa constrictor—a honey when it comes to snakes. Besides being gentle when she's out of her cage for an airing, she has other attributes in her favor—such as sleeping most of the time and not kicking up a row when the pantry goes bare.

Leda, of course, is a lady. She has been in the Lovness family three years, arriving in a burlap bag inside a cigar-like wooden box from Guatemala. About 14 inches long when she first saw St. Paul, she has grown to be about 5½ feet long and Mr. Lovness says that in another two years she will grow another three feet.

Some of the Lovness' friends have long forgotten the old superstition that all snakes are harmful and insist on fondling her when they go to call. Others stay their distance, and no coaxing can make them pet her.

Their snake is a very rare specimen, they tell me, and already the very fine Lincoln Park zoo in Chicago is counting on having her as a part of their snake family. Mr. Lovness isn't so sure when that will be, certainly not while there is cold weather.

At no time has Mr. Lovness been in awe of a snake. Even as a small child, his wife said, he always was in possession of one or two.

In addition to Leda, they have two beautiful cats, one Siamese and one solid black, who have become pals of Leda. They are such good pals that Mrs. Lovness says, when Leda is out of the cage they can't wait to take a little nip or two, or sit directly in front of her, watching. The nips bring a slight hiss

...O PLAYING—That seems to be the order ...iamese cat, Sinbad, and their pet Imperial ...ave been friends for several years and Si...

Doris Bock wrote again a year after her first story about the snake appeared.

I HAD NOT HEARD, UNTIL a few days ago, what became of Leda the imperial boa constrictor, pet of Donald Lovness, Belle-air, White Bear lake, which made the front page of the Sunday Pioneer Press two years ago. Well, I got a chance to talk to Mr. Lovness, who told me Leda grew by leaps and bounds and was eating so much he had to find a new home for her, so off she went to Milo Perkins at the Chicago zoo, where she is now living the life of Riley.

At the time of the story Leda was about five feet long but Mr. Lovness told me that when he gave her to the zoo Leda was eight feet long.

Of particular interest to Wright was the idea of a simple yet functional and pleasant home for the American everyman: the Usonian house. (The name was taken from an alternative name for the United States that differentiated it from the South America or Canada: Usonia.) It was his vision of the true American home. Usonian houses were generally small and built of inexpensive brick or concrete blocks, often with plywood and other modest materials, adhering to a grid layout. The blocks could be put together in a variety of ways but were a simple and easy-to-work-with alternative to rock. By the 1950s dozens of these homes, each different, had been built across the country's heartland.

My mother had already begun an interest in Wright's work when she met my father and in their first married years they made a point to visit some of his homes nearby. "We used to go around and look at houses all the time," my father said. On a business trip to Wausau, Wisconsin Don took along his bride for a chance to visit the Charles L. Manson home there. Finished in 1941, it was typical of Usonian homes with brick, a concrete floor and cypress boards and battens. Although built on a grid the floorplan jogs slightly at angles as it rises from a terrace and living area to the master bedroom and a carport in two sets of steps, matching the rise of the lot. Wright drew plans based on topo maps—having never seen the actual site—but it was a perfect example of a home fitting into and complementing its site. This lesson was not lost on the young visiting couple who recalled being "overwhelmed."

Mr. Manson was an insurance agency owner (and later insurance commissioner for the state) and his wife Dorothy was an activist in women's causes, a strong and accomplished woman. They were enthusiastic patrons of the arts and music, entertaining often in their Wright home. They raised two daughters, just as my parents did, but each had their own small bedroom, a luxury my sister and I did not have.

The Henry Neils house on Cedar Lake in Minneapolis was built in 1950 and '51. It was unusual in that the materials used were not the normal local "organic" components, but rather, exotic stone and marble along with larch for trim and aluminum window framing. One element that was shared with my parents' home was the placement of the heating system behind the fireplace where it generated hot water for the in-floor heating. It also had a huge hearth and much exposed stone inside the house, elements that surely influenced my mother's later insistence on stone rather than blocks or bricks for the Woodpile Lake studio. Although the Neils house had sweeping pitched roofs, my parents home was flat-topped. That dramatic wing-like covering must have made an impression, however, and the second house they built had a steep, cantilevered covering.

The Neils provided advice and moral support for the young couple as they were building their own Wright home. One of their daughters, Patricia, was married to Cedric Boulter, a professor at the University of Cincinnati. The Boulters engaged Wright to design a home for them in 1954 and it was on the Taliesin drawing boards at about the same time as my parents'. One

Don and Virginia made a hobby of sorts out of visiting Prairie School buildings and Usonian homes whenever possible. He took photos they could use as a catalog of ideas for the future, and she was never reluctant to pose for his camera.

The Charles L. Manson House in Wausau, Wisconsin was finished in 1941 and had three levels. With strong horizontal surfaces, this and other Usonian houses seemed to grow out of the land they were on. Primary materials were concrete, plywood and brick, simple and easily formed, fulfilling Wright's idea of "affordable, beautiful housing for a democratic America."

Wright designed the Manson house using topographic drawings and never saw the site in person. The same is true of our house but its site is relatively flat. On their visit, Don took several photos including one of Virginia. Having seen the brick and wood in this Wright design, then Taliesin a few years later, it's not surprising she opted for stone in our house.

Responding to a lack of work during the Great Depression, Wright originated the Taliesin Fellowship in 1932, where young aspiring architects could live and learn while working at the master's elbow (and in his kitchen and fields, as well). Among the first apprentices were William Wesley Peters and John Howe, who later became close friends of my parents. Wright also published his 600-plus page autobiography that year, a book that inspired Nancy Willey to contact him. Their home was the first commission for the new fellowship, a milestone. Steve Sikora describes its other significance: "This small and entirely new kind of commission for Wright, became an incubator for forward-thinking ideas related to housing the emerging middle class. Ideas Wright developed for the Willey House—while specific to time and place—were employed, expounded upon and refined over the next 25 years of his architectural practice."

Like my mother, Nancy Willey had a "determined enthusiasm" that drove the project forward.

significant similarity between the Boulter and Lovness houses is the framed clerestory windows above french doors and a patio with mitered glass corners, although little else is the same. It's an example of the cross-pollination (or you could say mix-and-match) in designs among Wright residences. The bottom line, however, is that it works. It's hard to find fault with or claim that any of his designs are without integrity even though they may be "pieced" together. Wright would often say he "shook designs out of his sleeve," and by the 1950s there were already quite a few up there to choose from.

It's doubtful my parents ever saw the Boulter home, although over the years they visited many others. One other Wright home in Minneapolis was well-known to Virginia, having been built in 1934. Malcolm Willey was a University of Minnesota administrator. His wife Nancy had read Wright's recently published Autobiography and wrote to him asking for a "creation of art". A caveat was that they had only $8000 to spend. A first design at two stories was deemed too expensive but a subsequent plan was built and became a bridge between the Prairie School and the Usonian "everyman's" home to come. The house blurred the lines between indoors and out with easy access to terraces, an open kitchen and rooms partitioned only by built-ins. The Willeys were thrilled with their new home and enjoyed it for many years.

As with many other Wright structures, however, it fell into disrepair over the years but current owner, architect Steve Sikora has restored it including original furniture designs and it is open to the public for scheduled tours.

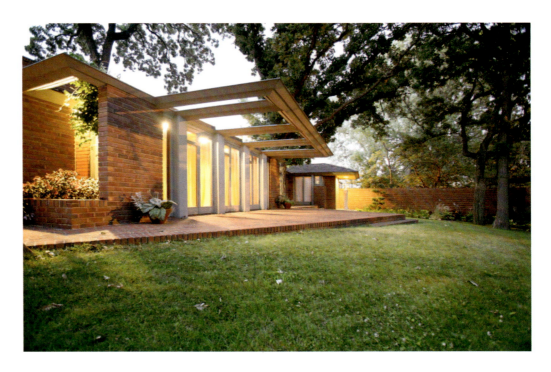

Prior to their meeting with Wright, Virgina and Don also visited the Frieda and Henry J. Neils house on Cedar Lake in Minneapolis. Neils was a distributor of stone and building materials and his home reflected an upscale approach to the Usonian concept. It was on a lake but here, Wright's concept of "Owning your view" over the water extended only through a few compass points.

Two wildly disparate Usonian homes: The Neils house on Cedar Lake in Minneapolis and the Boulter home in Cincinnati.

Neils' daughter Patricia and her husband Cedric Boulter built their concrete block and mahogany two-story home about the same time my parents were building theirs. Note the elaborately framed clerestory windows, tall french doors and mitered glass corners, very similar to the Lovness design. The Boulter home, however, is in a suburban setting, close to a street and on a steep hill.

CLERESTORY. NOT ACCESSIBLE FOR
MEASURING THIS INFORMATION FROM 1954 "AS
BUILT" PRINTS PROVIDED BY CURRENT OWNER

2ND FLOOR CEILING
elevation 18'-8"

2ND FLOOR
elevation 9'-0"

GROUND FLOOR
elevation 0'-0"

SOUTH ELEVATION
Scale 1/4" = 1'-0"

Two years later, in Madison Wisconsin, newspaperman Herbert Jacobs and his wife visited Wright with a challenge: can you design a house to be built for $5000? It was the Depression and money was tight, not only for working men, but for Wright and his newly-formed Fellowship of paying apprentices. The architect's response to Jacobs was that for twenty years he'd been wanting to build a low cost house but no one had ever asked him before. Maybe it was because commissions were few or because Wright truly was "the most democratic man", as my mother said. Probably it was both, and Wright took on the challenge. The Jacobs built a 1500 square foot home using brick, plywood, boards and battens. The L-shaped structure had radiant in-floor heating in a concrete slab, a flat roof and is designed on a module of 2 x 4 feet. It was described by Wright as a Usonian home, an example of what every family in America could have in his vision of the United States as "Usonia", part of a grand urban design called Broadacre City.

This first Usonian was followed by about 140 more before Wright's death in 1959 and the Jacobs family, having outgrown this home, built a second one in 1944. Mr. Jacobs documented his adventures in a 1978 book, Building With Frank Lloyd Wright.

While most Wright clients had some hands-on involvement, none that I'm aware of put the degree of effort into their project that my parents did. Mr. Wright called them his "Do-It-Yourself Couple" and the title was appropriate, although there was at least one runner-up. A few hundred miles south in Cedar Rapids, Iowa, Douglas and Jackie Grant built a Wright design beginning in 1948. While they employed masons, carpenters, plumbers and other specialists, they engaged in plenty of hands-on construction themselves. Most unusual, however, is that the couple quarried rock by hand on the property, even teaching themselves to work with black powder, blasting the limestone loose then hauling tons of it to the building site with a war-surplus Jeep and a trailer. Construction took place while Douglas held a job and Jackie tended to their three children. The oldest of those, Donna Grant Reilly, documented it all in her 2010 book An American Proceeding. My parents visited the Grants in 1959; I'm sure they had a lot of things to talk about!

Like Nancy Willey, the Grants approached Wright by admiring his work but asking if he might be able to suggest another architect who could possibly design something on a limited budget, a circumspect challenge that of course, he could not turn down. Unlike my parents, the Grants didn't have to go find land; they had 50 lovely acres with a home site perfect for the type of "of the hill" structure they had seen in a January, 1938 Architectural Forum magazine article about Wright. But like my parents the Grants were both fully engaged for a few years in the construction of a home they truly considered a dream, and enjoyed it for decades, never losing appreciation of the harmony with nature that it brought.

In a sketchbook filled with downtown buildings, Como Park amusement rides, sailboats on White Bear Lake and even a few portraits of her daughter, Mother made some shorthand notes about Wright, with sketches. She was a big fan long before she met the man.

Herbert and Katherine Jacobs built what is considered the first Usonian house in Madison, Wisconsin in 1937. Clear themes for future Usonians are evident. The opposite side of the building faces the street with a car port and very small windows just below the eaves, affording privacy in its suburban setting.

The Grant house in Cedar Rapids was unusual in having two floors. In 1975 my father told Al Drap two stories about the house: "The Grants didn't have enough money for lumber needed to support the forms for the concrete roof slab, so they cut down trees to use. A woman visiting the house with a forest of tree trunks in the living room said, 'I knew Wright liked to bring the outside in but this is ridiculous.'

"Mr. Grant worked very hard on his house along with some hired laborers. One time a worker— who didn't know who Mr. Grant was—told him, "Hey buddy, you don't need to work so hard, anyone who can afford a house like this has to be loaded."

Don took this photo when they visited in 1959.

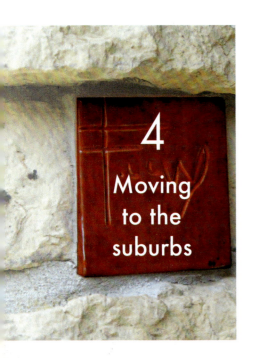

4

Moving to the suburbs

eing drawn to water is something inherent in the human psyche, I believe. It must have been for my parents, as they moved from a completely urban setting to a home (or what could more accurately be described as a hovel) on a large body of water some seven miles from downtown. While White Bear Lake had a yacht club and several opulent summer homes for the wealthy, the south end of the lake was made up of modest homes and the cinderblock walk-out basement they bought was possibly the most modest of all. In 1951 waterfront property did not have the appeal it does today, and a lake home didn't necessarily bring a premium price. Even so, Don and Virginia only invested a few hundred dollars as a down payment with a contract for deed for $7000. That figure left some financial breathing room for the improvements they planned.

My mother saw this simple space as a blank canvas, a basis for creating a dream home. She loved the water, the mature trees and the ducks and geese that would pass through. She had a vision and a willing accomplice; they would both begin to develop latent skills on small scale projects that—unknown to them at the time—would prepare them for the project of a lifetime a few years later. My father, for his part, saw things on a larger scale than most people. I think because he was six-feet-four he had an XXL view toward life. Building a rock fireplace was not daunting, and if you were going to have an aquarium, make it 75 gallons. He was unfazed by almost any challenge and was intelligent enough to solve almost any problem. Together, they started to improve the home for themselves, for me and soon, for my sister Ty.

Now with a yard and more space, they began to collect creatures in earnest. There's no other way to put it; there were dogs, cats, birds, snakes, lizards, fish. They started an accumulation of animals that went on for decades. A Great Dane was added to the menagerie, then a Scarlet Macaw. By now the snake, Leda, had grown considerably and was confined to her glass cage when Don wasn't home. One winter day she managed to break out and when my mother couldn't find her, she grabbed the cat and me, called the dog and got on the other side of the front door as fast as she could. Although Leda was usually gentle, my mother was taking no chance that she would mistake any of us for a squeeze toy or a meal. Peering in through the window, shivering and trying to keep me warm, she must have looked pathetic enough that a neighbor came over to investigate. The neighbor was able to help get Leda penned and my mother calmed down. When Don came home the discussion was about finding a new home for the snake. It was shortly thereafter that Leda went to live at the Lincoln Park Zoo in Chicago, an arrangement that had been agreed to previously. The director there, Marlin Perkins, was excited to have Leda since many Boas in captivity don't like to eat. That was certainly not Leda's problem, most likely because she'd been pampered with only the finest live mice for years. Marlin Perkins, like Don, had a fascination with snakes since childhood. He was a television pioneer with a 1950s show called *Zoo Parade*, and in 1963 began hosting a nature series called *Wild Kingdom*, which ran for over 20 years and gave many people their first exposure to the conservation movement.

Facing north to White Bear Lake, the house backed up to a hill on the southwest. By the time I came along there was a huge dog, a scarlet macaw, cats and fish. In the fall of 1953 the Lovness family car was now a practical used station wagon, as another child was on the way.

My given name Ilona was seldom used; I was Lonnie to family and friends. My sister was just "Baby Lovness" for a while before being named Tracy. That was later shortened to Ty.

Living on water and living with unusual pets were two consistent aspects of growing up in the Lovness family. At White Bear and later at Woodpile Lake, my sister and I loved the water - and the animals we lived with.

With Leda gone, her glass enclosure was turned into an aquarium. My father built a stone base for it and it became a room divider. Doris Bock of the St. Paul newspaper visited again in 1954 and described the fish in their tank and the "little show place" my parents were building.

Just as they had in the St. Paul apartment—and would for the rest of their lives— my mother and father worked diligently at improving their surroundings. The walls of the new house were painted bright colors, and Don built a rubblestone fireplace. It was just enough mason experience to make him think he was prepared for the challenge of building a rock home a few years later. They envisioned building up and outward from the existing walk-out, oriented northeast toward the lake. Wide eaves and stone walkways outside would complement the large hearth and ten-foot wide glass windows in the living room. Two bedrooms and a dining room were connected by a short hall and a few steps, following the contours of the property's incline. The plan was long on imagination but short on detail. It was at this point Franz Aust suggested a meeting, thinking Mr. Wright would be interested and have some suggestions. My mother recalled her mindset at the time:

I had all of Mr. Wright's books - there weren't many at the time, maybe half a dozen. I thought we understood his principles. So right away I started designing a studio to hang over the lake. The lake was at an angle to the house so I designed this studio at an angle as well.

In about 1953 the St. Paul newspaper carried a story by Doris Bock about our Bellaire home and what was at the time an unusual item: a large aquarium (Leda's former home). It read:

A little cement block house, painted the most beautiful red so you can't miss it, stands by the side of the lake-shore road at Bellaire, White Bear lake. It is the home of two former St. Paulites, Mr. and Mrs. George (sic) Lovness.

Under construction the past two years, the house is not yet completed but when it is will be one of the little show places around the lake. Much of the house is being built by Mr. Lovness which, of course, makes it slow business, but even today it is attractive and livable.

The living room with its large fireplace, which is kept burning most of the time and gives a cozy atmosphere, will be the dining room when the large room is built across the front of the house.

Right now the Lovnesses are contemplating getting a well-known architect to help them with this very special room which, no doubt, will be built before many months have passed.

Mrs. Lovness also has contributed to the building of the house because she told me she and her husband built the fireplace jointly and that the rocks used for it were hauled from buildings torn down for the Capitol Approach. An artist with much talent, she being a student in the art department at Hamline University, Mrs. Lovness has many of her impressionistic pictures framed around on the walls.

But what their friends are most interested in is the 75-gallon aquarium which has just been completed and separates the living room from the pretty red kitchen. About four feet long and two feet wide, the aquarium holds many interesting fish. While some are very fancy, I noticed several rough fish in the aquarium such as baby bullheads and a small dogfish, and a little later on they may have some large sunfish.

On the bottom of the aquarium is a layer of crushed quartz in which rest snails, clams and a large sea shell, together with weeds such as fish must have to keep alive. When you know that the aquarium weighs more than 600 pounds you know what an attraction it is.

I was excited to have a new sister!

Art Work At World Praised

By **JOHN H. HARVEY**

There's a profusion of well-executed water colors and a few oil paintings in the showing of work by Virginia Lovness, young St. Paul artist, currently running at the World art gallery, 494 Wabasha.

The artist has had good training at the St. Paul School of Art and Hamline university, and it shows in a feeling for color, crispness of line and freedom of formal design to be found in her water colors.

The case is not quite so clear in the oils on exhibition, which are all abstractions and seem to show an experimental diversity of style and method which suggests she has not yet established a direction for herself.

But even here the colors are lively and the execution has dash.

The water colors, which run from the representational to the semi-abstract, include street and industrial scenes, landscapes, buildings, and a variety of scenes from everyday life which testify to a wide and lively range of interest. They also show a good eye for patterns.

There was no grass growing under my mother's feet. While improving the lake home and drawing plans to expand it, she continued producing oils and watercolors, and worked hard to promote herself as an artist. This news clipping is from June, 1954.

She loved the property and the huge trees, "big enough for three people to link arms around the trunk". The one-story block house, of course, we just a starting point but could have been a showplace with a good design. The lake was and remains an attractive recreational destination, although its water level declined in the early 2000s before normalizing in 2017. White Bear has a long tradition as a sailing mecca and was the birthplace of the fast and sleek racing "scows" at the turn of the twentieth century. Summer sailboat regattas take place several times a week and fishing is popular all year long. It was and is a great place to live. My sister Tracy (who we always call Ty) was born in December, 1953 and from the time we could walk we were in the water all summer. But in spite of all its potential, the property would never have been right for a Wright home. After meeting the architect, in late 1955 my parents made plans to begin building a new home and effectively, a new life. They didn't know it at the time but they would soon be firmly in the orbit of the Taliesin fellowship, living in a Frank Lloyd Wright home and living a Wright-inspired life.

When an arrangement was made to sell the house soon after their June, 1955 meeting with Mr. Wright, a sense of excitement was combined with a real feeling of urgency. Now financially free to pursue their dream, the questions they needed to answer were first, where; then when and finally; how? My mother's notes recall that time:

It was unbelieveable. Mr. Wright had offered to design a house and now we had money to buy ten acres and rock, and to pay him. We had asked Gene Masselink and he told us the fee was 10% of the cost of the house. There were a lot of unwritten restrictions, both from Mr. Wright and some self-imposed: we had to have water in our view; the home would face southwest (Mr. Wright's favorite direction); and we had to "own" our own view. All this on ten acres.

Bolstered by the thought that they might actually be able to do this project, they piled my sister and me in the back of the car and went on a search for land. They hunted every day for weeks, fanning out to the north and east, away from the city. However, finding property they could afford and having enough money left for construction was beginning to look like an impossible feat. A water view was a pretty tall order with only a couple of thousand dollars to work with. Virginia's old notebook describes the quest:

For three months each morning I packed my daughters in our car upon taking Don to work and began our organized search for our new project. Right at the beginning, the obstacles were insurmountable. Although Minnesota is relatively unpopulated, our requirements for land seemed out of all proportion to what we could afford (which obviously was nothing at all!). We must have privacy. Water, whether stream, river or lake was immaterial, as long as it was beautiful, wooded and isolated from higher up. The homesite could face directly southwest and we could control our view, (since upon having seen the ultimate [at Taliesin], that became a necessity.)

2707 South Shore Boulevard
White Bear Lake 10, Minn.
June 13, 1955

Mr. Frank Lloyd Wright
Taliesin
Spring Green, Wisconsin

Dear Mr. Wright,

It's impossible to thank you enough for the visit we had with you
last Saturday. I haven't come back down to earth yet after your
most wonderful offer to build a house for us -

We have already located a fine site - 8 acres uite far out which
I am going to buy today. As soon as I can get a topographical
map made I will contact you. I am looking forward to seeing you
again as much as living in one of your houses.

Sincerely,

My mother's enthusiasm and excitement led her to exaggerate a bit when she wrote Mr. Wright to say they had found property within days of their Taliesin visit. In fact, it would take much of the summer and the purchase was not finalized until the end of that year. In the meantime, however, Mr. Wright and his draftsmen were working on the plans.

My father had the latest in cool cars when I was born, a 1951 Buick Super Convertible. Bebo the Great Dane enjoyed going for a ride. A few years later, a more pragmatic and older Ford wagon became the family car, and it was well-traveled, taking them to Taliesin and on more than one trip to Mexico where the roads and bridges were very basic; no impediment to my adventurous parents.

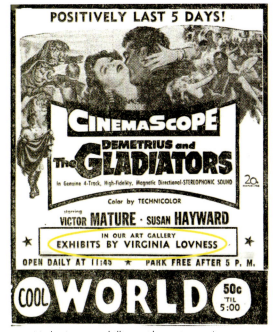

Mother's art got billing with movie stars!

Mexico was a favorite
destination for them over the years,
where Mother loved the colors and
the warmth of the people. She
exhibited at the Minnesota State
Fair until the mid-1960s

We started out looking at want ads. There were farms where we could accomplish this but the price of farmland was exorbitant. In our drives we would stop to ask farmers if they knew of a little lake anywhere. We found five acres but there was no water and not much view. Mr. Wright rejected this; he wanted more open space and little more hilly terrain with no view of other houses.

One of the parcels my parents considered was on the St. Croix River, twelve miles east and six miles north of their White Bear Lake home. The owner, Henry Van Meier was a physician who practiced in Stillwater. He and his wife Katherine lived above his office just a block off Main Street but they also had a summer home at Arcola, about six miles north. My parents knew them and discussed the idea of building on ten acres of their half-mile of riverfront property. Katherine, a genteel Southern Belle at heart, had visions of establishing an artists' colony on the property and Virginia, of course would fit perfectly into her plans. My mother recalls her asking, however, "Why would Mr. Wright design a house for you?" While the St. Croix is lovely - and in 1968 would be Federally designated as a Wild and Scenic River - the parcel my parents were considering faced east with poor access, a cliff above the river, a steep sloping hill to the west and heavy woods all around. Mr. Wright rejected this idea as well.

Twenty years later I would take up summer residence on the Van Meier property and eventually, the St. Croix became a place I love and have called home for decades. In 1955, however, the river bluff was not the ideal spot to build a Wright house. They looked at dozens of spots that were either too expensive or didn't meet their criteria. The search continued and my parents spread the word among friends that they were looking for a parcel with water, privacy, some trees, a view and of course, it had to be inexpensive. It was a Unicorn quest but my mother dutifully scanned the classifieds and trolled dirt roads with her two little girls almost every day. Then, a stroke of luck:

Good fortune was with us. 10 acres and a 25 minute drive to work. The most beautiful softly rolling wooded pasture, a long driveway on a narrow dirt township road and then a driveway with grass growing between the tracks between a lake and a pond to our site. Wooded with three kinds of Oak and Birch and all grassy and a private little lake of our own with a bay - and control of the opposite point, all wooded and full of wildlife.

Yet again, a relative of my father's came through; he knew a farmer who had some land outside of Stillwater so they raced over to see the property and it was perfect! Just three miles to the east from White Bear Lake, a section of the farmer's land had been used for grazing - a gently rolling, wooded parcel with a shoreline on the western side and marshland to the north. Woodpile Lake was small but quite deep with open land around most of it, a dirt road edging about a quarter of it and little chance of further development. The farmer, George Welander, was elderly but he knew of Wright's work. However, he didn't want to sell because his cows grazed in the meadow above the lake.

My mother always loved this Henry David Thoreau quote:

"A lake is the landscape's most beautiful and expressive feature. It is earth's eye; looking into which the beholder measures the depth of his own nature. The fluviatile trees next to the shore are the slender eyelashes which fringe it, and the wooded hills and cliffs around are its overhanging brows."

Woodpile Lake, at 13 acres is just big enough to be called one of Minnesota's "10,000 lakes." In fact, there are 11,842 lakes of 10 acres or more in the state, including White Bear at over 2400 acres. In spite of its small size (or perhaps because of it) Don and Virginia felt Woodpile was the perfect spot. This is one of the photos sent to Mr. Wright in 1955, taken from what would be our front yard, looking west. The house would be sited to the right and behind this vantage point, just uphill on the slight rise. Mature oaks were all over on the property and around the lake. Over the years my parents would buy more property around the lake from neighbors with the intention of building additional Wright-designed cabins.

We told him he could still graze his cows if he would just sell us 10 acres so we could build a Wright home, facing southwest. It took some convincing but he finally agreed. Topographic maps and photos were rushed to Mr. Wright. He called us and was enthusiastic, promising to start our design right away.

He asked us what materials we planned to use. "Rock, absolutely," we told him. "Rock inside and out." Don said the only thing he couldn't do is plaster, so he asked Mr. Wright if we could have a wood ceiling. "No plaster!"

I mentioned that since this would be a studio, we didn't need any hallways, just open space; no need for a hall gallery! We would also need a carport and a storage building. And all this for $10,000.

There had been some near-misses with the property search. Years later, every time they would drive past a local Technical College my mother would say to my sister Ty, "Thank God we didn't buy that spot." In 1955 it was open land but within a dozen years a freeway and major development had overrun the area. There was also one apparent near-miss with the design of the house. Mother had written to Mr. Wright in August about their needs, and also to promote their abilities - and in the process making some significant exaggerations. The letter read:

In accordance with our talks this morning I am sending a few thoughts, dimensions and prices: Structural cypress here is $140/1000 (perhaps enough for only part of the house at this price). Quarry limestone is $5/ton delivered. Red ceramic floor brick is $110/1000 (4x8x1-1/2 deep).

Don is chemical engineer, but spends all of his spare time on his own projects. In our present house we did all the stonework ourselves. Don also did all the heating, wiring, plumbing and building himself. Actually, he is able to do anything and everything along those lines and likes nothing better than working with materials. With your house, he will have to have the well dug, concrete slab laid, cesspools dug. And perhaps help to rough the whole structure in. But all the stonework we will do. Also much of the wood building and certainly all the furniture building, window frames, etc. We truly believe we will love much more greatly a house and the land for having built it with our own hands.

With this in mind, I sincerely hope you won't be too hampered and that we can have:

1 large living room, studio, 2 small bedrooms, kitchen and dining. Enclosed are the measurements for the kitchen equipment.

Washer and dryer, 31" wide x 30" deep by 40" high.

Refrigerator 33" wide x 30" deep x 70" high.

The reason I ask for a separate studio is that I make such a mess when I paint and I like to leave the litter for the next day. And if this mess is in the living area, I can't relax when reading or listening to music or when friends come in. A studio adjacent to the living-dining area, but somewhat secluded would be so much more practical.

Space for a phonograph turntable should be about 24" x 24" x 24". Record space 3' at least of shelving for 12" and 10" records.

The speaker should have at least 10-15 cu feet of space behind it. Usually Don can find a place to put the speaker in a wall with cupboard or closet space sufficient behind it.

In addition to her time spent painting and drawing (and traveling), Virginia was a dedicated mother to Ty and me as well, and a loving caretaker for the ever-changing menagerie which in 1955 included our Siamese kitten.

Stillwater Minn.
Dec. 23, 1955

Dear Mr & Mrs Don Looness:

You were not home when I stopped ~~it~~ yesterday so will drop you a note.

If we are to make a deal on the land we will have to have some understanding soon.

In regard to prices it depends on what you want. I am sending several layouts with prices and whatever you do about it will suit us. Even if ~~you~~ you don't want any land at these prices.

There will be some expense to us, surveying, fencing and a new road besides the papers that will have to be made out.

I know these prices are high but everything considered It is not ~~much~~ out of line.

Wish you all a Merry Christmas and a Happy new year.

Sincerely yours,
George Welander

Farmer Welander was informal and quite flexible in the size of the parcel he would sell, but not inclined to give anyone a bargain. Don and Virginia opted for a ten acre piece of land, and just as they had with the White Bear Lake house, put only a few hundred down. When their home closed the following March they paid the balance and moved to the new property.

In 1957 they bought another small parcel to improve access and in the 1980s, more land around the lake was acquired in order to make sure they "owned their view".

An early, somewhat generic drawing of a Usonian Automatic on a grid was provided by Taliesin and included two bedrooms and a studio, as Virginia requested. Most likely it was deemed too large and expensive to build, and it certainly was associated with a different piece of land, as the north orientation would not have fit the woodpile lake site. (Note the mis-spelling of the name, a common initial mistake people make.)

If at all possible we would like to have the house composed of limestone and wood, as both are fairly inexpensive here and easily obtainable. Is it possible to have a red brick floor - would seem so ever-lasting with cypress and stone?

We particularly want to emphasize that we have made all of our present furniture and will make all of the furniture for your house. Would it be possible for you to include in the furniture plans one of your outdoor picnic tables?

Don and I are so much more capable than the "Do-it-yourself" widely publicized trend suggests, that you can be sure we are quite capable and very sincere about doing a terrific job on something we are so en-thusiastic about. I feel confident we can do justice to one of your freest designs. Please let us know if we can help in any way by coming down to Taliesin again to see you.

Mr. Wright called from Taliesin to discuss the design. He said they had come to the con-clusion it was best if my parents built a "Usonian Automatic." Mr. Wright had developed this style in the 1930s, a simple and adaptable construction form on a grid using concrete blocks,

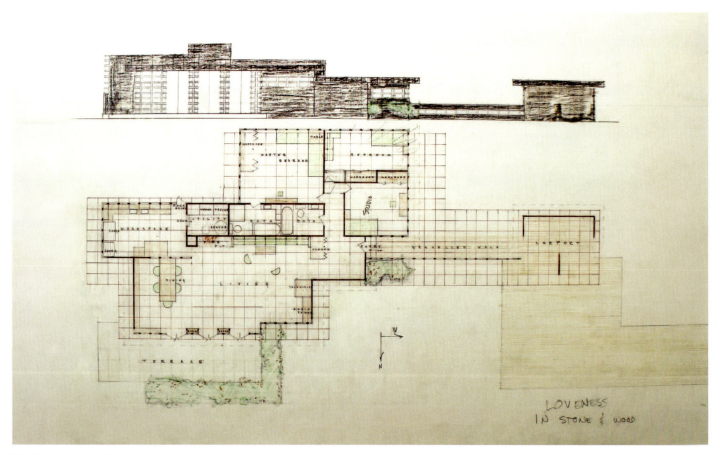

2707 So. Shore Boulevard
White Bear Lake 10, Minn.

Mr. Frank Lloyd Wright
Taliesin
Spring Green, Wisconsin

Dear Mr. Wright,

We are enclosing the photographs and the topographical map of the site. The area is about 6 acres of rolling wooded pastureland 15 miles from town. It is very secluded--cannot be seen from the road. The site requires a well and cesspool. There is about 6"of topsoil over sandy gravel. Don is already hauling limestone.

When not painting and working, reading, we spend much of our time listening to music, but imagine that somewhere there will be ample space in a bookshelf or closet for records, phonograph and speaker.

I am still in awe over the feeling of naturalness, spontaneity and shelter that Taliesin possesses. And it stimulates me even to think of living in a structure that can be so earthbound yet spiritual -

If we have overlooked any pertinent or vital information, please let us know.

                    Sincerely,

In early fall 1955, photos and topo drawings were sent to Taliesin, where Mr. Wright immediately approved the site. Work on the plans began shortly afterward.

Virginia Lovness
2707 South Shore Boulevard
White Bear Lake 10
Minnesota

Dear Mrs. Lovness: Your plans are well under way and it should not be too long before you will have blue prints of the complete working drawings and specifications.   Good News!!

TALIESIN WEST

                    Sincerely,
                    Eugene Masselink
                    Secretary to Frank Lloyd Wright

                              December 1st, 1955

Virginia's concern about having working drawings was answered by Gene Masselink in December from Taliesin West in Arizona.

bricks or "textile blocks" of textured or formed concrete with plywood and other simple, inexpensive materials. This suggestion caught my parents by surprise. Mother later wrote about the inital confusion and her subsequent emphatic reply.

> *I couldn't even think. After we hung up I asked Don if Mr. Wright was saying what I thought he was saying. Don said he was talking about perforated concrete blocks. I immediately called Mr. Wright back and asked if that's what he meant. He said, "Yes. You can spend the summer making the blocks and start on the building the following summer."*
> *I told Mr. Wright that I really loved rock. He answered that he understood but we couldn't afford to build with rock.*
> *"Isn't there any way that we can use rock?" I said.*
> *"No," he replied.*
> *Then I told him, "I won't live in it unless it's rock!"*
> *There was a hesitation but he finally said, "All right. Rock it is."*

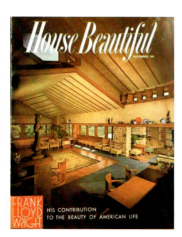

My mother wrote, "We were with Mr. Wright when the November, 1955 issue of House Beautiful came out. We were telling him how good it was and he said it was alright but had a 'bushel of advertising'. He also said how difficult it was for him to be 'going downstream' when his whole life he had been swimming upstream."

This insistence on using stone was only the first expression of the naiveté the young couple brought to their project. At that stage they still held a belief that they would hire a contractor and invest some sweat equity. Virginia had no idea about the effort and complication she was adding. With no experience in construction and no clear plan in her head about how the house would be built, the difference between using the lovely cut stone she had seen in other Wright houses and the simple bricks or concrete blocks that were a basis of the Usonian design must have seemed abstract at that moment. It's likely that looking over Mr. Wright's shoulder when they spoke initially, she sensed the solidity and permanence of the native rock walls at Taliesin, and felt how the other materials harmonized with the limestone. Or maybe she was just trying to butter up the old man who clearly was taken with this "spitfire" - as he later described her.

Whatever her intentions, the decision to build with rock would have effects she could never have foreseen, and present challenges that would bring her close to a breaking point, physically and emotionally, more than once.

Plans underway

With his approval of the site, to their surprise Mr. Wright started designing a house almost immediately. With many other clients he had a reputation of taking a very long time to produce plans, but not with the plans for our house. In September the presentation drawings arrived and my mother described them as "absolutely inspired". The plans were highly anticipated but the timing could not have been worse. When the package arrived my mother was in the hospital suffering from peritonitis, a painful infection of the abdominal wall, something that is often life-threatening. When Don brought the drawings to her in the hospital he laid them out on her bed. She remembers the moment well:

VIEW FROM NORTHWEST

H O U S E   F O R   M R.   AND   M R S.   D O N   L O V N E S S
WHITE BEAR LAKE MINNESOTA
F R A N K   L L O Y D   W R I G H T   A R C H I T E C T

The color original (copy below) was lost but a new drawing (above) was made years later.

A perspective drawing of the proposed plan from Taliesin (drawn by Jack Howe) was based on photos and topographic data of the property. It was common for Mr. Wright to design homes and buildings without having visited the site but unlike some properties that posed challenges with steep terrain or watercourses, the gentle contours of our pasture were easy to deal with.

While dramatic in its presentation, the drawing is short on detail but does show rock on the north end, as my mother insisted on having.

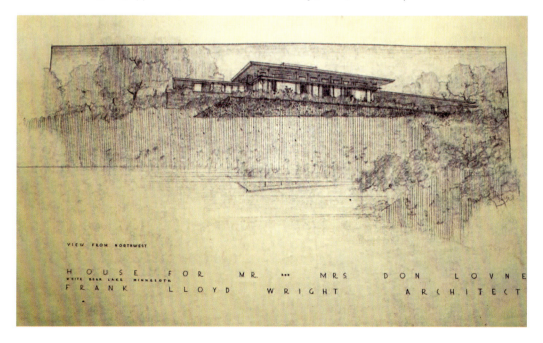

VIEW FROM NORTHWEST

H O U S E   F O R   M R   AND   M R S   D O N   L O V N E
WHITE BEAR LAKE MINNESOTA
F R A N K   L L O Y D   W R I G H T   A R C H I T E C T

I just cried and cried, it was so beautiful and unbelievable. A very large studio, forty feet long. The tall french doors that I had so admired that day with Mr. Wright on three sides. Two bedrooms, a high ceiling, huge fireplace and the whole design snuggled into the earth and looking like it was born there, overlooking Woodpile Lake. We asked Mr. Wright to go ahead with the working drawings, with no changes at all, no alterations whatsoever.

The only thing we told him is that we'd like to have working drawings so we could start in the spring. We were really cut for time because we had sold our house, bought property, and it was all just handshakes. No contracts. Mrs. Neils had told us, "Oh, you've got to wait a couple of years for those working drawings." And by gosh in March those drawings came and we just went out in the snow and started laying things out.

The drawings gave a tantalizing glimpse of what could be, but when four contractors were asked to bid on construction, two declined and the lowest of the other two was $83,000. At this point my father pored over the plans at work, determining material costs. After a few days of calculations it became clear the only way they could afford the house was to build it themselves. Many co-workers, all engineers and phDs, tried to dissuade him from the project, explaining that as an engineer it wasn't really socially acceptable to do common construction work. He had a bright future at 3M and it wouldn't look good for his advancement opportunities. But with a fearless naiveté and no building experience, they decided to press on, anxiously waiting for the spring thaw.

My mother's response to Mr. Wright, composed while bedridden, was still upbeat and enthusiastic. This is a transcription of the original note which was written in a shaky hand.

October 10, 1955
St. John's Hospital

Dear Mr. Wright,

Our plans arrived last week and we think they are the most beautiful in all the world. The day they arrived I was taken to the hospital and couldn't call to thank you right then. But I did get a chance to take a small look - how can we ever thank you for doing such a perfect home -

I'll call you when I get home and see if we can go over a few minor details on these before you leave for Arizona. Kindest personal regards to you.
      Sincerely,

      Virginia Lovness

P.S. I hope you will forgive the sad-looking penmanship, as I'm unable to sit up and write yet.

November 6, 1955
2707 So. Shore Boulevard
White Bear Lake 10, Minn.

Mr. Frank Lloyd Wright
Taliesin West
Box 157
Scottsdale, Arizona

Dear Mr. Wright,

We still can't believe our good fortune! Your plans for us are perfect!
We are very enthused about the house, interior and exterior, and do
believe we can keep close to our $15,000 figure by doing much ourselves;
also we would like a rough natural interior to complement the rock,
much like Taliesin North which we admire so.

The only alteration we can see is changing the studio to a studio-bedroom.
Our two daughters could have the other bedroom. We will leave everything
up to you.

There were a couple other small arrangements we were wondering about. We
spend several hours every day listening to records so we do need a place
in the living room for record equipment, record storage and speaker.

Then there is a fence for cattle around our land. We were wondering if a
car gate would not be a welcoming entry into the driveway. Also we do
enjoy eating outside; would it be possible to include an outdoor picnic
table with the furniture plans?

Again we thank you and hope you are enjoying the southern climate. We
have had our first real snow today so are hibernating with our books and
painting and music for a long cold winter up here.

                              Sincerely,

                              Virginia Lovness

We mailed the Preliminary Sketches back to you yesterday and hope they
arrived safely.

November 23, 1955
2707 So. Shore Boulevard
White Bear Lake 10, Minn.

Mr. Frank Lloyd Wright
Taliesin West
Box 157
Scottsdale, Arizona

Dear Mr. Wright,

Just a note to see how the working plans are progressing and let you know
the latest developments up here.

The people who bought our house have possession March 1 and we can live
here until then. Then we intend to move into a trailer at our new site to
expedite building. We are very hopeful that we can have the working plans
before then in order to study them have electricity brought in, well dug,
etc. to make our temporary quarters feasible. Also, building materials are
much more readily available in the early spring before all the housing
projects get in full swing. We have one more obstical--road restrictions
go on about the first of May so all the rock should be delivered and the
slab laid before then.

Incidentally, in your plans, we loved the ornamentation in the eaves and
clerestory windows. I hope you can repeat it in the furniture, wooden
screen that separates the kitchen area from the living area, the gate, etc.
Somehow, all that detail art work, so expensive and difficult to have done
today, makes the difference in a house being complete and finished to its
fullest. The detailed art work throughout the house we will particularly
enjoy doing ourselves, and can be our winter project after we get the house
closed in.

Do you think we can get started by March 1? Could Mr. Masselink drop us a
note to let us know how the plans are progressing?

Best wishes to you.

                              Sincerely,

                              Virginia Lovness

By November the near-final sketches were in my parents' hands.
Even at this early stage a pattern was beginning to develop, where
Virginia would sweetly ask for additional items. Some she got, some
she didn't. The bedrooms and "studio" noted in this letter were never
combined; Virginia's painting area was the living room. A record
player spot was later included in the plan, near the entrance to the
main bedroom, with record storage beneath. A gate was designed
and built years later, after the driveway access had been moved away
from the farmer's property. Ironically, what would seem to be the
simplest request never came to fruition. We never did have a picnic
table.

Two weeks later, a note of desperation has crept into her letter and
she makes a compelling case for getting the plans before spring truly
arrives. Road restrictions are in place during the time that the ground
thaws in the spring, when the moisture trapped in the frozen ground
allows it to be soft and pavement is liable to shift and crack under the
weight of heavy trucks - like those carrying rock and cement supplies. For
builders in Minnesota it is a real concern.

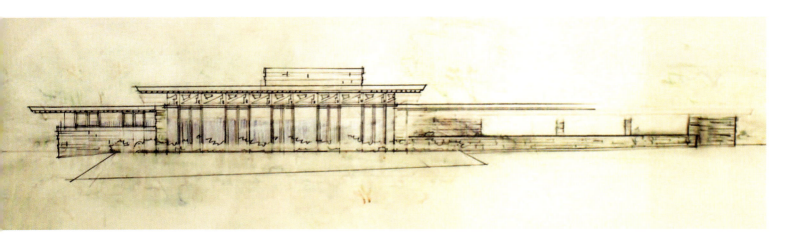

West (above), north (right) and south elevation sketches accompanied preliminary plan views. Virgina sent a hand-written thank you to Mr. Wright mentioning that she would like to change a "few minor details". In fact, she and Don were very happy with the plan. After making it clear to Mr. Wright that native limestone was what she wanted, she sent preliminary plans out for bid to stonemasons for the rock work. The least expensive estimate to build their house came back at $83,000. At the time, the median price for home in Minnesota was around $10,000. She said later, in something of an understatement, "That was a little steep considering we had bought the rock, and we had the land. So we just went ahead and started building it ourselves."

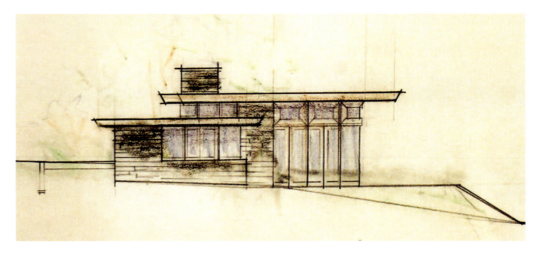

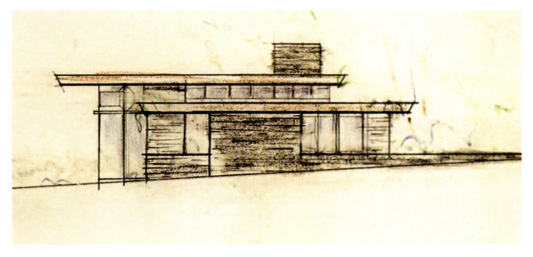

February 15, 1956
2707 So. Shore Boulevard
White Bear Lake 10, Minn.

Mr. Eugene Masselink
Taliesin West
Box 157
Scottsdale, Arizona

Dear Mr. Masselink,

We hate to bother you again, but we're wondering if you can
let us know how the plans are progressing now.

Yesterday we finished hauling 150 ton of rock to our site. We'd
like to bring the electricity in and have the well dug, but are
stimied without bulldozing. We have to leave our present house the
first part of March and living in the trailer will be pretty
rough without well and electricity!

Road restrictions also can set in anytime around March 1 and out in
the country where we are really can tie us up after that. We had
the whole site plowed but has been rough going with so much snow.
I'll bet we are the only people who ever built a Wright house that
built under such circumstances! Wish we were in a more temperate
climate like you this time of year.

If at all possible can you give us any idea when the plans will
arrive?

Thank you for taking the time to answer our letters. We'd certainly
like to have you come to see us next summer and see this fine site
of ours and how beautifully Mr. Wright's house will belong to the
rolling hills and ponds and oak trees. Needless to say, we can
hardly wait to get started!

Sincerely,

Virginia Lovness

In February, anxious to get a start, she sent a letter to Gene Masselink. Enthusiasm for the project was now tempered by the reality of weather, having to soon move out of their White Bear Lake home, and so much to do before construction could even begin.

March 5, 1956
2707 So. Shore Boulevard
White Bear Lake 10, Minn.

Mr. Frank Lloyd Wright
Taliesin West
Box 157
Scottsdale, Arizona

Dear Mr. Wright:

We were delighted with our working plans. I can't thank you enough
for sending them right on schedule. If we had waited many more months
for them, we still would have understood how busy you were with more
important projects. We shall always think of you as Democratic in the
strictest sense of the word!

The blueprints are very complete and very enlightening. Don says he
shall have no trouble following them, tho it is going to take some
studying. We particularly like the ceiling pattern, the 2x12 mullions
by the doors, the phonograph space and are delighted by the table
design. May we also have chair and gate design? Also the rest of the
carport as Don thinks now we may as well put the roof on the entire
structure all at once, completing all rock work this summer.

We'll contact you at Spring Green as problems arise.

Very sincerely,

Virginia Lovness

The lantern design is a Masterpiece! As is each and every detail as we
delve into the plans!

Enclosed is check for $800.

The working drawings arrived in early March with a bill for them. In this note, a follow-up to the invoice sent March 1st, she mentions that Mr. Wright is the most democratic of men, something she would repeat many times over the years. Something else she would repeat is requests for more designs.

THE PERSONAL ARCHITECTURAL SERVICES OF FRANK LLOYD WRIGHT are available to clients for a fee of ten percent of the cost of the completed building which invariably includes the planting of the grounds and the major furnishings considered as part of the building scheme. The fee is the same for a million dollar project or for a low-cost dwelling. The fee is divided into three parts as follows:

1   5% of proposed cost of the building payable when preliminary studies are presented to the client. These, however, subsequent to original payment, may be modified without additional charge until satisfactory to client and architect.

2   4% additional for the working drawings and specifications payable when, in the architect's estimation, they are complete and ready to be presented for bids but with the understanding that should the proposed building costs be more than the client is willing to incur, the architect will do his best to so modify the drawings as to bring costs within reason. If the project is abandoned the architect's fee, minus the fee for supervision, is to be paid by the client.

3   1% additional to complete the fee of ten percent which includes the architect's **supervision** only is payable from time to time during construction or when the building is completed. Final adjustment of the fee to accord with the total cost of the completed building bringing the architect's final fee to ten percent of cost of completed building (furniture and planting included) is to be made when requested by the architect. The client in accepting the architect's services agrees that no changes in connection with the project shall be made unless authorized in writing by the architect. The architect's decision in these matters shall be final and binding upon the parties to this agreement. Plans and details are instruments of service, therefore remain the property of the architect to be returned to him upon demand.

In addition to supervision by the architect, superintendence satisfactory to architect and client, if so desired, may be arranged at the client's expense. Also traveling expenses incurred by the architect or his agent in direct connection with this work are to be paid from time to time on architect's certificate.

.   .   .   .

The architect, where general contractors are not desirable or available, will undertake to itemize mill work and material for the building at cost—let contracts to subcontractors for piece work and, so far as possible, eliminate the general contractor by sending a qualified apprentice of the Taliesin Fellowship at the proper time to take charge, do necessary shopping and hold the entire building operation together. This apprentice will check cost layouts, bids, etc., refer proposed changes to the architect and endeavor to bring the work to successful completion. Lodging and board of this apprentice is to be arranged and paid for by the owner. The necessary traveling expense of the apprentice is to be paid by the owner who also pays the apprentice the sum of $50.00 per week for his services so long as the apprentice is, in the architect's estimation, required on the work. This arrangement may save most of a general contractor's fee. But both client and architect are better assured of the results of such simplifications of detail and extensions of space as characterize the new methods of building we employ.

.   .   .   .

Before the architect proceeds to design any building an **accurate** topographical survey of the property showing all natural slopes and features such as rock outcroppings, trees, etc., roads, neighboring buildings and service lines for water, sewer, gas and light together with as complete a list of the client's requirements as is feasible, should be on record. Dwelling-houses upon urban lots are usually not accepted. Acreage is indispensable to the type of dwelling we like to build.

The services of Frank Lloyd Wright are exclusively owned by The Frank Lloyd Wright Foundation.

T A L I E S I N

Mr. Don Lovness: On account for Preliminary Sketches according to terms above:

5% of $20,000.00, proposed cost of house $1,000.00

The Frank Lloyd Wright Foundation
Frank L₁oyd Wright   Architect
Taliesin. Spring Green. Wisconsin   October 7th, 1955

type of dwelling we like to build.

The services of Frank Lloyd Wright are exclusively owned by The Frank Lloyd Wright Foundation.

T A L I E S I N

To Mr. and Mrs. Don Lovness: On account for Working Drawings of house according to terms above:

4% of $20,000.00, proposed cost of house . . . $800.00

The Frank Lloyd Wright Foundation
Frank L₁oyd Wright   Architect
Taliesin West.Box 157.Scottsdale.Arizona.March 1st, 1956

Check mailed March 4, 1956

When the White Bear Lake house was sold, a good portion of the proceeds went to pay for architectural services, the inital charges (as noted, above opposite, preliminary studies) being five percent of the construction cost, which by now was acknowledged as realistically being $20,000. Working drawings (below, opposite) were an additional four percent which was paid on receipt just as construction began the following March. At that time, Mr. Wright signed and endorsed the checks himself.

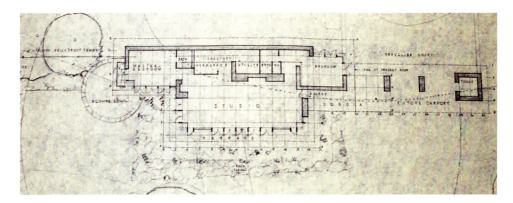

Working drawings included a plan view of the house grid and the position of pillars, whose construction would occupy my parents for two summers. Wright originally envisioned a plunge pool at the north end of the house, and specified a layout for a rock garden surrounding the terrace. Initially the carport was slated for "future" construction, giving them the option to delay some of the work until later.

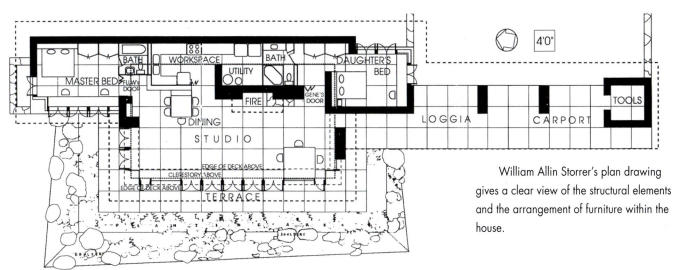

William Allin Storrer's plan drawing gives a clear view of the structural elements and the arrangement of furniture within the house.

The longest journey, as they say, starts with a single step, and that step was to buy a trailer to live in, shelter from the elements while our new home rose, stone by stone. "It was one of the first trailers ever made," my mother would say. An old, small one-bedroom affair that was stored in White Bear Lake then dragged to the Woodpile Lake property as the snow was still melting in early 1956. Other necessary improvements to the land immediately were a well and electrical service. A septic system would come later but at the outset a donated outhouse was our bathroom. It didn't have a door and my father, with his usual gruff sense of humor would tell people, "If you want some privacy put a grocery bag over your head!" After a year or so a door was installed, a bar room-style swinging door, which only made the outhouse look that much more ridiculous.

The next order of business was building materials for the project. Southeastern Minnesota's bedrock is mostly limestone and dolostone (limestone with the mineral dolomite), similar to what was available locally in Sauk County, Wisconsin when Taliesin was built. A quarry just across the St. Croix River from Stillwater in Houlton, Wisconsin was a source for the cream-colored limestone my mother loved, run by a man named Clarence Jonk who delivered 150 tons of "wall stone" to the property early in the year. Ten dollars of his February invoice was for "snow plowing" to get to the site. At six dollars a ton, the young couple stretched their budget by paying out $900. As we moved onto our new property that spring, almost a tenth of the entire budget was lying there in a huge pile, more of a liability than an asset.

Harvey Moulter, a local excavating contractor, brought in gravel and sand and spent a day with his bulldozer to build a driveway, at $8 an hour. Martell Well Drilling added $850 to the project's cost, and all before construction even began.

If that mountain of rock wasn't daunting enough, it was joined by ten yards of gravel and ten yards of sand, each of those being a full dump truck load. White Bear Lumber and Coal would have a steady stream of delivery trucks bringing hundreds of sacks of Portland and Masonry cement, ten or twenty at a time over the next two years. A bag of cement was not the kind of thing you could leave out in the elements, and at the start we had no storage shed to protect it so only "just enough" was kept on hand.

With the building materials in place and excitement about starting at a fever pitch, the great adventure began. My mother describes those first days and weeks:

We surveyed the site, laid it out and decided we would start with the fireplace footing. We dug it by hand, 21 feet x 5-1/2 feet x 12 inches. We had no tools, we mixed the cement by hand in a box. I can remember when we finished I dragged myself out of the footing and laid down on the ground. I didn't think I could ever get up again. But it got worse.

The next Saturday we were going to start building the fireplace, the core of our new Wright home. It was a momentous occasion; we were inspired and renewed. Our daughters cheerfully ran around in their stiff new blue jeans, thrilled at their new country freedom. I, being the artist of the family, would pattern and lay the rock while strong Father mixed cement and chiseled.

The mountain of raw rock slowly began to form the fireplace. Steel beams were braced in place as the overhanging lintel was built. During the hot summer months the working uniform for these two masons was as little clothing as possible. Note the lack of steel-toed shoes on my mother's feet. During the hard work, they only had to glance west over the lake to be reminded why they were doing this.

Don said, *"Well, let's get started. What do you want me to do?"* expecting me to supervise.

"I don't know," I moaned. And that was the understatement of the year. For half an hour neither of us could do anything.

Don then started piling rocks, one on top of another, with layers of mortar in between. The rock from our local quarry was not like layer cake sections, but more like boulders of all sizes, and had to be chiseled so its horizontal edges were flat along with its sides, which all had to be at right angles to the face. Upon presenting Don with these facts he said, *"Absolutely not. We'll never get done."*

I argued. He was adamant. There was no turning back. There was the land and the mountain of rock, that wreck of a trailer and two little daughters. It was more than overwhelming to look at that huge pile of stones and the piles of sand and gravel. It was defeating. There were tears, remorse, accusations of who had been the most stupid and who had gotten us into this mess. What could we do?

While we were still arguing fate stepped in, once again, in the form of Franz Aust. Franz drove up to see how we were progressing. He asked Don, *"What are you doing?"*

"Building a fireplace" was Don's reply.

"But where are your tools? Your pitching chisels?"

Don told him, *"We don't have any, just the wooden box and a hoe to mix mortar."*

Franz said to us, *"Don't do anything! Just wait for me."* And he rushed off and bought a few of the necessary chiseling tools for us.

After the fireplace had progressed a few feet we sent photos to Taliesin and spoke to Mr. Wright who asked if all of our rock was this thick. We didn't have the narrower, paver-like pieces that were used for projections at Taliesin. Our quarry just didn't produce rock of that type. He told us he liked our rock work and that we should continue using it to its *"best advantage"*, meaning large, thick projections.

At every stage we usually contacted Mr. Wright, calling him at Spring Green station-to-station in the evening when long distance rates were cheaper. (Taliesin West didn't have a phone at that time, only a radio for communication.) There were many calls that took Mr. Wright from his dinner table at the house in Taliesin but he always knew exactly how to remedy any problem. He never had to go to the drafting room at Hillside to check our plans.

Developing a pattern

As the spring and summer wore on, they became more proficient, developing a work pattern that was intense, but efficient for the situation. Up at 4 or 5 every morning, they would lay rock until Don had to go to work at 3M. They had purchased a used cement mixer for $60, and before leaving he would mix a huge batch of mortar that my mother could use to lay more rock. She would lay it up as fast as she could, racing the clock before it set up by itself. Then there would be a little time to attend to us, the girls, and maybe get supplies. When Don rushed home from work they would continue laying rock until 11 or 12 at night, working under the light of a few bare bulbs, swatting at the bugs. Mother remembers that part with no fondness:

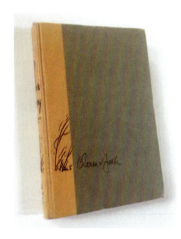

Building a Wright house connected my parents with many interesting and unusual people over the years. The man who delivered their "mountain of rock", Clarence Jonk, was more than just a quarryman. His books of poetry were published while in college and in 1964 he wrote a fascinating book about his adventures living on a home-built raft on the Mississippi during the Depression.

There was nothing fancy and no protruding courses on this side, as this section would be where the furnace, well tank and electrical panels would be located. The "window" at right was the cutout for a new oven.

Photos like this, of the back of the fireplace, were sent regularly to Mr. Wright. He responded encouragingly:

"Dear Eminences, Stonework good but suggest more horizontal and larger protruding courses. All very level. FLW."

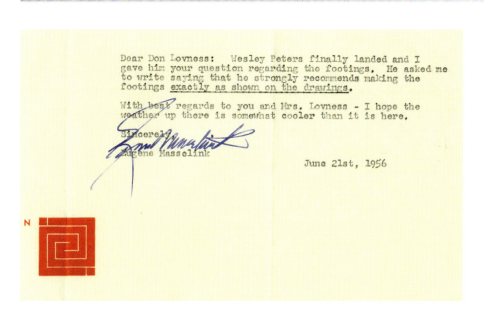

Dear Don Lovness: Wesley Peters finally landed and I gave him your question regarding the footings. He asked me to write saying that he strongly recommends making the footings exactly as shown on the drawings.

With best regards to you and Mrs. Lovness - I hope the weather up there is somewhat cooler than it is here.

Sincerely,
Eugene Masselink

June 21st, 1956

My parents' inexperience as masons must have prompted a question and most likely Mr. Wright was in New York at the time. Gene Masselink replied via letter.

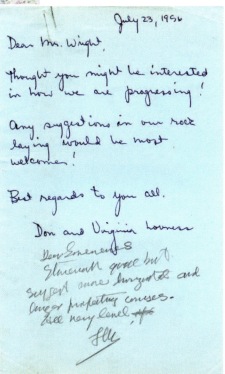

July 23, 1956

Dear Mr. Wright,

thought you might be interested in how we are progressing!

Any suggestions in our rock laying would be most welcome!

Best regards to you all.

Don and Virginia Lovness

Dear Eminences
Stonework good but suggest more horizontal and larger protruding courses.
All very level.

FLW

Finally we were able to buy a cement mixer! Working late at night the mosquitoes were fierce. I don't remember ever having a repellent that was good enough. Some nights they were so bad I'd be thinking it might be better to just jump off the scaffolding and get it over with.

Aside from the rock itself there was steel to support the lintel, firebrick on the back wall, clay flue liners, a damper, plumbing venting and electrical conduit built into the fireplace. Between the front and back walls, the void needed to be filled. That's where Ty and I came in, filling our little beach buckets with rubble from the chiseled stone. This was tossed into the open area with cement to make a solid center. The whole process was described in Mother's notes:

We found that between us Don and I couldn't lift many of the larger rocks, so we would "walk" them up a 2x10, twelve-foot-long plank. Then there was always the problem of keeping everything level. With such rough rock, using a level wasn't really much help. So I'd have to step back and eyeball our progress regularly. As we built higher and higher it became more of a problem, climbing down off the scaffolding to check, then back up to continue work.

I am deathly afraid of heights but there was nothing I could do but be up on the scaffolding when necessary. I would call down to Don what size rock was needed and he would find one, chisel it and lift it up to me. Once I asked Don for a 5" x 20" rock and he kept lifting up the wrong size, telling me, "Make it fit!" I began throwing mortar down at him and he retaliated in kind, just as some friends drove up. I wonder if they thought we'd ever finish at that rate.

When it came time to do the smoke chamber, Don was too big to fit in the space, so he lowered me down on a rope to cement in the chamber - about the size of a coffin, and it felt like it. Watching this, both little girls cried; they didn't think their mommy would ever get out!

Shortly after we started laying rock an architecture grad from the University of Minnesota stopped by and said he was interested in working with us. We told him the reason we were building the studio ourselves was because we couldn't afford to hire anyone, and we couldn't pay him. He told us he didn't need to get paid if we would just feed him. We could do that! He set up a tent. It seemed like another act of fate.

But after a few weeks of chiseling and laying rock with him it became evident it wasn't going to work. Everything went fine when Don was with us on weekends, early mornings and evenings. But our helper would put electrical outlets in upside down or lay rocks in a weird pattern or with too small projections. It just wasn't acceptable. Don would have to chisel out the mistakes every night. It's very difficult to let someone go who's volunteering their services - to fire someone who's working for free. But we had to do it.

The "helper", according to my mother, had somehow divined the mysteries of the universe and was writing a book about it. He had explained all this to her and then said, "Don't tell anybody!" After being let go, he was disappointed but still fascinated with Wright's work so he decided to go to the source - Taliesin. My father called Gene Masselink to warn him of this

Building masonry skills took time but my parents caught on fairly quickly. Raking the joints was tedious work but Don discovered that an automotive tool made the job a little simpler and faster. This drum brake adjusting tool worked great!

By mid-summer 1956 we had developed a routine for life in a construction site. The trailer was our sleeping quarters, and mending and other chores could be done on the "porch". Baths were either in the lake or in a bucket, and the rest of the time Ty and I would keep busy chasing the goat, playing on our swing set or just amusing ourselves while Mother worked.

strange person but Gene said, "It's too late, Mr. Wright already let him come." It wasn't long, however, before he wore out his welcome there as well. He wasn't the last unusual character to be attracted to our project.

Another complication in building the fireplace arose as they studied the plans for the kitchen. As in almost every Wright home, the kitchen was little more than a galley, a place to cook, clean and store dishes, nothing like the huge areas in today's homes. Even so, my mother was keenly attuned to how it should look, and the long "aisle" between cabinets was narrow enough that an open oven door would be a hazard. It was resolved with a phone call, as Mother relates:

Our old porcelain stove was going to be too shabby to put in the kitchen when the time came. A cooktop burner would have plenty of room in the long countertop, but where to put an oven (even if we could afford it)? We didn't want to ruin the long line of the cabinet doors with an oven hanging down. So again I called Mr. Wright and told him about our dilemma.

When he knew it was me calling, Mr. Wright always answered the phone not with, "Hello," but, "How much money do we have to work with today?"

I told him we might be able to swing the purchase of a new countertop burner and even an oven, but where would we place the oven? Immediately he said, "That's no problem. We'll put it in the fireplace!" We would never have thought of that, but it was a perfect solution. And as ever, Mr. Wright didn't need to reference the plans; he had them in his head.

By late summer 1956 the fireplace and much of the back wall was almost complete. There now was a tool shed to store bags of cement and supplies; it also housed the well and was our electrical "service center". Our trailer was cozy enough but it didn't have a place to take a bath, so all through the summer we would swim in the lake or Mother would warm well water in a bucket for us. (We never used the terms "Mom" or "Dad". From the time Ty and I got past baby talk it was always "Mother" and "D", or "Big D" as we sometimes called our father.)

Ty and I had a Siamese kitten and a baby goat. We would play king of the mountain with the goat on top of the gravel and sand piles, but he usually won. Mother told the story of when winter came and we brought him in the trailer and put him in bed with us. He relaxed and got comfortable, then all of a sudden started regurgitating his food. We didn't know that goats are ruminants like cows, and chew their cud. Out he went, to remain an outdoor pet until one evening much later, unbeknown to Ty and me, he ended up as dinner.

Other animals were present as well. The agreement with Mr. Welander was that he would be able to graze his cows on our property, so all during construction there would be cows coming and going. According to Mother, Welander did all the milking so the cows were unaccustomed to women and they would give chase whenever she got close to them. The good news was they kept the grasses short but you always had to watch where you were walking.

D worked day and night, literally, but there still was time for an occasional break in the action to hug his daughters.

Sunday was not always a day of rest for the family, but sometimes we would dress up for a visit with friends or family. When my grandparents visited one weekend in 1956, Mother wore a bright Gypsy outfit. She reveled in wearing bright colors after a week of hauling cement and laying rock.

Friends from 3M would sometimes stop by after church, as this family did in 1957, as the framing was just beginning. Some only visited once, discovering that dress shoes were not the best idea, even in the middle of our "living room".

Custom Design-Engineering existed mostly on paper, but it allowed my parents access to wholesale prices.

Below, being serious about music and records, D the chemist developed a line of record-care products in conjunction with 3M.

For an out-of-the way place, there were a lot of people who were interested in seeing what was going on at our construction site. Some of D's friends at work would visit and even help but another group of skeptics at 3M were making bets on whether my parents would ever finish. Among the visitors to show up unannounced was a man in a suit who knocked on the trailer door, and said he was looking for a company called Custom Design Engineering. He apologized, assuming he was at the wrong address and stated that he was from Dun and Bradstreet. Mother explained that was their company, showed him the plans and took him around, enthusiastically describing what they were doing. He was impressed, and very gracious. He told Mother that enterprising young couples like themselves would often be successful - and gave Custom a triple-A rating. Mother wrote about other visitors:

People would come out to see the place. I'm afraid we were already a little notorious. When I was up on the scaffold I could see them driving around our little lake and I'd think, Oh, no! You can't stop working. Later there were the little foreign sports cars driving around Woodpile Lake. They were usually more architecture students from the U of M who had heard about the Frank Lloyd Wright house. They would always have interesting comments to make and questions about a woman building a Wright house. As the pillars began to form it was a little easier to explain: rock walls inside and out, wood ceiling and framework to hold the french doors, that's it! Oh yes, and the cement floor. Later, people would kick the floor and say, "What do you think they're going to do with this? Carpet it?" Sometimes when I was up on the scaffold they'd talk about the strange house as if I wasn't there.

Other visitors came, especially on weekends. Our favorites were the local farmers; we could almost hear their thoughts as they shook their heads over these city slickers who should have stayed put. Several times we heard the comment, "But I thought they were building a house!"

Another skeptic was my Grandfather Lovness. Al would come out on Sundays, along with friends and other sight-seers, kind of a ritual. He had been concerned about the fireplace hood, believing it would never be supported on its own. "I don't know, that will never stand up!" he'd say. It was held up by concrete blocks while the rest of the fireplace took shape. One Sunday afternoon D casually walked over to the posts and knocked them out with a sledge-hammer as Al looked on. "I thought he might have a heart attack right there," my father said as he would tell this, one of his favorite building stories. The lintel, of course, was perfect. No cracks then or now.

There was one problem, however - at least in my mother's mind:

When we started on the lintel Don put in a rock that wasn't so nice. I said it should project, but he said it can't, there isn't anything to hold it. But it always bothered me and the further up we went there were more arguments about the design. He doesn't know anything and I had to have my way!

As we got toward the ceiling it became perfectly obvious that this rock had to project. But he wouldn't

With the flue and smokebox complete, the fireplace underwent some testing. Here Mother takes a break on the shelf that would get much use over the years, a cozy spot by the fire. Note the notches at top for ceiling beams and the horizontal slot at right, where a wooden beam would frame the doorway to the south bedroom. They included a whimsical triangular rock in the design, something that would generate many comments.

take it out, saying, "If you take that rock out the whole fireplace is sitting on it. You can't. We're stuck with it." But I couldn't live with it. So one rainy day I got a friend to come over and he chiseled it out, working under a tarp in the rain. We put a few little temporary stones in its place. Don came home and we yelled, "Surprise!" I don't think I've ever seen him cut a rock faster to fit. But now we have patterning the way it should be.

My father was one of those men who just intuitively knew how to do things. A chemical engineering degree gave him a good grounding in subjects like elements and molecules, but beyond that he had a sense of how pretty much everything worked, and he wasn't afraid to try his hand at anything. He explained, many years later, "No matter what you did yourself you could buy the tool to do it with, and then throw the tool out afterwards and you're better off than hiring someone to do it." At the same time, he knew his limitations and recognized that expediency was sometimes more important than saving money. Plumber LeRoy Smith was called in to do some welding (at $2.50 an hour) and supply parts for the heating and plumbing system incorporated into the fireplace and its foundation. Electrical work however, seemed simple to him - just a matter of using common sense. But common sense sometimes is at odds with bureaucracy. He related this story in an interview with Taliesin years later:

When you think back, we must have been nuts. We wired the place ourselves and the inspector was nasty. Those inspectors were part of the union, and if you wire your own house they look for everything. He red-tagged the job, saying, "You can't get electricity until you re-wire the thing, and I'm not going to tell you what's wrong, either. You've got to go through the whole thing and find out for yourself."

So I thought about it for a little while and finally said, "The hell with it." I went out and jumpered the whole system. They didn't have a meter on it yet, so we were getting free electricity. About a week and half went by and the Northern States Power meter reader came by, making his rounds. Virginia was the only one home. He went up and looked at the jumpered wires and he ran out of the yard! This happened in the morning and by two o'clock in the afternoon there was a meter in place. The inspector didn't come back, and this happened several times with inspectors. The Township was going to do something to us one time and I went and looked at how much money they had in the kitty and there wasn't enough to sue anybody. So I went ahead and did it anyway.

The next year, when the house was nearing completion, an electrical inspector did come back, and was no less hard-nosed about the situation. My mother told this part of the tale:

The electrical inspector came to the trailer door and I said, "Won't you come in and have a cup of coffee?" He told me we would have to take all the built-in light boxes out of the upper valances because of the temperature allowed inside them, and we would have to have more outlets. Apparently by the time we started and the time we finished the code had changed. He said we'd have to tear down the fireplace and put in so many more outlets.

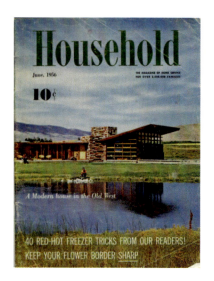

The June, 1956 *Household* magazine featured a Wright house on its cover. It was the Quintin Blair home near Cody, Wyoming, finished three years earlier. Seeing this feature in a national magazine must have been a shot of adrenaline for my parents while they were in the midst of construction. Years later they visited the Blairs.

Hard at work, my sister and I help Mother by collecting stone chips as the goat looks on. My mother may have been the only mason around who wore sandals, a tube halter top, and short shorts on the job.

"We can't tear the fireplace down!" I said

"Well, you could do something artistic with conduit," was his answer.

In the end he insisted we put in a dozen or so outlets, high up above the valance near the lights, where you can't reach them, to meet the requirements. We wouldn't possibly use them, ever, but we didn't have enough money to battle so we just went along with this idiotic plan.

That first summer was one of intense work and good luck to boot, considering the type of work they were doing for 12 hours each day. There was little illness to set them back and no disasters, although my mother did tell of one close call:

Nearing fall the fireplace was finished. All that rock, and only a beginning! We worked even harder - if that was possible - on the long back wall of the studio. There was only one accident during the two years we worked on that rock pile. I was putting on the top layer of rock on the back wall; the cement was still wet. I slipped off the scaffolding and fell backwards, grabbing at the top rocks to hold on. They immediately came loose and fell. Just then Don was coming by with a wheelbarrow and he caught me before I hit the ground and the rocks crushed me. It had to be fate, once again.

We worked until a fierce snow storm came and our mortar would freeze. That put a stop to rock work for the season. Winter, however, was a welcome break. Our oldest daughter Lonnie started kindergarten, so Ty and I were enjoying our tiny trailer. I'd haul water from the well in our tool shack, boil it on our two-burner stove and give Ty and Lonnie a sponge bath. Tea and baking powder biscuits with honey was what we served to anyone who stopped by. If we were invited to a party, I'd accept on the condition that our hosts would let me take a bath there before the festivities!

Winter furniture projects

During that first winter I started kindergarten. Mother would walk me to the bus stop, which was at the end of our long driveway. There was no building going on at the site; we were just occupied keeping the snow and cold at bay. By this time there was ongoing discussion with Mr. Wright and the people at Taliesin about how to furnish the house, even though we were a long way from needing tables and chairs. While my parents were visiting Taliesin over a weekend Mother asked for high-backed chairs for the dining room table. Mr. Wright suggested that they use Danish, as his son had done. He said his furniture wasn't very good and that high-backed chairs were old-fashioned, the style going all the way back to his Robie house in 1910. My mother argued that they would be perfect for the high-ceilinged room, and she didn't want Danish. When Mr. Wright didn't respond to that, she assumed the matter was closed, but later he seemed to change his mind, came over and whispered to her, "We won't call them old-fashioned, we'll call them regal!"

Unlike my mother, D was never a slave to fashion, especially in his choice of work clothing. Considering that these photos were taken a year apart there's a startling similarity. It's the same hat and pipe; maybe even the same pants. If so, I hope they got washed occasionally.

This photo shows the beginning of framing during the second summer, and one of the vertical members attached to a stone pillar at the north end of the living room. The plumbing behind him served both the kitchen and my parents' bedroom. Where D is standing, his beloved hi-fi system would live in a custom-built cabinet, tucked into an L-shaped pillar. That pillar presented special challenges and seemed to take forever, according to my mother. The rock had to be faced top, bottom and two sides for every other piece.

Note the joints in the foreground have yet to be raked, something that needed to be done after the mortar had begun to set, but not yet hardened. Timing was everything.

Winter put a halt to all work except furniture building, through the kindness of friends.

He sent table designs that were based on the house's four-foot module. There was one large work table in the studio (living room) area, and two dining tables to be used together in the dining room. Designs for four hassocks also arrived. When a coffee table design came Mr. Wright asked how Mother liked it. She said it was a perfect shape although maybe a little small for the size of the living room. He agreed immediately, and a similar but larger design was sent. None of the designs were unique to our house; like many of Wright's creations they were based on or simply copies of pervious ideas. They fit perfectly into the space, however.

During that winter a golden opportunity arose. A number of 3M engineers and managers lived on or near White Bear Lake, where there were enclaves of upper-income homes. One of those belonged to friends of my father's. Mother tells it:

Some friends of ours from 3M were going on a three-week cruise to South America. They asked if we would be their guests in their newly-redecorated home in Mahtomedi during that time. That seemed like such a tremendous offer, especially since they had no children of their own and we had two small daughters. And Don could use their shop and tools to build our furniture while we were there.

We worked night and day for those three weeks and got the large work table, the double dining room tables and the eight high-back chairs along with four hassocks built. We also sanded and varnished them. When our friends returned we had cleaned every inch of the house because of the sawdust. They were kind to say it had never been so clean.

We then we were able to store the furniture in another friend's attic until we could finish the house, which would take all the next summer and well into fall.

The three-foot wide coffee table was joined by a larger work table of the same design, situated near the front door. That table became Mother's painting and sewing table.

We hunkered down for the remainder of winter, anxiously waiting for the cold to subside. The raw pile of stones had been transformed into a sturdy hearth and with a back wall in place—even under the snow— we could just envision what was to be. It still took faith to believe it could all happen, but Mother and D must have felt like veteran masons at this point. Spring could not come soon enough.

COFFEE TABLE
HOUSE FOR MR. AND MRS. DON LOVNESS
WHITE BEAR LAKE, MINNESOTA
FRANK LLOYD WRIGHT ARCHITECT

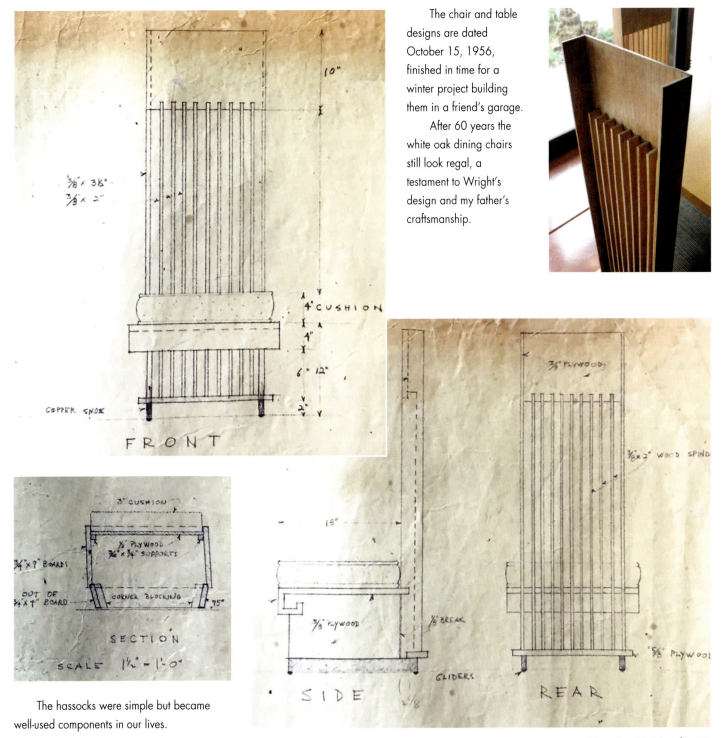

The chair and table designs are dated October 15, 1956, finished in time for a winter project building them in a friend's garage.

After 60 years the white oak dining chairs still look regal, a testament to Wright's design and my father's craftsmanship.

The hassocks were simple but became well-used components in our lives.

My mother had originally asked for a separate studio room for painting and other art pursuits. That idea was quickly shelved, however, after the first rough drawing showed an extra room would be too costly. The solution was to make the large main room into a dining-living-studio space with a work table for her.

While she had often painted huge non-objective pieces on canvas, now, with limited space for work and even less for display on the rock walls of the new home, Mother had to be content with small watercolors and oils, often painted plein air.

The easel design was a consolation prize, kind of an inside joke with Mr. Wright. Almost useless as a painting easel, it could be used to display art but even in that form it had limitations, being so low.

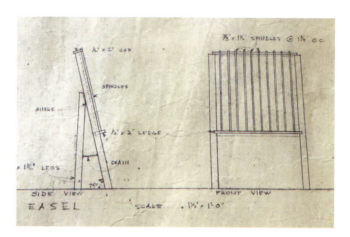

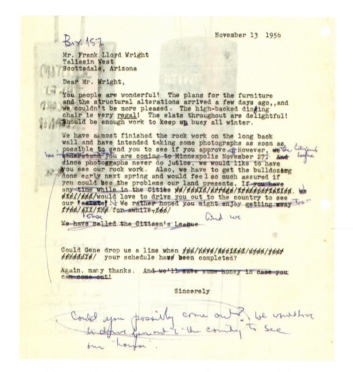

November 13 1956

Mr. Frank Lloyd Wright
Taliesin West
Scottsdale, Arizona

Dear Mr. Wright,

You people are wonderful! The plans for the furniture and the structural alterations arrived a few days ago,,and we couldn't be more pleased. The high-backed dining chair is very regal! The slats throughout are delightful! Should be enough work to keep us busy all winter.

We have almost finished the rock work on the long back wall and have intended taking some photographs as soon as possible to send you to see if you approve. However, we understand you are coming to Minneapolis November 27. And since photographs never do justice, we would like to have you see our rock work. Also, we have to get the bulldozing done early next spring and would feel so much assured if you could see the problems our land presents. If you have anytime while in the Cities we would love to drive you out to the country to see our "estate". We rather hoped you might enjoy getting away for awhile too.

We have called the Citizen's League

Could Gene drop us a line when your schedule has been completed?

Again, many thanks. And we'll have some honey in case you can come out!

Sincerely

November 13, 1956

Mr. Frank Lloyd Wright
Taliesin West
Scottsdale, Arizona

Dear Mr. Wright,

You people are wonderful! The plans for the furniture and structural alterations arrived a few days ago and we couldn't be more pleased. The high-backed dining chair is very regal! The slats throughout are delightful! Should be enough work to keep us busy all winter.

We have almost finished the rock work on the long back wall and have intended taking some photographs as soon as possible to send you to see if you approve.

However, the Citizens' League has informed us that you are coming to Minnesota November 27. Could you possibly come out? We would love to drive you out to the country to see our "house". Since photographs never do justice, we would like to have you see our rock work. Also, the backfilling and bulldozing has to be done soon and we would feel so much assured if you could see the problems our land presents.

Could Gene drop us a line when your schedule has been completed?

Again, many thanks. Our best wishes to you.

Virginia Lovness

A letter to Mr. Wright in mid-November 1956 invited him to visit and see the building site. At left, a draft, showing that they carefully crafted their correspondence (on the back, a sketch for D's record cleaner label). At right, a re-creation of the final sent to Mr. Wright.

Furniture was built in the winter of 1956, almost a year before the house was ready for occupancy. The high-back chairs were used with the two square dining tables. Hassocks were not used as foot rests, but rather for occasional seating near the fire and in the bedrooms. Mr. Wright probably never considered a coffee table as the perfect place for a little girl to play but it worked fine for me.

The couch my father built for their St. Paul apartment did living room duty for a few years until a Wright design was created.

A near miss

My mother and father had written, telephoned and visited Taliesin that first year of construction to get advice about their rock work and ask questions. They had written to acknowledge receipt of the furniture plans and expressed hope that Mr. Wright could see their progress. But in spite of some promising opportunities, he was never able to get to Woodpile Lake. The closest he came was in late fall 1956 when he visited Minneapolis. By this time Mother and D were on a first-name basis with Gene Masselink, and his response to their letter about a visit had a little humor and was now signed simply, "Gene".

Mr. Wright made a stop at the Henry Neils house in Minneapolis during his visit.

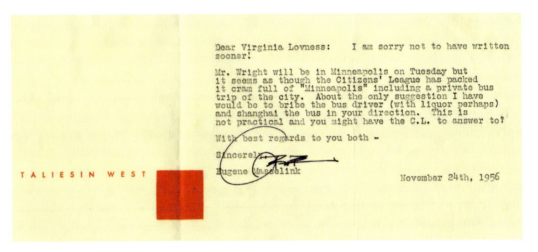

Dear Virginia Lovness: I am sorry not to have written sooner!

Mr. Wright will be in Minneapolis on Tuesday but it seems as though the Citizens' League has packed it cram full of "Minneapolis" including a private bus trip of the city. About the only suggestion I have would be to bribe the bus driver (with liquor perhaps) and shanghai the bus in your direction. This is not practical and you might have the C.L. to answer to?

With best regards to you both -

Sincerely,

Eugene Masselink

TALIESIN WEST

November 24th, 1956

She recalled a story about that Minneapolis trip, and an encounter that took place during a visit to Taliesin North the following year:

We had brought a photograph from a Minneapolis newspaper, taken at Southdale, that we asked him to autograph for us. We never had enough courage to bother him to take a photo with us. He took one look at the Star/Tribune photo and said, "That's my favorite overcoat!" The coat was hand woven and it was a great photo of him. He took it from us and seemed to forget we had asked him to autograph it. We really wanted it but what could we do?

In the spring of 1957 Mother took advantage of late cold weather to work on a softer pursuit. The furniture had been built during the preceding months, with Mother sanding and staining as the pieces came together, but now she began planning cushions for the chairs and hassocks. She had sewn her own clothes for years and was not daunted by this simpler, yet heavier construction. She must have been suffering some color fatigue after two seasons of working with gray cement, and she wanted some bright colors for her new interior. She told this story often over the years:

Wright visited Southdale in Bloomington, Minnesota, the nation's first enclosed mall in November, 1956, before giving a talk to the Citizens League of Minneapolis. Described by Minneapolis Star writer Frank Murray as the "Stormy Petrel of American architecture", Wright had nothing good to say about the new Mall: "Who wants to sit in that desolate-looking spot?"

Mr. Wright was absolutely great. Anything I asked for, he gave me. And I remember after working in the mud, the cement, I wanted shocking pink velvet throughout the main house for my upholstery. I called Taliesin to ask and Gene Masselink answered. I explained my problem, and he said, "Oh Virginia, you don't want shocking pink, do you? Mr. Wright never chooses something like that. He likes organic colors. Don't you want moss green or rust?"

"No," I said. "I want shocking pink."

So he asked Mr. Wright and later we got a note saying, "You win. Shocking!"

The cushions were sewn late that fall after the house was closed in; they weren't needed before then and of course she had lots to do beside sewing. But there was some irony to her efforts to get her way this time. In the finished house, with the large windows and sun blazing into the living room, the cushions faded almost immediately. She dyed them moss green.

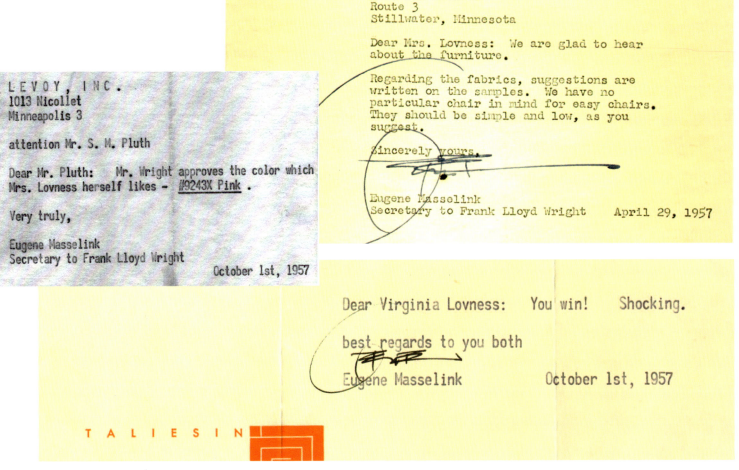

Mrs. Don Lovness
Route 3
Stillwater, Minnesota

Dear Mrs. Lovness: We are glad to hear about the furniture.

Regarding the fabrics, suggestions are written on the samples. We have no particular chair in mind for easy chairs. They should be simple and low, as you suggest.

Sincerely yours,

Eugene Masselink
Secretary to Frank Lloyd Wright   April 29, 1957

L E V O Y , I N C .
1013 Nicollet
Minneapolis 3

attention Mr. S. M. Pluth

Dear Mr. Pluth: Mr. Wright approves the color which Mrs. Lovness herself likes - #9243X Pink .

Very truly,

Eugene Masselink
Secretary to Frank Lloyd Wright

October 1st, 1957

Dear Virginia Lovness: You win!   Shocking.

best regards to you both

Eugene Masselink   October 1st, 1957

TALIESIN

```
                                        April 12, 1957
                                        Route 3
                                        Stillwater, Minn.


Mr  Frank Lloyd Wright
Taliesin West
Box 157
Scottsdale, Arizona

Dear Mr. Wright,


We hope you and yours had a pleasant and productive winter.
We've been following your career via publications and your
project in Baghdad sounds very exciting.

We finished building all the furniture you designed for us a
few weeks ago.  The furniture is white oak, perfectly natural
with only a filler and clear finish--no platinums or stains to
mar the natural grain.  The results are even better than
anticipated:  the dining chairs are very regal; the 6' x 6'
work table is tremendous; and the slats in all are poetic--
no less.

Enclosed is a brochure of material a friend can get for us
for the dining chair cushions and bedspreads and hassocks.
Our preferences are marked.  Have you any suggestions?  We
have been wondering what type of chair and fabric you are
contemplating for comfortable seating in the living area.
Could it be something that one could curl up in--or almost
recline in?  I even toyed with the idea of something actually
on the floor level with arms and backs.  What do you suggest?
Don can build almost anything so you needn't be hesitant on
our account!

The material for the heating system has arrived.  The price
was almost identical between the 2" and the 1½" pipe so we
decided to use the original 2" layout.  The boiler is the
Kewanee 189,000 BTU #OW5U.  Please let us know if this is not
satisfactory in any way.

In betwixt snowstorms we have started laying rock again.  We
are planning to put the roof on around August 1 so have much
chiseling and rock laying to do before then.

Our best to you all.

                          Very truly yours,



P.S.  Saw the plans of your proposed capitol for Arizona in
Architectural Forum this month.  It is the most beautiful
public office building we have ever seen.  If there are any
complications about the building of it, send us up the plans
and we will build it ourselves on the back forty!
```

Mother wrote this progress report to Mr. Wright in the spring of 1957. Early April is notorious for being unpredictable weather-wise in Minnesota, so she was planning ahead before the construction resumed in earnest.

6
A roof over our heads

As usual in the Twin Cities, it was the middle of April, 1957 before the temperature was consistently above freezing and mortar could be mixed and used without resorting to tarps or other protection. There was still a lot to do, however. Supplies were ordered. The steady flow of cement sacks resumed - five to twenty at a time and by early May the lumber began to appear on site, number 3 pine for framing and ten and twelve foot long planks of number 1 clear fir for exposed finish work. More re-bar was brought in for foundations of the pillars yet to be built. The driveway had so much truck traffic that in late June it had to be reinforced with 34 tons of traprock, a hard blue crushed gravel from a quarry in Dresser, Wisconsin. At $4 a ton the charge was $136.00.

The costs were adding up and the bank account was going down. Money from the sale of the White Bear Lake home had carried them, but now it was necessary to get a mortgage. My father tells about working with banks at the time:

One of the hardships was that we had to get a loan, obviously. By the time we paid for the land and paid Taliesin and then bought the rock we didn't have any money. So we went ahead and laid rock for two years, and then we needed a mortgage. And here we had the land and the plans and the major portion done. So we went to the bank thinking, well, this shouldn't be a problem. And they just looked at us as though we were out of our minds. I remember after I had exhausted all the banks I went to a farm credit place which lent money for building in the country; you had to have so many acres (later we also became a tree farm, we put in 26,000 pine, by hand). So anyhow we thought this would be the place to get a loan.

Then everybody else rejects you if you're doing it yourself. I remember sitting down with the plans and the photos of everything we'd done. The man said, "Well, all of you do-it-yourselfers do poor jobs." This was his introduction! "We really don't like to handle those."

And so I said, "No, we're doing a wonderful job. Take a look at what we've done, and all we need is money enough to finish. And we've got the major portion done."

"Well, you should have come to me before you started!"

"But we didn't need money before we started."

"Well, I can't help you now until the place is finished."

So we had just one hell of a time. I don't have a lot of faith in banks. Not only that, but we had our original blueprints—that we'd bring to Mr. Wright and he'd scribble on, telling us things to do. The bank said, when they did give us a loan for the first house finally, "You'll have to leave a set of plans with us, that's customary." Well, when you're young, you don't know any better so you say OK, you do what you have to do - you're glad to get the money. But then they lost the plans! Or they threw them out or something. These were blueprints, but Mr. Wright had written all over them. And they were very special to us, but we thought, we'll let the bank have the very special, good plans. When you're living in a trailer you think they're safer in a bank. You assume banks are safe; the bank would keep the nice clean set, and we'd keep the others, which had gotten rained on and gotten pretty dilapidated. Anyhow, they built a new bank building and when we came to ask for the plans no one knew anything. What can you do?

Rock patterning became more interesting as Mother went along. On this pillar at the north end of the living room there were tall rectangles, triangles and a wide variety of sizes. She was taking to heart what Mr. Wright had told her: use the rock to its best advantage. She also was now wearing "sensible" shoes rather than huarache sandals when handling the chunks of stone.

The loss of those blueprints would not be discovered for a few years, and there were other things on their minds in that summer of 1957. With a new infusion of money in the form of a hard-won mortgage, my mother felt a break was needed for their mental and physical well-being. She put an ad in the paper for help, a boy to mix cement. Having another worker didn't actually allow them to work any less but the pace picked up and the stones rose faster than they had the previous summer. D churned out cut stone like a machine, keeping both Mother and the young man busy. The remaining pillars went up relatively quickly. They had a self-imposed "deadline" of moving in by the time winter winds blew once again; none of us was enthusiastic about spending more cold weather in the trailer. There was no time to waste.

Pillars for the car port and the blocks and stone veneer of the tool room at its far end went up, and it was exciting for me to see my (and my sister's) bedroom take shape. As a six-year old, my impression of the whole project was simply that it was taking a long time. Like so many people who visited, I didn't have a real sense of what it would be; it just seemed like my parents were building a big fort - and to me that was a lot of fun.

Some of the roof framing along the back wall could be done while the pillars were being finished but for the most part by early July my father turned his attention to a necessary step before the floor could be poured or wall framing could be built: the in-floor heating system.

In-floor heat

While building, D had quickly become adept at reading and interpreting the plans. In addition to the blueprints, each aspect of the project was covered by a set of written specifications for layout, plumbing, electrical, concrete, masonry, carpentry and millwork, roofing and flashing, and heating. These spec sheets were meant to be guidelines for contractors, and my father's ability to interpret and follow them showed what a truly talented man he was. In fact, his analytical approach sometimes proved superior to what the structural engineers provided. Wright's warmed floor heating system, first used in Herbert Jacobs' Usonian house in 1938, had been improved and updated to the point that it was almost mainstream. My father, however, was skeptical of the testing procedure outlined in the spec sheet. He described his concerns in a Taliesin interview in the 1990s:

Sometimes I disagreed with Mr. Wright's specifications. For one thing I didn't agree with charging the heating system to 100 pounds of air pressure for 24 hours. What I did is get hold of a hydrostatic pump and filled a tank full of water and pumped it up to 500 lbs per square inch. And then we found pinhole leaks all over the place and one by one we fixed them. Those pinhole leaks you can't tell with air pressure, and it might take 25 years for them to break as pipe leaks. And it's happening all around: it happened in the Neils house; it happened in the Palmer house.

As it turned out, it also happened in the Lovness house, but not for about 45 years. In 2003 a new, modern boiler and some sections of the piping under the kitchen floor were replaced

Looking north from the tool room, the stonework of the second car port pillar nears completion. Our front door rough framing is in place at left.

Below, stonework is mostly complete and the first boards are put in place.

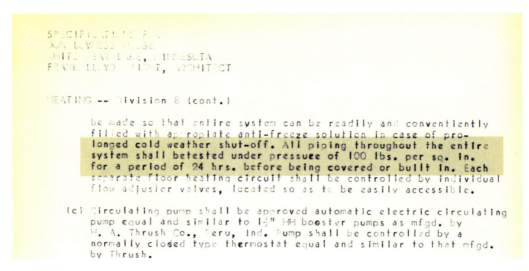

along with some valves and air vents. Generally speaking, the system has served its purpose admirably and I loved living with a cozy warm floor.

To get that cozy floor, however, took a lot of effort and considerable cost. In-floor heating was not unheard of, but it was at the very least unusual in the northern climates for a residence. I'm sure the tradesmen my parents contacted for help were skeptical at first. A local welder, Palmer Edwins, spent almost a week welding seams at $2.50 per hour. Oxygen and Acetylene totaled $17.64 and welding rod came to $3.00. The boiler and its controls and connections were overseen by Jim Breedlove and Allan Stoltzman. That took a big chunk of the budget at almost $1500.00. Another thousand dollars went to other specialists and suppliers.

It must have seemed ironic to be putting in heating pipes under a blazing summer sun, but the work went on.

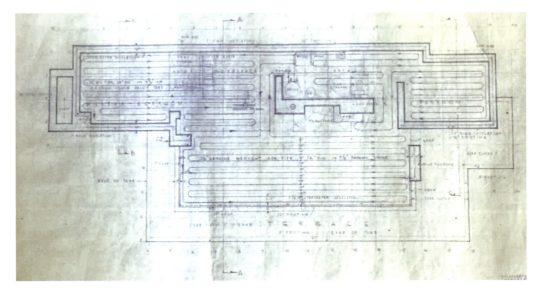

```
SPECIFICATIONS
DON LOVNESS HOUSE
WHITE BEAR LAKE, MINNESOTA
FRANK LLOYD WRIGHT, ARCHITECT


H E A T I N G  -- Division 8          (Revised October 15, 1956)

1. Work included:
   Provide all labor and materials to install a complete and
   perfectly operating system of automatic circulating hot water
   floor heating as indicated in the drawings or as specified
   herein, or both, including work as follows:

     (a) Automatic oil-fired hot water boiler-burner unit.
     (b) Floor heating pipe coils laid in broken stone fill below slab.
     (c) Circulating pump
     (d) Compression tank
     (e) Automatic mixing valve
     (f) Flow control valves
     (g) All other piping to properly connect system and all its parts
     (h) Pressure relief valves and pressure reducing valves
     (i) Air vents and vent cocks
     (j) Underground fuel storage tank and fuel oil supply lines
            to boiler and water heater
     (k) Manual valves throughout to properly control system,
            including gate valves, globe valves, hose bibbs,
            drainage, etc., and balancing fittings
     (l) Complete thermostatic controls
     (m) Electrical wiring for power and controls for heating
            system, starting from power outlet in heater room
     (n) All smoke pipe, breeching, draft hoods, dampers, etc. for
            boiler, water heater
     (o) All mountings, hangers, supports, etc., to properly
            support in correct place all parts of heating system
     (p) Do all excavation and filling required for proper
            installation of all parts of system
     (q) Drawings
     (r) Schedule of parts
     (s) Guarantee

2. Materials and workmanship and general description of items:
   All items shall be as indicated in drawings or as described
   as follows:

     (a) BOILER-BURNER UNIT shall be a complete automatic oil-fired
            hot water unit having an approved output capacity not
            less than 189,000 BTU/hr., equal and similar to Kewanee
            OW-5U (water) oil-fired boiler-burner unit as manufactured
            by the Kewanee Ross Corp., Kewanee, Illinois. Unit shall
            be complete with insulated enamelled metal jacket,
            approved burner, thermometer, head gauge, built-in burner
            control, automatic pilot, limit control and automatic
            shut-off, etc.

     (b) Floor heating pipe coils and other piping for the heating
            system shall be genuine wrought iron pipe (Byers or equal)
            with welded type fittings, main supply and return lines
            shall be 1-1/2" with 1-1/2" feeder lines, laid in
```

The specification sheets contained explicit instructions for the contractor and listed equipment and materials to be used by brand name.

This section was revised in the fall after the first summer of construction, before any heating pipe was laid. The original plan called for 1-1/2" pipe and was changed to 2" size. The boiler was originally sized at 243,000 BTU/HR as a boiler. This revision calls for a boiler/burner (hot water heater). In the first draft an electric water heater was noted. Other small adjustments were to call for "broken stone" fill (b) rather than the original "rock" fill. Perhaps this was due to the fact that after a summer of chipping away (literally) we had plenty of "broken stone on hand. The word "thermostatic" was added to (l).

My father was on site as much as possible and worked with these craftsmen. As noted earlier he was concerned about the long-term integrity of the system, since repairing a leak meant ripping out a portion of the floor. Careful prep work was done with a bed of crushed gravel and broken stone. (I like to think Ty and I contributed to that effort.) The wrought iron pipes were measured and bent, then cut to perfectly align at their edges for efficient welding without any small gaps.

It's interesting to compare the photos here with the original heating plan. D rarely took a shortcut but it appears he dropped the number of lines in the main room from twelve, as shown on the plan, to ten. Same in the parent's bedroom zone (which also included the bath, kitchen work area and dining space. There were also a few gaps where our dining table would be and rather than add another bend, he ran a line under a pillar nearby. He was, however, using 2-inch pipe rather than the 1-1/2 inch specified so we can assume there was a method to his madness.

The hot water was routed to the outside of each zone first; from the boiler pump behind the fireplace along the back wall to each bedroom, then zig-zagging back to the return. The living room circuit started with a run under the short hallway into the "kitchen", assuring that this well-travelled spot would always be warm. It then jogged to the north and went around the outside perimeter before starting a back-and-forth across the large room, ending with a run around the base of the fireplace.

I doubt that D planned it this way, but that outermost pipe was very close to the windows. Those huge window/doors on the west never fogged, and any snow or ice against the outside of that wall didn't last long. In fact over the years our pets (and some wild animals) would find that exterior edge of the slab a cozy place to lie in cold weather.

That slab became another new adventure for Mother and D. They were now accomplished stone masons, the plumbing was mostly complete, furniture was built, carpentry was well underway and almost all electric wiring was in place. But one thing they had not attempted was concrete finishing, so they brought in a ringer. My mother remembered it this way:

The worst thing of all though was pouring the cement floor. We didn't know how to lay cement that would be slick. So we found an old German cement finisher who had retired, and he showed us how to do the scoring and the slicking. We divided the house into three sections and then the logia. Early in the morning, we would pour the cement, adding iron oxide, so it was an integral part of the cement. But you have to keep trowelling with boards until you bring the water up to the surface, so you get the smooth effect, and then you have to score it. Meanwhile you're standing on narrow planks on top of this. This all went well. But one day we started to do one section and the humidity was high and it didn't set up. We started early in the morning, and at midnight or so we were still trowelling trying to get the thing right. That was the trickiest thing.

In the end they had to break up that section of floor and start over. Since the red floor was

The plumber is using a heavy tubing cutter while Don holds a reamer. It was important to clean the inside ridge after a cut to ensure smooth water flow.

The heating pipe had to be cut, bent and laid out so the ends were perfectly square and matched prior to welding. These photos from July, 1957 show some of the pipe already welded while the rest is in place but still separate. Carpentry went on concurrently with the plumbing; the car port roof was already framed (it was the easiest part). By this time there were only three, at the most four months of good construction weather left.

As the west wall is framed, the house takes shape and the dream begins to come into focus. The top layer of concrete floor, infused with red oxide, had yet to laid down.

being done in sections, they had to be careful to mix the colorant evenly in different batches. Iron oxide is a fine powder, commonly used to tint paint, coatings and concrete. It's even used in cosmetics but in this case D bought it in bags of 50 or 60 pounds. As a tinting agent it's extremely potent and will turn anything it contacts red: your clothes, hands, lumber. It must have been a mess to work with but ultimately they managed to produce a floor that was consistent in color and smoothness. Part of that success is due to D's deviation from the specs, as he explained:

(Mr. Wright) also specified using A.C. Horn iron oxide for the cement. And A.C. Horn stuff is very

The car port was considered by Wright to be a future project, and its construction could have been pushed back to a later date. My parents, however, were on a roll and built the pillars along with the rest of the house. Its roof was framed with nailed 2x8s, with an open span of over five feet on the west side.

When the lumber was delivered it gave Ty and me (and the goat) another place to play.

expensive. And being at 3M at the time we dealt with tons of iron oxide. So I took some iron oxide and some cement in the laboratory and I measured to see what the saturation point was. And I found it to be about between 2 and 3%. So I figured if I put 4% in it will be even all over the whole thing, which we did, and it worked like a million dollars.

Walls and roof

What would be the walls already existed for the most part in the stones and block so laboriously laid over two summers. The remaining vertical wooden construction was simply framing for the glass that would dominate the living room. Each bedroom had half-high stone walls and above that would also be mostly glass. So the majority of the wood would be in the roofs, upper and lower, and the elaborate patterned ceiling.

D was happy to be working with material that was familiar and easier to deal with than limestone. However, just as when the fireplace began, he didn't have many tools. A friend loaned a power saw and from that point the framing went up quickly.

Mr. Wright had some unusual methods for long spans. Some of the beams were constructed

Seen from the northeast corner, the roof is framed in before the window frames are installed. At this point the rockwork begins to make some sense to those who had been watching the building go up.

Below, the master bedroom begins to take shape.

of a 2x6 nestled into a "C"-shaped steel beam, bolted to another 2x6. The main supports of the upper ceiling were flitched beams consisting of 2x12s sandwiching a 10 inch tall, 1/2 inch steel plate. These beams, on 4' and 8' centers, formed shallow coffers with the ceiling boards patterned in concentric rectangles 10 feet above the living room floor. In each bedroom the pattern was similar but at a height of 6 feet, 8 inches. The ceiling beams themselves were made of several layers, with a dentil lower finish. Then there were the light decks around the perimeter of the room, the fascia with dentils and framing around the upper clerestory windows.

Much of this lumber had to be secured to the stonework, where slots had been left as the pillars were built. Each time an attachment was made was a moment of truth, when D found out if their learn-as-you-go masonry was good enough. It was.

A friend would hold one end of the longer planks while he got them in position, and a crane was called in for the biggest beams, but otherwise D worked until dark, and sometimes later, to finish the framing. Care had to be taken with the fir mullions that served as door frames to the french doors, as they were "finish" exposed. The rest of the interior was a lot of fussy work that would have taxed an experienced finish carpenter but he did an exceptional job.

The bags of Portland and Mason cement kept coming all during the summer, now joined by #1 fir and some lesser quality material for framing, from their main supplier, White Bear Lumber and Coal. In early September D had to go further afield for some specialty lumber and plywood from Stewart Lumber in Minneapolis. The S4S (surfaced on all 4 sides) fir for the living room "door frames"and other interior wood was "milled to their detail" according to the invoices.

Cabinet work was farmed out to Virgil Vangsgard, whose cabinet shop was near 3M's East Side plant in St. Paul. Kitchen cabinets - upper and lower, bath vanities, a wardrobe and assorted plywood cost well over $600 in October and November. Virgil charged $4 an hour for labor, the going rate for a first-class craftsman at the time.

By late August the upper and lower roofs were framed, the diagonal decking was in place and it was important to get some weather protection in place so the interior could be finished. Berwald Roofing applied a 5-ply pitch and gravel covering and did the metal work around the perimeter. That total was $790. The mortgage money was going fast.

With weather protection above, D concentrated on the interior, building the framing for the windows. Autumn was slipping away and there was much else to do beyond just pounding nails. In mid-September the phone lines were buried from the pole to the new house. It was time to order appliances, and just as they had for a number of years, every effort was made to get it wholesale. A letter to Sears on offical "Custom Design"stationery (remember, the "company" had an excellent Dun & Bradstreet rating) asked for a 10% discount and alluded to more needs in the future. The letter, certainly written by my mother—but of course signed by my father, as no business would consider a woman's request for the same discount—described a

When the studio was renovated in 2017 the original steel channels were retired. They had not failed but there are better modern alternatives to ensure the house lasts another half century and more.

It seemed like the rock pile would never go away. Masonry work on the chimney continued even as the roof framing took shape. It was exciting to see our "girls'" bedroom get a roof and window frames.

D takes a break with his girls under the newly enclosed carport roof.

12-acre landscaped paradise with an orchard. It's unlikely that many of the items mentioned in the letter were even handled by Sears, but the tone implied that Mother and D would throw a lot of money in Sears' direction if they would just play ball with a discount. It was brash and almost outrageous; in other words, typical Lovness.

A washer, dryer, stainless sink, mattress and bed frame were noted with stock number and price in the letter. Four days later, appliances and a medicine cabinet were delivered, although there's no record of other items being purchased from Sears. Generally, things like hinges or casement window cranks came from specialty suppliers (there were no big-box home improvement centers) and D became very good at finding and developing relationships with them.

Pittsburgh Plate Glass had a local branch in downtown Minneapolis, back when what's now called the North Loop was a thriving commercial and manufacturing area. From them in October, a 56 x 44 inch bathroom mirror was ordered, drilled with four holes, with screws and metal rosettes. The invoice noted, "Wrap in heavy paper, they will pick up in their station wagon Thursday, 31st."

D had already developed a relationship with the company, who had supplied all the single-pane glass for the house. Double-pane or thermal glass was readily available but only in standard sizes, and this project was anything but standard. My father stated that thermal glass would have cost $6000, about eight times the cost of our "regular " glass. Those glass sheets were brought to Payne Avenue Woodworking in St. Paul—again, close to 3M— where they built the sash and mounted the glass. Back at Woodpile Lake, installing the window sash in the framing wasn't easy but the biggest challenge was the mitered corner glass. D remembered it well:

Mr. Wright always used to say, "To close the house in doesn't take a long time, but finishing it does." It was almost winter, the snow was blowing when we were putting in the mitered glass windows. Boy, do they take a long time to put in, because they have to fit perfectly. Every time you went to take a measurement you'd have to wipe the snow off your face. And we must have been heating all of St. Paul because we had the heating system going!

Since there was no sash involved, the corner glass was mounted "bare". But before that could happen, it had to be delivered to the site, which proved to be problematic. After more than one piece was broken in handling, the owner of the company drove out personally to deliver the glass. It may have been one of the first, but by no means the last instance where a company took an interest and a lot of pride in being a part of this Frank Lloyd Wright-designed project. In years to come that attitude would be beneficial to my parents in their projects, to the point where they no longer had to use "company" stationery to get a deal.

At this point my mother was still completely involved in the project. Before and as the windows were installed her job was to apply a finish to the woodwork, inside and out. Before starting that, however, my father expressed some concerns about what to use on the wood; he

D was taking no chances with the large mirror for our girls' bathroom. We picked it up in the Ford wagon.

Custom

DESIGN - ENGINEERING
1550 EDGEWATER DRIVE
SAINT PAUL 13, MINNESOTA

September 22, 1957

Sears
White Bear Lake, Minn.

Gentlemen:

Enclosed is a list of the articles we would like to buy
immediately from your company if we are allowed the 10%
contractors' discount.

Also, in the near future we will be needing a water softener,
a garbage disposal, 2 outside doors, 2 flush inside doors,
6 doors for 3 wardrobe closets, hardware for entire house
including 16 French door hinges and knobs for the living room,
14 French door hinges and knobs for bedroom windows, plus other
inside and outside door hardware, and hardware for kitchen
cabinets and built-ins throughout; medicine cabinets for 2
bathrooms, mirrors to cover 1 wall of one bath, ceramic tile
for 2 bathrooms (one 10½' ceiling with floor to ceiling tile),
etc.

In addition we will need a freezer and furnishings such as
linens, bedspreads, rugs, dishes, a vacuum cleaner. Also
we will need a quantity of shrubbery, fruit trees, evergreens,
etc. as we have 12 acres to landscape and plant an orchard.

Inasmuch as we are doing our own contracting, we have been
receiving contractors' prices on all our building supplies.
We would appreciate being given a similar courtesy by Sears.

Thank you.

Very truly yours,

Donald Lovness
Route 3
Stillwater, Minn.

STUDIOS - 2707 SOUTH SHORE BLVD. WHITE BEAR LAKE 10, MINNESOTA

It's unclear whether the Sears branch in White Bear Lake jumped to accomodate D's request, but if they had checked they would have found that Custom Design - Engineering had an excellent Dun and Bradstreet credit rating!

was thinking about longevity and after two years of intense labor was not inclined to want to do anything over again, anytime soon. He recalled his ideas in a Taliesin interview with Indira Berndtson:

I checked with Mr. Wright. He had specifications for a type of varnish to be used on the woodwork. I told him that as a chemist I disagreed with that. I thought water gets behind it and it spalls off and the wood can't breathe. I said, "How would you feel about creosote?"

And I'd never seen this - his eyes lit up and he said, "That is my favorite thing, creosote." He said, "I creosoted everything at Oak Park. All the architects used to laugh at me because they would smell creosote." But it only smells for about a week or two. But you know, the creosote has been on for fifty years and it looks just like brand new. It's got a nice reddish color.

My mother was charged with applying the creosote finish. Her fear of heights had been tamed somewhat by months of masonry work on a scaffold, but now she was working above her head and breathing heavy fumes. She recalled getting used to the smell and even beginning to like it. What she—and most other people at the time—didn't know was that this coal tar distillate was probably a carcinogen and could cause respiratory, nervous system, skin and eye disorders, among others. My father the chemist was a pragmatist and would use whatever material did the job including DDT to keep the insects at bay. We all survived, however, including the woodwork which certainly lasted longer than it would have with other treatments.

With the house now enclosed, there were still a number of trim areas to complete but in mid-November the offical move was made to our new home. My parents were thrilled and Ty and I now had a real room of our own, albeit small and shared. She hardly remembered the White Bear Lake house and when the old trailer was dragged away we both cried. The cozy home we'd known for two years was going away!

Greening the space

The interior was a work of art, the furniture was complementary (except for the long "sofa" that was a carryover from the St. Paul apartment) but to Mother there was still something missing. The house needed, she felt, a connection with nature that would carry her through the long months of winter. Indoor plants would do the trick but like her choice of pets, these would not be just geraniums. Rather, she put an ad in the newspaper asking if anyone had an exotic houseplant that had outgrown its space. There was a surprising response and in short order the house filled with scheffleras, philodendrons and huge rubber plants. She made a call to the Como Park Conservatory and after explaining the situation the director told her, "I'll send a truck." Mother wrote at length about it in her notes:

Once in the studio it seemed to need nature inside too. Without money to buy plants we had to improvise in the local newspaper with a want ad that proved almost too successful: "A good home for your over-

The roof was an important prerequisite to all the interior and glass work. The tar and gravel surface was applied over several layers of membrane, with metal edging and drains.

Once covered, the interior and window work began. In this view a friend admires the sunset over the lake looking west.

grown indoor plants." Calls came in fast and furious. After putting plants outside for the summer, the realization of how big they had grown was sad for people; lots of them hated to throw them away and called. Chasing them all down was a big job! Some turned out to be little shriveled-up specimens whose demise was imminent, but most were too large for a normal house. Our Wright home, however, was so conducive to foliage that we went wild!

We soon had more than the house could hold; on the deck, under the clerestory windows, grouped on the floor. Rumors got back to us that students on a tour from the University of Minnesota thought the house was breathtaking - but the woman who lived there went overboard with foliage.

Detail work went on into the winter months and when the interior reached a point of near-completion my parents, ever the self-promoters, invited the Minneapolis newspaper to visit and interview them. A story appeared on March 6th.

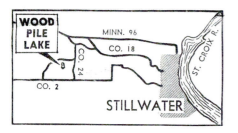

A small map accompanied the article to give readers some geographical context. Over the years, however, even people who had a map had trouble finding the place, as the house was not visible from the road. That was just as well; we had enough "walk-ins" as it was.

★ Neighborhood and Suburban News **THE MINNEAPOLIS S**

THURSDAY, MARCH 6, 1958

MRS. LOVNESS STANDS BY PARTLY COMPLETED FIREPLACE
Their dream house was designed by Frank Lloyd Wright

★ ★ ★ ★ ★ ★ ★ ★ ★ ★

COUPLE FEELS KINSHIP WITH ARCHITECT

Do-It-Yourself House
Built to Wright's Plans

THE LOVNESSES ENJOY THE HOUSE THEY BUILT THEMSELVES
Huge fireplace sets off ultramodern living room

By GENE NEWHALL
Minneapolis Star Staff Writer

Woodpile lake, a tiny pond in the oak-cloaked rolling country between White Bear Lake and Stillwater, isn't on most maps — but a house built stone by stone by a young St. Paul chemist and his artist wife may soon put it there.

It may be the last house to be designed by 88-year-old Frank Lloyd Wright, world-renowned architect now busy with plans such as his mile-high office building.

The Washington county home of Don and Virginia

Lovness is believed to be the first do-it-yourself h o u s e built to plans from Wright's drawing board.

"We could never have had a Wright home without building it ourselves," the Lovnesses explain. "We couldn't even pay the taxes on it if it were valued at what it would

OUTSIDE VIEW OF COMPLETED HOUSE

The first of many stories that would appear over the years in both the Minneapolis and St. Paul newspapers. The full text follows:

Above, by late fall the clerestory window frames were in place, along with upper glass. The first of the french doors awaits placement and ceiling and soffit boards are stacked inside. A "lantern" is completed on both ends.

Left, the finished house in winter. Note that the floor area just outside the windows is free of snow thanks to the in-floor heating system. A rubber plant thrives in the southwest window near Mother's work table.

By GENE NEWHALL, Minneapolis Star Staff Writer

Woodpile lake, a tiny pond in the oak-cloaked rolling country between White Bear Lake and Stillwater, isn't on most maps — but a house built stone by stone by a young St. Paul chemist and his artist wife may soon put it there.

It may be the last house to be designed by 88-year-old Frank Lloyd Wright, world-renowned architect now busy with plans such as his mile-high office building.

The Washington county home of Don and Virginia Lovness is believed to be the first do-it-yourself house built to plans from Wright's drawing board.

"We could never have had a Wright home without building it ourselves," the Lovnesses explain. "We couldn't even pay the taxes on it if it were valued at what it would have cost if commercially built."

The Lovnesses, with their two small daughters, moved into a trailer two summers ago at the construction site on the 12 acres of lakeshore they bought from a farmer. The couple first ordered in truckloads of rough stone from a Stillwater quarry, only a six-mile haul. They cut each stone with hammer and chisel. They didn't count the hundreds of stones. Just weighed them - 175 tons.

Construction started with the mammoth fireplace, a "centerpiece" for the house. Skeptical neighbors wondered what sort of Pueblo dwelling would emerge. Don and Virginia just kept mixing more cement and laying up more rock, then spidering wrought-iron pipes out from the all-weather furnace hidden behind the fireplace—the pipes to form the radiant heating in the concrete floor.

Fir lumber and glass complete the walls, in integrated panel-patterns matching Wright's symmetrical designs in the floor. The front of the house, toward the little lake, consists of 18 French doors. The whole house can be opened like one great porch in summer. Rich red wax rubbed into the floor heightens the oak-leaf tones of the yard and steadies the bright pink-and-yellow cast of the Oneona dolomite, which is the native stone used.

The stone gives the Lovnesses a geologic as well as artistic link with Wright's own far larger and more elaborate home, Taliesin, some 250 miles southeast in Wisconsin. "We've built from the same vein of rock," they explain.

Much of their happiness in their self-built masterpiece fitted into the lakeshore is in the friendship built with Wright during progress of the work.

Mrs. Lovness likes to quote Wright's maxim: "There can be no separation between our architecture and our culture. Nor any separation of either from our happiness."

By the spring of 1959 there was time to attend to the yard, with birch trees planted and a few boulders arranged near the patio.

Mr. Newhall took some liberties with the story, probably because the details were supplied by D and Mother. Our home was certainly not the first "do-it-yourself" project Wright had penned, nor was it his last house, even though he would pass away the following year. It wasn't wax that gave the floor its rich red tone and saying the Stillwater dolomite was from the same vein as Taliesin's rock was a considerable stretch. Facts, however, should never get in the way of a good story and over the years my parents would tell theirs over and over again, with only a few variations on the theme.

Two of the Star article photos were supplied by my parents but this living room image by their photographer shows a comfortable fire in the huge hearth, a perfect image of domestic tranquility, Wright-style. The furniture and built-ins were essentially complete although the doorway to the bedroom (beyond the dining table at center) did not yet have a screen. Another later addition was a light sculpture above the dining area. At this time the dentiled ceiling beam coverings were not yet in place. Reflecting the fact that her original "painting studio" area was now just a corner of the main room, my mother made sure one of her watercolors was shown in the foreground on her work table.

Unforeseen hazards

The construction saga was interesting and had several twists and turns, but we were barely into our new home before a really crazy thing happened. Just as the stone pillars had attracted people curious about what was being built, by the time the house was almost finished (and actually looked like a house) it still aroused interest - and in the case of a neighbor, anger. It was late fall in 1957. Mother related the tale in an interview:

The valances were a key element in the large living room, but the design was not completely self-supporting. Over the years, D had to add small cables and turnbuckles to keep them from sagging. It probably didn't help that sculptures, speakers and plants were placed there.

Lonnie had started kindergarten by then. And in the middle of the afternoon if I could I'd lie down for a little bit, because I was exhausted! Day in and day out at heavy manual work - when I hate anything that sounds like exercise. It was the middle of the afternoon and I heard gunshots. At that time there were no residences nearby, just a very successful farmer a little ways away, and the rest of it was old farms, 100 acre farms. So the buildings were far apart, you couldn't see them. But there was one old shack way back in the woods - Katie's. I was in the bedroom at one end and our youngest daughter was in the other. And to get from bedroom and bath to the other bedroom and bath you had to cross this 60, 70 feet of glass with a ceiling. And I heard what I thought were gunshots, and our windows going! We didn't have them all in, but I heard windows going. So I ran and looked out and here was a woman, just crazy, waving her arms and singing. I mean, I thought it would be a kid out there, shooting with a gun. But it was a woman, throwing our Japanese landscaping, our rocks, through the windows! Mr. Wright had designed all kinds of piles of rock and she'd taken them up and thrown them through the window. It was a woman and she looked crazy, her hair flying. Because it was cold! I couldn't get to our daughter without being out there, and I thought, I need help. So I ran and called the sheriff and said, "I need help, there's a woman destroying our house!" I was terrified, you know. I ran and got my daughter. I called Don and said, "You'd better get home, I don't know what's happening. I called the sheriff." So they came and got Katie, the pickled pigs feet packer from Swifts, and locked her up.

She was our next door farm lady back in the woods. We didn't get to meet our neighbors other than the one who sold us the property, because we were too busy! And evidently she was an alcoholic and bonkers, and she came to see what we were doing, because she could hear the building. She was inebriated and couldn't find the front door, so she got mad at the house! But when she got to jail they said her language was worse than any man there - she'd been a frequent inhabiter of the jail and she'd shake the bars and swear.

Don wasn't far away, maybe half an hour. By the time he got home the house was filled with neighbors, and the police and deputies. And he came barreling in the front door, yelling so that everybody heard, "She didn't get the mitred windows, did she?"

We told that story to Mr. Wright and he thought that was the funniest thing he ever heard. He said, "Your wife is much easier to replace than those windows."

So then we finished and moved into the house.

Our new home was a cozy but secluded spot. Woodpile Lake on the right and a shallow slough on the left meant we were surrounded by water on two sides. The nearest houses were a quarter mile away and there were few of them. The long driveway meant a plow was needed. Local farmers would use their tractors but D bought a war surplus army jeep and rigged up a snow plow. This photo was taken before thousands of pines were planted. Most of the trees around the house were Oaks.

Quid pro quo

By the time the house was finished my mother and father had gotten to know Mr. Wright and many of the Taliesin people quite well. In the first moments after meeting, Mr. Wright asked my father where he worked. When he replied, "3M Company", the architect's interest was piqued. He knew 3M made a wide range of products from office supplies to construction materials, many of which would be very useful to the members of the Fellowship. For his part, D was happy to supply items that Taliesin could use at whatever discount could be arranged, or in many cases, for free. My mother and father both grew to greatly admire Mr. Wright and she became something of a pet to him; he would always joke with her, calling their new home the "Love nest". They also became close to Mrs. Wright over the years, my mother acting as an assistant hostess at Taliesin events and my father, the chemist, a consultant on subjects as wide-ranging as mosquito control and wood preservation. The relationship would be mutually beneficial for many years, but perhaps the most important exchange took place during a Taliesin visit in the fall of 1958, after the house was completed.

D described a meeting with Mr. Wright that was pivotal:

We'd no sooner moved in than we went back to Taliesin again. Mr. Wright had been sick that summer of '58, right after his birthday; I think he had a slight stroke. So we went down to the drafting room at Taliesin in September. He was sitting at his desk and we started talking about the house. We were telling him how much we liked it and he said, "How much did it end up costing?"

I told him $18,000 (he had estimated it would cost $20,000). Under budget!

He said, "You know, I've been practicing architecture for sixty years and this is the first time this has ever happened to me!

Mother continued the story:

He was happy, rubbing his hands and said, "Well, what are we going to do next?"

You know, he never said anything straight to me, he always teased. So I thought he was teasing because he knew how hard it had been to get the house built. But as a matter of fact we had been thinking that we wanted barges like Lake Tahoe and little cottages all around our little lake. So when I told him what I'd been thinking he said, "It's yours, you deserve a bonus!"

"We'll design some cottages for you and we'll get them done as fast as we can," he told us. We got down to the drafting room where he was working on the Seth Peterson cottage - but he didn't like Seth Peterson very well.

"This is a nice design," he told us. "Why don't you build this one. He'll never build it!"

But he did build it, so Mr. Wright designed two other cottages for us.

Mother's request for barges was based on a design from 1923, when Wright's career was somewhat stagnant. He had proposed to a wealthy developer that a resort on the steep slopes of Lake Tahoe's Emerald Bay would encompass not only a main resort building and cabins among the pines, but floating cottages on the lake. It was never built but as a student of Wright's

Part of the plans for a hanging light; this one lit the living room near the front door and a similar design was used near the dining room table.

January 13, 1958
Route 3
Stillwater, Minn.

Mr. Frank Lloyd Wright
Taliesin West
Box 157
Scottsdale, Arizona

Dear Mr. Wright,

A Belated Happy New Year!

Here are a few very poor pictures we took ourselves of the house. It really is very beautiful--and living in it is delightful!

The weather here has been as cold as-10° and the 1/4 inch plate glass does not frost at all. The radiant heating is extremely comfortable. But most of all, the house itself is inspirational.

There are a few small details--we ran out of plans! We hateeto bother you but can come to no conclusion as to what to do about lighting the dining area. Even with all the lights on and as many candles as we can mueter, it isstill dark. Can you give us a light design? We enjoy your theatre lights--the tall ones at Spring Green, unless you have something else in mind.

Also, we would like to make the perforated folding screens that close off the bedrooms. Could you possibly send us a sketch for these?

Many thanks.

Sincerely,

In the middle of our first winter it was clear more light was needed at the table. When Helen and Mag visited a few candles were all we had. A year later D had built a hanging lamp for the dining area, and another near the front door, based on the theater lights at Taliesin. Below, Bernard Pyron and his friends had stopped by to see the house and were invited for dinner. They were among visitors that would number in the thousands over the years.

work, Mother was intrigued by the idea and envisioned a smaller-scale version on Woodpile Lake. Mr. Wright probably recognized that idea as impractical and instead produced drawings for two small cabins. She wrote about Wright's initial burst of energy for the project:

Mr. Wright went right ahead with our designs and got carried away. He gathered the Fellowship around him and drew buildings with 100-foot tall spires, lights and a bridge across our bay. One of the apprentices piped up and said, "It looks like Broadacre City!"

The designs he finally settled on were rock - two flat-roofed versions of the studio. One-room cottages with sleeping area in the living room, kitchen bath and patios.

In the winter of 1957-58 photos of the finished house were sent to Mr. Wright, who was pleased to see them.

Then Mr. Wright gave us the cottage design he had created for his sister Maginel, which had never been built. This was a triangular battered-wall, high-ceilinged tiny cottage, with a bedroom, bathroom, living room, kitchen - again with patios. Together with Mr. Wright we earmarked where the cottages would be built on our topographical map. We wanted to do that (the Maginel cottage) on the point right across from us; it's so steep you can't walk up. We would do it right on the edge so you can look down.

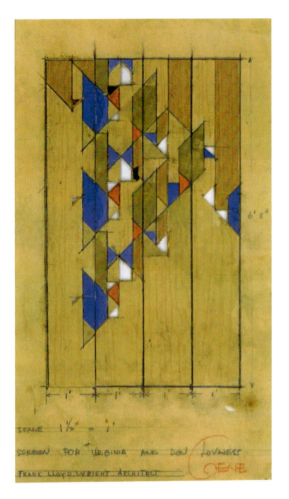

The other request Mother made in that January 1958 letter to Mr. Wright was for a means of achieving some privacy, especially between the living room and master bedroom. Doors would have been out of place and required a lot of room for swinging. A folding screen would be perfect: compact and a vehicle for an interesting design. In early 1959 Gene Masselink sent a drawing for the divider going into our "children's wing". My father executed it (in a mirror image) in enameled metals, stained wood and gold leaf.

A similar screen for the parents' bedroom doorway was designed by Mr. Wright.

Gene Masselink's reply in February 1959 had an long list of requested 3M products, and in another note later that year he offered help with any other designs.

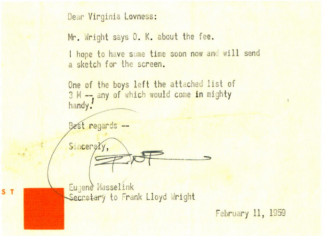

Dear Virginia Lovness:

Mr. Wright says O. K. about the fee.

I hope to have some time soon now and will send a sketch for the screen.

One of the boys left the attached list of 3 M — any of which would come in mighty handy!

Best regards —

Sincerely,

Eugene Masselink
Secretary to Frank Lloyd Wright

February 11, 1959

Dear Virginia and Don . . . . So sorry I did not have a chance to see you while you were here — but glad to hear you liked the little screen design. Let me know how it works out — and wasn't theresomething else you mentioned? Let me know what and if you want me to do so — I'll work it out.

TALIESIN   Thank you again for the SCOTCH

Below, in September, Mother again exaggerated about being ready to build. And rarely did a letter go to Taliesin without her reminding them that Don was ready, willing and able to pick up some products.

Cottages A, B and C (the Maginel cottage) would never be built, even though my parents' enthusiasm was high and their letter to Mr. Wright in the fall of 1958 indicated they were ready to begin the following spring. However, the seed of an idea planted during that visit in September would lie dormant for over a decade, and bear fruit when they did indeed begin building the Seth Peterson cottage (in fact, an improved version of it) in 1972. Mother's dream of a Wright "colony" of cottages would be limited to just two, although decades later a third structure—an adaptation of "Cottage A"—would be built on the site. She would live just long enough to see that, but in 1958 there was energy and excitement in the air. A new life in a Wright home had just begun!

September 15, 1958

Dear Mr. Wright,

Thank you for the usual enjoyable visit we had last week at Taliesin. Naturally we are very excited about the 2 cabins you are going to design for us. We are already hauling rock again and would like to start as soon as the frost leaves the ground next spring!

Do you suppose in a tiny bathroom a shower would take less room than a tub? We can hardly wait to see what you come up with!

If someone can drop us a note and let us know what size reels and type recording tape you use, Don will send some down.

Again - our sincerest thanks and Best Wishes

Love

D , V

The Lovnesses

February 3, 1959

Dear Jack,

Many thanks on the very speedy and very beautiful little cabin plans! We're thrilled! Don has a lot of things he'd like to talk over with you - probably questions - on it! It seems to be perfect, but Don thinks he may be able to put radiant heating in so it could be used year-round, etc.

We are going to try to finish all the little touches on the house before starting a cottage. We've written several times but have had no answer on a poker design for the fireplace and on a comfortable chair design. (Mr. Wright marked on your set of plans where they were to be put around the studio--7 of them I believe he figured out.) Also still need the kitchen stool Mr. Wright said he'd fix us up with! And the picnic table (which would be good on the cabin terrace also!) All we would need is a rough sketch.

Can you help us?!

Hope you and Lue can come up to see us this spring. Best regards to you both.

Right, by February the plans were received but the fever to begin had subsided. Of all her requests in this letter to John Howe, only the pokers would come through later - and in spades!

It's amazing to think that having just completed a project that took two years of sweat and blood, this pair would even consider another building spree. Mother indicated in her letter that they were ready to roll come spring, however. I'm not sure why they didn't go forward immediately; maybe sanity prevailed or maybe the huge projects in Iraq and Marin County were draining energy away from the drafting room at Taliesin. At Woodpile Lake, it would be 12 years before any more serious construction took place, and in the meantime there was much to keep them busy.

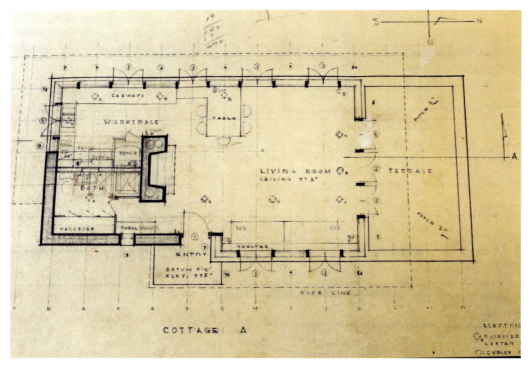

COTTAGE A

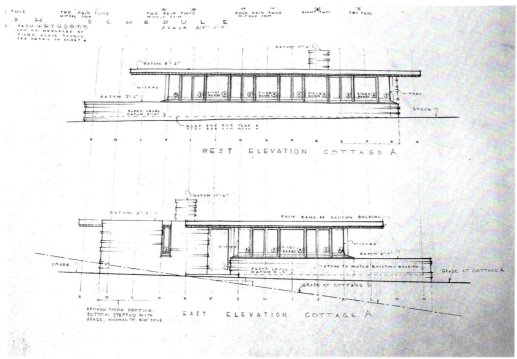

WEST ELEVATION COTTAGE A

EAST ELEVATION COTTAGE A

Cottage A was pretty straightforward as Wright designs go, but simplicity was what it was all about for this guest cottage. Cottage B was a variation on this theme.

Sixty years would pass before the design—adapted and modified —would rise just east of the studio. Those who see it today agree it complements the other buildings and is a worthy addition to the property.

Maginel (Maggie Nell) Wright Enright was Frank's younger sister, by ten years. She was an accomplished illustrator and artist who illustrated many successful children's books plus magazine covers and articles. She also designed shoes, clothing and fabric. She often summered at Taliesin and in 1948 Frank designed a home for her to be built nearby. She was hardly ready to retire to her ancestral home, however, and while she continued working in New England the idea of a house for her in Wisconsin quietly faded away. New life was breathed into it a decade later as "Cottage C" for the Lovnesses. Working drawings, produced a few years later, were slightly different than the original presentation drawings but in the end, it was never built.

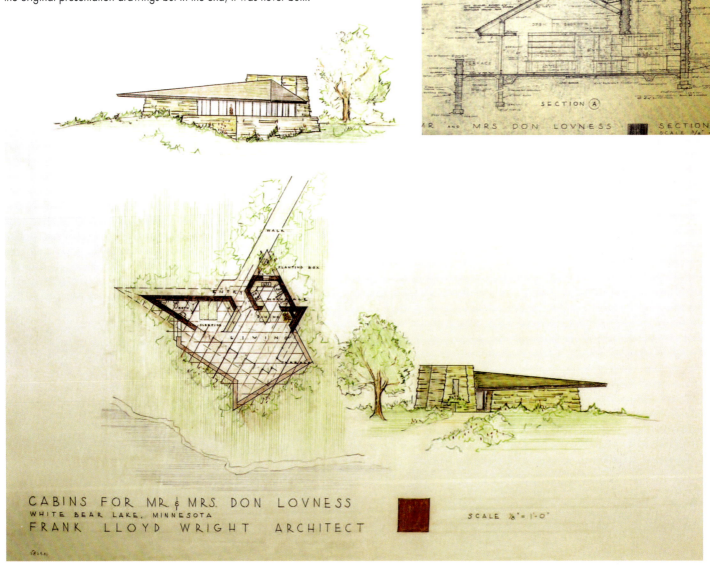

CABINS FOR MR. & MRS. DON LOVNESS
WHITE BEAR LAKE, MINNESOTA
FRANK LLOYD WRIGHT ARCHITECT
SCALE ⅛"=1'-0"

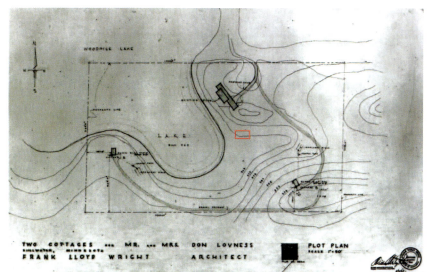

The two cabins were sited in a specific manner, some distance from the main house, allowing privacy for each guest and taking advantage of rises in the terrain. Cottage C would be on a point directly across from the studio, where Mother could see it across the lake. These drawings by Wes Peters are dated February, 1963.

The red mark indicates the approximate location of the cottage they did build in 1972-75.

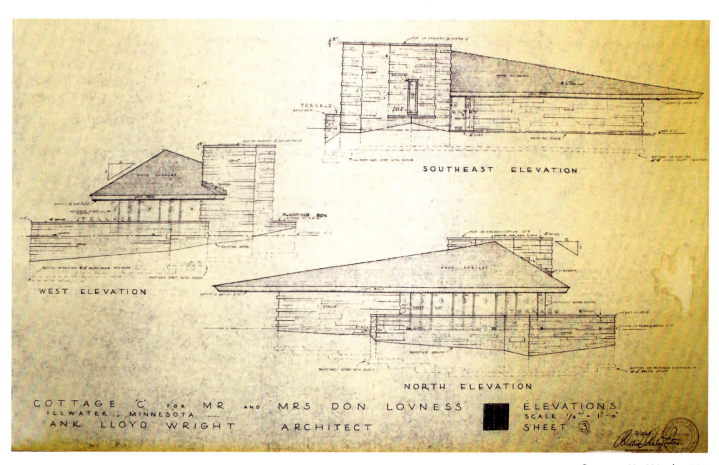

A 1980s view from the entrance looking north, and at left, evidence that the sun faded the red cushions. Mother later made beige covers.

D built a planter table based on the Little house furniture.

Over the years things would change in the house. The chairs and sofa were built by D in the 1960s based on designs from the Little house in Minnetonka. He also built floor lamp versions of Taliesin lamps. Art, sculptures and pottery came and went, and would move around the house. And always, there were plants; sometimes more, sometimes less but Mother loved her greenery.

Left, in the bedroom Ty and I shared there was a built-in desk with a chair and three drawers for each of us. We had a closet where Ty remembers she hung her clothes while I piled mine on the floor.

At the age of six it's easy to transition from what most people would consider privation into a living space that was a work of art. White Bear Lake was a distant memory and our trailer had been home - nothing special but nothing awful, just home. And now we had running water, a bathroom, a bedroom of our own and space to play indoors. Because the house had slowly risen around us, literally, there was no moment of awe when it was finally finished. Ty and I were just two little girls who had a new place to live, although it felt familiar since we had witnessed its creation.

There was, of course, no discussion about paint colors or wallpaper for the girls' room. There was rock and creosoted fir, oak trim and glass. There was red concrete and a built-in desk, with three drawers for each of us. We had a built-in closet although our clothes shared space with overcoats, as the front door was just steps away.

7
Ordinary and extraordinary

With the studio finished, Ty and I show off our matching outfits, probably made by Grandma Gladys. Mother was certainly capable of making our clothes but she had been a little preoccupied for the previous two years. One of her paintings hangs from the wall where a folding screen would be a few years later. There was precious little space for artwork on the walls, although pottery and figurines later filled the shelves.

In the summer of 1958 the newsletter "Inside 3M" featured a story about the house that roofing granule chemist Don Lovness and his wife Virginia built. Professional photographer Harlis Anderson documented "a day in the life" of the family including this touching scene of D reading to us at bedtime. Other than this posed moment, however, that never happened.

For her part, Mother was content with her new role of housewife although she continued with her painting, printmaking and other artistic pursuits. She reluctantly accepted that the huge canvasses she had often created were completely impractical for her new studio, which now consisted of the six-foot-square work table in the corner of the living room. But she was just as proficient on a smaller scale, making paper dolls for us.

Her own clothes had always been attention-getting and she not only sewed many of them, but created the designs or adapted something she had seen or a pattern she had. In later life she would wear expensive designer clothing but in her 30s there was no budget for that. Nevertheless, she always looked fashion forward, with her slim figure complemented by her clothing, jewelry and hairdo. She had already proven that being petite didn't keep her from being a hard worker; masonry wasn't objectionable, but having muscles was something she dreaded and for a while during building, she felt the need to wear long sleeves.

During our first few summers we had no screens - like thermal glass, Mr. Wright didn't seem to think they were necessary. My mother wrote about it:

Along with recommending plate glass windows Mr. Wright said it wasn't necessary to make screens. He said he'd lived for years without them. So we spent several years living with all the doors and windows wide open all summer. Our studio was an open pavilion and it worked fine. Breezes came through; also animals and turtles - lots of big snappers lived in the lake. There were skunks, raccoons, and often our

St. Paul newspaper columnist Doris Bock commented on Virginia's look in a 1953 piece. Five years later she is shown relaxing in her new home.

The original concept of a home which incorporated Mother's painting studio ended up allowing her only a corner of the living room for her work. By this time she had given up large canvasses for watercolors and the occasional linoleum print. This photo shows another side of her creativity: the patterning of the rock she laid. It's similar to that at Taliesin (right) but with a little more whimsy and flair. This wall would have been built near the end of rock work, when Mother and D had polished their craft and developed a style. Note that much of the limestone in Spring Green was thinner, requiring less work to dress and form the rock pieces.

In his home designs Wright sought to erase the distinction between indoors and out. With huge expanses of glass (and no screens), indoor plants and earthy tones in wood and stone, on a warm day the house was at one with nature.

cats would drop a live mouse in our bed at night. But that wasn't what was bothersome. It wasn't the mosquitoes - spraying controlled them. It was the black flies in late summer that bit and stung. Finally, screens were added!

The windows in our new house really brought the outside into the living space. They also brought a chill when the winter temps hit well below zero. Mr. Wright had said they would not frost up, and they didn't (at least until we got a dishwasher several years later). But when the winter wind blew sometimes we would have to stay several feet back from the glass to feel comfortable. Ironically, when the huge hearth was stoked and blazing (my father didn't use "logs", he used tree trunks), heat would be sucked out of the living space and up the chimney at a prodigious rate. We moved further away from the windows.

With the construction finished, Mother was happy to be tucking in bedclothes rather than tuckpointing masonry joints. She sewed the moss green velvet bed cover herself, along with all the upholstery like the hassock cushion at left. The large handmade Mexican rug in the parents' bedroom was the only floor covering in the house. Just below the far foot corner of the bed was a drain / vent valve for the in-floor heating system. The closet door, like the one in our bedroom, was creosoted plywood. The desk shelf at left was where our TV was located so the parents could watch from bed. Ty and I would sit on the floor and act as a remote control to change channels.

SCHOOL DAYS 1958-59

On my way to school in 1958, lunch bucket in hand. We were all bundled up for the cold, including the goat who had put on a layer of fat and some long fur. His summer job was to be the lawnmower. Mother and D had planted native prairie grasses which grew pretty tall but after the snow came he had to work a little harder at getting his lunch.

I was now going to school, hiking to the end of the driveway where the bus would stop. Mother and Ty walked with me along the sometimes muddy track, where we had to watch for big snapping turtles crossing from Woodpile Lake to the slough, and were often startled by ducks or herons who were feeding in the weeds or water. The Stillwater school district boundary ran through the middle of Woodpile, so this was the far end of the bus route and the ride was a long one. Ty started school three years later and for the next three years of elementary school we took the trip together.

Domesticity day-to-day

While D "brought home the bacon", Mother would prepare it. She was as bold in the kitchen as she was in her dress and her art. She loved to experiment with new dishes and her favorites were things like Miso soup with shrimp balls; the Japanese bowls she kept on the open shelves were not just for show. She would shop at an oriental market in the Twin Cities and prowl the butcher shops for things like Rocky Mountain Oysters. These exotic dishes were tried out on the family (with varying degrees of success), then served to guests, such as the stream of apprentices from Taliesin that came through for years.

Our everyday fare, however, was a little more pedestrian. Fish sticks were easy, as were Swanson TV dinners and pot pies. For lunch it might be peanut butter and honey sandwiches. These menus suited us girls just fine, although we drew the line at having D cook for us. Once when Mother was away he served us dinner consisting of a frozen weiner each. Nothing wrong with that except he was so unfamiliar with cooking he didn't know they had to be heated first.

In summer the driveway could be rocky or muddy or both. In some years the lake level would rise and new fill had to be brought in.

Minnesota winters are nothing to be taken lightly. Snow can accumulate many feet deep and on a flat roof, the weight can be significant. Shoveling the roof was a regular chore. For our long driveway we had a war-surplus jeep with a plow.

Inside our cozy home we enjoyed the Christmas holiday. Our stockings (two each) were hung with care, usually filled with hand-made gifts. We knew Santa would have no trouble getting down this chimney! On winter days the small table was a center of activity for Ty and me. For the cat the warm floor in front of the hearth was the center of inactivity.

At one point Mother entered a phase of eating for fitness after hearing Jack LaLanne on TV and tried to get us to eat brewer's yeast in shakes, which we hated, almost as much as we hated yogurt. She would chase us around the house with a spoonful of it, so in the end it worked out: we all got some exercise. Ty also hated eggs, but there was no running away from them. D was convinced an egg was necessary at least once a week, so every weekend for breakfast we would be served eggs with strict instructions: eat your eggs or you don't leave the table. We tried putting them in napkins or feeding them to the cat, which didn't really work. I could choke one down but not Ty, so there she sat. I don't think our parents had any idea how stubborn she could be. Hours went by. People would come and go. She was not about to eat an egg, however, and they finally had to give up.

Something else Ty and I both dreaded was the weekly Sunday trip to Welander's farm next door where Art would fill a metal can with fresh, raw milk. After sitting a bit the cream would rise to the top, something we thought was disgusting. The parents would put it on their cereal and in coffee. We avoided it completely.

Kitchens were something that Frank Lloyd Wright seemed to see as a necessary evil. He effectively refused to acknowledge their existence, instead calling the food preparation area a "workspace". There was no pretense of eating in this area unless you were standing up, and countertop space was at a premium. Open cabinet doors could be a hazard. Our state of the art refrigerator had doors that swung in the wrong direction—away from the sink and prep area—and blocked the aisle when they were open. The oven was as much in the dining area as in the kitchen, so removing a prune pork roast (one of Mother's favorites) could be a delicate safety operation. We didn't use rugs because they would keep the radiant heat from rising, so comfortable shoes were a necessity if you were cooking or cleaning for any length of time.

Mr. Wright showed genius in many aspects of his designs, but one that was particulary effective, especially in a residence, was the passage from low to high-ceiling spaces. Entering our front door a guest transitioned from an almost claustrophobic loggia—a connector from the car port— into an airy and breathtaking room, made larger by the glass that seemed to extend the space into the outdoors. Many people didn't consciously acknowledge the change but coming into that living room always had an effect on them, either conscious or unconscious. It was part of the "wow" factor that made you realize you weren't in an ordinary house.

Although we knew the house was somewhat different, Ty and I didn't at first realize just how different it was from an ordinary home. Until she started school Ty was, like me, pretty naive about other kids and their lives, as we had no close neighbors. She remembers in the second or third grade after the teacher had arranged a field trip to our home so the class could see a Frank Lloyd Wright house, Ty kept wondering when the group would tour the other kids' homes.

Joyce Welander still runs the family farm although she now raises Llamas instead of cattle. The old milk shed is still there, along with much of the equipment from years gone by, like this steel milk can. It may even have been one that D used to bring raw milk home.

Our shiny new oven was built into the stone of the fireplace. Countertops were bright red.

Cooking wasn't Mother's favorite thing to do but she went at it with gusto. The kitchen was small but efficient, and by the standards of the day, quite modern.

The low ceiling gave the kitchen a comfortable feeling of scale, although my father's head had only a few inches of clearance.

Just behind this camera vantage point was the warm spot near the furnace where my mother and I would meet on sleepless nights, sitting on the floor and reading cookbooks and stories by food writer M.F.K. Fisher.

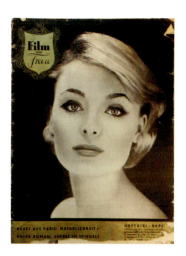

The new Frank Lloyd Wright-designed home was something of an international sensation. The German magazine *Film und Frau* featured the same photos as the 3M article and a slightly adapted text in an early volume of 1959 entitled, "Stone on stone, self-built."

Film und Frau was an upscale periodical that featured fashion, entertainment and regular articles about architecture.

Consider for a moment what a new home in America was like in 1955. Usually under 1000 square feet, with every room separated by walls, doors and hallways. Standard height ceilings, table in the kitchen. Wall-to-wall carpet was a new luxury and a garage was pretty much standard. Most roofs had short or no eaves at all. If there was any exterior ornamentation it might be faux pillars or non-functional shutters. On a small lot with close neighbors, the mid-century house was completely different from what we knew. Visitors to our home might have thought it was weird but we felt the same way about the typical suburban home. Stillwater was also full of large Victorian houses that were just as foreign to us. Our sense of "normal" was highly distorted!

Becoming tree farmers

Both my parents worked hard, but they also worked the system when it was to their advantage. A few years after the house was complete they made a significant change to the land around our home, with help from the state and federal government. Our acres were a remnant of old oak savannah, a balanced ecosystem with large oaks and minimal smaller trees and undergrowth, as opposed to pure prairie or heavy woods. The balance was maintained primarily by fire, either natural (lightning) or set by humans, something Native Americans had practiced regularly. Undergrowth was also kept in check by grazing, which is what Mr. Welander's cows had been doing for years. The oaks could withstand some fire, and a few grazing animals were beneficial. But the cows were now fenced out and we weren't about to burn the yard every spring. The oaks were stately and beautiful, but by nature they weren't numerous. Ever since construction began, curious people had been stopping by and the oaks didn't do much to shield the house from the road, especially in winter.

It's likely that Mother and D were looking not only for privacy, but a way to save money on taxes. Planting evergreens would certainly give us some natural screening, but also qualify for tax breaks if we planted enough of them to become a tree farm. In the spring of 1960 the first little trees arrived, four-year-old Norway (Red) Pines about a foot high. We tromped out into the fields and started planting. D would heel his shovel down into the soil, tilt it back to expose a hole and Ty and I would put the baby trees in place and pack the soil back down. Over the next few springs we planted thousands more and when they were older we would trim the candles each year, until they were too tall to manage. The only real setback in this program was the cows. A condition of purchase from Mr. Welander in 1955 was that his cows could graze on the property. They chased Mother when she was attempting to do some plein air painting, but she had come to terms with that. But now it turned out the cows found these seedlings quite tasty, so a talk with Welander was arranged. By this time, after seven years his herd had thinned as he got older, so he agreed to keep the cows away. As the trees grew, the look and feel of the property changed, with a "curtain" of trees now surrounding us on three sides. Later, when they were mature it was always pleasant to walk through the trees on a soft carpet of pine needles and of course the smell was lovely.

The Wright-designed furniture had not all been built in the summer of 1960. Our "cool" sofa from the St. Paul apartment served for several years in the living room. While the adults ate at the dining table on "regal" chairs, the coffee table was a just-right height for kid meals while we sat on the warm floor. Our cousin Leslie joined us for dinner which Mother served on Blue Willow plates. Like most everything in her life, even the dinnerware had to be beautiful.

The first of thousands of small trees came in the spring of 1960. Becoming an offical tree farm didn't require a lot of paperwork. Even the guidelines for planting were fairly informal, as seen on this hand drawn section map.

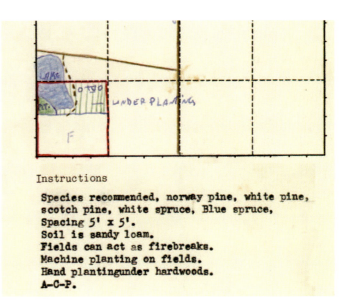

Instructions

Species recommended, norway pine, white pine, scotch pine, white spruce, Blue spruce, Spacing 5' x 5'.
Soil is sandy loam.
Fields can act as firebreaks.
Machine planting on fields.
Hand plantingunder hardwoods.
A-C-P.

A design for the yard

Franz Aust was an occasional visitor, maintaining an interest in the young family he had helped launch into the orbit of Mr. Wright and Taliesin. In 1962 the idea of a landscape design began to take shape, something my parents had always planned (more or less) but delayed out of necessity. The first page of Mr. Wright's original blueprints was a "plot plan" which included a site layout with a plunge pool, rock garden and specifics about the edge of the mowed areas. It was somewhat generic and they never went beyond the rock garden part of that plan. Franz Aust's ideas however, were exciting, with a 20-foot terrace, steps leading toward the lake, redwood planters with plastic domed covers and a fountain. An armillary sundial would be centered in the fountain, through which the water would spray. Our depleted bank account was rebounding enough to now consider an arrangement for the exterior that would complement the house.

Unfortunately, the plan never came to fruition, and some boulders and plantings made do for years. It wasn't that the gardening Mother and D did over time was not attractive, but it wasn't quite as inspired as Franz Aust's plan would have been. It would be 55 years later that a real yard and terrace design was created.

FRANZ A. AUST & ASSOCIATES

LANDSCAPE DESIGNERS, CONSULTANTS AND ENGINEERS
MADISON 5, WISCONSIN
2202 COMMONWEALTH AVENUE

November 23, 1962

Mr. and Mrs. Donald Lovness
Stillwater, Minnesota

Dear Don and Virginia:--

Under separate cover I am sending you two prints showing a proposed development of the terrace on the lake-side of your home.

The ideas shown are purely suggestive and should be checked in regard to levels, amount of excavation and fill required, etc.

The plan follows the same modulus as Brother Wright's plan, and the design is in keeping with the interior of the home and the exterior elevation. The terrace would tie onto the existing slab which, if I remember correctly, matches the interior floor and is red. The new slab would be of a brushed finish and darken the cement to lessen the reflections. There would be (2) two flagged areas 8'x 8' and three areas 4'x 6'.

The reflecting pool with its playful water jets and central feature of the armillary sun-dial as well as the "heap-big-injun" at the SW corner are the dominant and individualized features of the plan.

The planters C-D and E are important in the composition as a whole. Planters A and B are optional but would be interesting from the Studio, or shall we say the living room end windows?

The planter and step development I would want to check after the terrace is finished.

The pool provides 6 ceramic tile plaques 26"x 26" enclosed in a red-wood frame. (I was thinking of Virginia--for these would be her creations--should be very colorful and daring.)

Perhaps the two central ones would suffice. I have a feeling that Planters A and B plus the ceramic plaques at the end of the pool might be omitted. With them the terrace would loose some of its simplicity.

The areas adjacent to the terrace would consist of low plantings of ground cover, spreading evergreens and alpine currant.

Now for a few questions: (1) Is the Section A-A possible or are there too many steps? Can be reduced to 4 or 5. (2) Is the terrace too large as shown? Looks about right on paper. We would find a place for most of the existing boulders at the edge of the new cement.

Now mark up the blueprint--plenty of marginal comments--and return same as soon as possible. (I may not be able to work after the Minnesota-Wisconsin game tomorrow.) We are leaving for California Dec. 15, and I want to finish the construction plans for you before I go.

As ever,

Franz A.

f:F
r:A
l:A

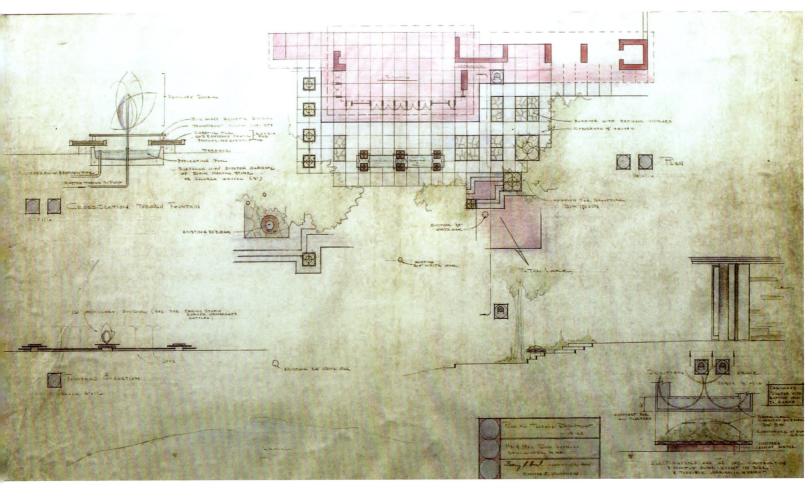

Franz Aust's initial drawing for a terrace almost doubled the size of the existing floor area. It would have further emphasized the idea of the house connecting with its environment and provided a lovely place to relax and entertain. The fountain pool, at 4 feet by almost 30 feet, would have been impressive. All these remained "would-haves", however. The plan was never carried forward.

Although the Franz Aust plan never came to fruition, we did have some large rocks on the lake side of the house, and Mother planted hosta and some flowers. D put in a few birch trees. One ornament there was a concrete "Sprite " that D cast; a simple and somewhat crude take on the Midway Gardens figurines. Years later he would cast some stellar reproductions.

D was a big-time jazz fan and in 1960 spent $75 on a single Lansing speaker for the hi-fi. He took his music (and Wright speeches) seriously.

Kid-sized spaces

For us children living in the house, the smaller spaces were the most inviting. Ty and I would play with our paper dolls or play games on the coffee table in the living room but that spot wasn't the center of our life. We would make a fort under the dining table with blankets and pillows (again, a small and cozy space) but for the most part, our bedroom was where reading and homework was done, games were played and even an occasional meal was taken. The cozy factor was important but as we got older, having a distinct separation from the parents entered into the equation. Mr. Wright had given the house a parents' wing and a children's wing at opposite ends. We have to give him credit for understanding how important that truly was.

One of Mother's skills that we loved was an ability to create paper dolls and clothing at a moment's notice. It was great incentive for us to behave and do our little chores around the house. As a special treat she would draw pretty ladies and cute girls on heavy paper, cut them out and then create lovely dresses, pantsuits and coats with tabs for them to "wear". Two or three of these dolls were worth hours of peace for her, but beyond the bribery aspect, she really enjoyed doing girly things with her girls.

When Barbie dolls arrived in the late 1950s she did the same thing in three dimensions, sewing fabulous little outfits that were much higher quality and—at least we thought—better looking than the commercially made pieces.

The party pad

The parents (for Ty and me, it was never "Mom and Dad" - it was "the parents") would have parties on a fairly regular basis. They had a wide circle of friends and people always enjoyed visiting the house. With a huge living area and the inviting hearth it made for convivial gatherings. The drinks flowed freely and things got boisterous as the evening wore on. Our girls' bed was the guest coat repository as there was never any free closet space. Since there was no other place for us to retire, we would climb the rock wall near the entry hallway and spend the night above the valance. From our perch there on pillows and blankets we would listen to the chatter and laughter, and peek down and watch the guests, with Mother holding court. D's booming laugh would echo around the room and he would talk about the house, explaining to architectural novices Mr. Wright's philosophy. Often we would nod off to sleep but we always heard the definitive signal that the party was ending: the jazz music would be replaced by a scratchy recording of Wright giving a speech or interview. After a few scotches D was sure everyone was interested in what the great architect had to say, but the usual result was a flurry of leave-taking.

The parties were memorable for our guests I'm sure, and usually booze-fueled, but on a day-to-day basis, D and Mother rarely drank. He was not one to come home from work and have a martini or even a beer, and Mother was kind of a lightweight when it came to putting it away. She was practiced at engaging in a party conversation with a glass in her hand but that

Mother was a fashion-forward, trend-setting woman and it couldn't help but rub off on her daughters. We were never adverse to dressing up and posing for the camera. The "Sprite" in the background is an early creation that D made, a rough replica of the figurines that had adorned Wright's Midway Gardens in the 1920s.

A couple of Barbies and Ken modeling some of the creations Mother made for them. There were always lots of fabric leftovers and sometimes Barbie would be wearing the same clothes Mother made for us.

Birthday parties were the same at a Frank Lloyd Wright home as anywhere else. Girls in dresses and bobby sox, with special hats and party favors. Mother was a consummate hostess to everyone, from children to celebrities.

The boulders and lillies were the extent of our landscaping in the first few years.

champagne or wine would last a long time.

What D did do regularly is smoke - a pipe or cigars, and like most other kids at the time, we put up with second hand smoke, not knowing any better. His pipe tobacco was sometimes sweet and enjoyable but those cigars were just stinky.

Ty and I were always three years apart in our school grades, so between elementary, junior high and high school we didn't often attend the same school. During the school year we didn't take part in sports but I was involved in some extracurricular activities such as editor of the school literary magazine. Unless an after school event would still allow us to catch the late bus home, we didn't stay, as there was no way Mother or D were going to drive 15 minutes to school to pick us up. We were free-range kids, pretty much on our own to amuse ourselves but limited by the distance to many school friends' houses. In the summer our playmates were the neighbors across the lake. Margie, Lorna and Judi were close friends who attended a different school district and, consequently, we didn't see them much otherwise. In addition to the school boundary, Woodpile Lake also was the outer limit for local calling in that section of the Twin Cities. We had a White Bear Lake exchange phone number (initially on a party line shared with two other homes) and it was long distance to call our school friends in Stillwater. This telephone situation further isolated us from the school pals but gave us the opportunity to have two different sets of friends. Summers were spent without ever seeing any of our Stillwater schoolmates but we played with our Mahtomedi friends swimming in the lake or horseback riding. We loved having overnight sleepovers at Judi's barn where we told each other scary stories well into the wee hours of the night.

Winter

There was plenty to do close to home. In the winter D would drive the Jeep down to the lake and plow a rink for us, plus a skating oval around the perimeter. One of our neighborhood boys, Clellan, could skate backwards, spin and do "Ice Follies" moves, something we all admired and envied. (Clellan was quite a bit older than me or my sister and loved to tease and harass us, often chasing us at the bus stop with dead animals or salamanders in the spring.) Although D didn't spend a lot of time or effort maintaining the rink after that initial plowing, Ty ad I would shovel snow off and revel in those cold clear days when the sun would briefly melt only the very top of the ice, creating a smooth, hard surface. Especially in winter, the lake was a focal point for local kids, a conduit to friendships for us. The neighbor kids from across the lake would come and join us for a day of skating followed by returning to our house and sliding our half-frozen feet under the rugs to let the radiant heating in the floor thaw them out.

When the weather was so bad the schools were closed, Mother would sometimes take us in the four-wheel-drive Jeep to Minneapolis where we would shop and have an exotic lunch at a Chinese restaurant. In those days most people in the eastern suburbs would only venture as far as St. Paul if they were going to "the cities". Minneapolis was just that much further and I

The fashionistas are at it again, in Mother's clothes that are only a little too big. A few years after the house was finished there were some ornamental bushes and decorative boulders around the patio. D let the "lawn" go native for the most part.

think it was even a little scary to them. The bigger city had more interesting places to visit and shop, however, and my parents always thought of St. Paul as being a little provincial in comparison. And for some reason D had a bug up his butt about Stillwater and didn't like to take his business there.

Winter offered all kinds of other opportunities for outside play, especially when the snow was high. We would build snow forts by digging into drifts, creating comfortable and quiet little spaces where our imagination ran wild. That peace was sometimes shattered when our dog Sugarfoot—always eager to keep us company— would burst on the scene with a treasure offering. Sometimes it was a dead skunk she had found, sometimes an unidentified but very bloody stump of an appendage from some large animal.

Sugarfoot Cheyenne Bodie was a Doberman named after two western TV show heroes of the day. Ostensibly she was a guard dog but in fact, way too sweet and friendly for the job. She was the first Dobie of many to come. We loved her.

Years later when she was suffering from cancer D took her out in the woods to put her down with his rifle. He could be a gruff, matter-of-fact guy, a pragmatist when it came to taking care of business - and this was a straight-forward case of putting her out of her misery. We waited and after a while saw him walking back toward the house. He looked a little choked up, as we all were. Then we saw Sugar, walking behind him. He couldn't do it after all, at least not that day. Tough guy, indeed.

Dogs were pretty much a constant at our house. Mother and D liked having Dobermans because they put the fear of God in strangers who would drive in to see the place unannounced. Not that they wished any harm to the tourists, but it was good to know when someone was ap-

Mother's look would change regularly and she had an eclectic wardrobe. At nine I was not all that enthusiastic about new hair styles but soon enough I would be following in her fashion footsteps.

Sugarfoot always wanted to play with us; there was no way she'd do anything else if we were around. Here cousin Leslie joins us for some romping in the snow.

proaching and with a dog as a greeting party at least there was some barking in the driveway instead of a knock at the door. The parents tended to pad around the house in underwear; D in his boxer shorts and Mother in her bra and panties. If visitors made it to the front door (which had no window) without warning it was pretty awkward to meet them in that state.

Since we were pretty isolated, D would work around the yard in whatever clothing (or lack thereof) that was comfortable. If he was dressed in his usual raggedy work clothes and someone drove in to see the Wright house, he would just say he was the hired help and they'd have to come back when the owners were home. Once or twice he was in minimal clothing on a hot day and had to hide behind some trees. In spite of being in the country, in a way it was like living in a fishbowl.

Woodpile Lake

In the summer Ty and I would push a wooden raft out to the middle of the lake, paddling hard to move the 55-gallon drums that kept it afloat. It was our spot to sun, lounge, talk about boys and listen to the top 40 hits on our little Japanese transistor radio. We would spend hours swimming and diving; I was so proud of being able to dive off backwards. After a storm the wind sometimes moved the raft to one shore or the other, so we would spend much of the day "rescuing" the raft, swimming it back into position to re-anchor it with a cement block. Mother would occasionally look out at the lake to count heads, only mildly concerned.

At certain times of year the bloodsuckers came out and we would jump into the water from shore in huge tractor inner tubes, trying hard to keep from getting wet, paddling out to the raft. Other times we had a contest involved sitting on opposite sides of a tube, then rocking back and forward with increasing force until one of us was launched off into the water. It was great fun but these tractor tubes had long metal inflating stems and it's amazing we never got impaled.

We had a wooden row boat that D used occasionally for fishing, and sometimes he would get big snapping turtles. He would bring them to shore (carefully), and hang them by their tails after slitting their throats to let them bleed out. Mother made turtle soup but Ty and I wouldn't touch it after seeing those creepy carcasses.

He would take the boat out occasionally to control the weeds that grew in the lake, spreading chemicals as he rowed around. Copper Sulfate was a herbicide that would control weeds but it was also toxic to fish. Like so many other chemicals used at the time, we were all a little naive about their long-term effects. D kept a 55 gallon drum of DDT and he would spray it around to keep the mosquitoes in check. God knows what other nasty concoctions he would use. As a chemist he was aware of exactly what he was doing but to him, these were simply tools. He kept large heavy glass containers of chemicals half-buried in the woods across the driveway from our house, and drums of chemicals in his shed. It made some sense: if you were going to keep the stuff around, don't put it on a shelf where it can fall off. Years later we joked about his stash, referring to it as "Love Canal".

Snapping turtles with shells the size of manhole covers had to be respected. They could snap a thick branch—or a finger—in half with their powerful jaws.

At Taliesin, the lake below the main house was weed-free for years thanks to our father; it wasn't just tape that he supplied to the Fellowship. At D's direction they would come with a truck to the Twin Cities to pick up sacks of herbicide. In the early 1970s when Wes Peters was working on the Pearl Palace for the Shah of Iran's sister, princess Shams Pahlavi, he wrote to D asking for suggestions about how to clear the waters in the man-made lakes around the palace. We don't have a record of D's response, but when it came to deadly chemicals, Wes knew who to call. He referred to my father (with affection) as "Silent Spring Lovness".

Living past the end of the garbage truck route, we would pile our refuse up in bags against the side of D's work shed. In the spring we'd have to load it all onto a trailer and bring it to the local dump. After months outside, the bags were falling apart and it was a messy, awful job.

Dressed up for some summer occasion (it wasn't church) Ty and I looked cute in our pink dresses and D held Algae the Siamese cat.

A teenage rite of summer for us was relaxing in a tube or our raft on the lake.

Mr. Wright designed a folding screen for the parents' bedroom, which my father built.

Mother's specialty was quick sketches with brushes. Some of her favorite subjects were Taliesin buildings like the Midway barns.

Summers stretched on and we enjoyed finding adventures in the woods or down the dirt road, sometimes just hanging out at the two-room Grant town hall on the roof of the outhouse. One summer when it had rained a lot, the blacktop road flooded a half mile away and Ty and I would head down there and swim, daring each other to swim where cars had driven earlier. We loved to try to spend the night outside in a hammock but the mosquitoes always chased us inside before the night was done. We resorted to using my father's old oilcloth war surplus tent with a little clear plastic window. We brought pillows and blankets and were happy to sleep in the front yard where the mosquitos buzzed outside. Sometimes, however, it would rain, the tent would steam up and smell old and moldy and the adventure would lose its excitement.

D helped us build a treehouse high in an oak tree in the woods. We would love to climb up there to survey the world and pretend we lived there. Fifty years later, the oak is still alive and rungs to the treehouse survive!

Being isolated in the country meant we had to invent things to do. We had a swing set since before the house was completed and a game we developed involved swinging as high as possible and at the outer edge of the arc, launching our flip-flops as far as we could. At Halloween, there were no nearby houses so some years we would each put on a sheet, go outside, then knock on the door. Mother would answer and give us Butterfingers (our favorites). We would repeat a few more times, with Mother expressing surprise (and a little horror) each time she opened the door: "Oh my goodness, ghosts!" Other years we would go to Uncle Paul and Aunt Donna's house in the suburbs and trick-or-treat with our cousins, happily filling our bags with candy.

Unlike most homes, our television was not in the living room or a den. The black and white set was on a shelf along the windows, across from the bed in Mother and D's room. We would all gather to watch Gunsmoke, Perry Mason and other hits from the '60s with Ty and I at the foot of the bed on the floor. We were the channel changers and volume controllers, according to the parents' wishes. We were also called into duty as massagers and hair brushers while they watched. Dinner was not a formal affair at our house; sometimes it would just be popcorn in front of the tube. And that was fine with us.

We would sometimes go to a movie, but usually at a drive-in theater. The parents liked horror movies and often these would come packaged as a triple-feature. Ty and I would be so scared. I think I'm still emotionally scarred from seeing Hush, Hush, Sweet Charlotte in 1964.

Virginia the artist

Mother continued to paint but on a smaller scale. There was no room to create large canvasses, and nowhere to display them when complete. After a while most of her artistic efforts were directed toward teaching, and she had a number of enthusiastic pupils who would join her for plein air expeditions. Her favorite medium was watercolor and in demonstrating the techniques, she was always exasperated by the small, tentative dabs of color they would apply to the paper. "It's water," she would say. "It's meant to flow!"

Like many artists, she went through a period of non-objective painting, often with heavy layers and bold strokes of oil paint. Many of these were done on masonite board in the years following the studio's completion. Some mysteriously disappeared and it was not until 2017 that it was discovered D had used the boards for covers over the lights in the upper valance around the living room. They were trimmed to size and a few had holes cut for electrical boxes.

She didn't give up on big projects altogether, though. They had many friends among the higher-up management at 3M and it was some of these wives who came to her for classes - and in one case, a special assignment. North Oaks is a private residential enclave in the suburbs of St. Paul, at the time a gated community. Friends who lived there hired Mother to paint a mural in their swimming pool area. Another large work was a canvas featuring a single rose, a commission for Elisabeth Ljungkull. Payment was a used pink Cadillac; it was a deal that worked out well all around. Elisabeth was known as "Peter" to her friends, and she and husband Rolf were good friends, having loaned the parents money when construction of the studio was nearly finished. At that time, so was their bank account!

All dressed up for a shopping trip in the pink Cadillac, Ty and I pose with Mother at Grandma Helen's house.

North Suburbia Goes 'West Bank'

ARTIST VIRGINIA LOVENESS, pointing out a detail of technique, was one of many artists who displayed their work at the Annual Autumn White Bear Art Fair,

Sept. 15 and 16. The woman with artist Loveness was one of many city and suburban residents who attended the fair.

Any artist will tell you that art fairs are a tough way to make a living, but Mother was willing to slog through these weekend events, smiling and charming her customers. This 1962 local news headline refers to the U of M art dept. on the "West Bank" in Minneapolis, where I would later attend.

American Horticultural Society

From the March, 1991 journal edition: Don Lovness' "pioneering research into the life of the soil" has earned him this year's G.B. Gunlogson Award, which recognizes the creative use of new technology to make home gardening more productive and enjoyable and to benefit people/plant relationships.

Lovness spent 20 years with the 3M Company conducting new product research before joining the Ringer Corporation as a senior scientist. He helped Judd Ringer organize the company in 1961 and became a member of the board of directors in 1965. Ringer specializes in research, development, and sales of natural gardening products.

Lovness developed Ringer's proprietary fertilizer technology and holds nearly a dozen patents relating to soil biotechnology.

From shingle granules to soil supplements

In the mid-1960s D made a career move, and not just within his industry. It was the kind of change that would terrify many men who had worked in a large corporate structure like 3M, and D had been with that company for two decades. Our family would drive to Minneapolis in the evening, after work, where my father had business meetings while Mother, Ty and I would have dinner and wait for him at a large Chinese restaurant on Hennepin Avenue. His move was to join Judd Ringer in his eponymous company that sold lawn and garden products. Judd was a college football star, a Marine fighter pilot in WWII and a high-profile member of several boards and organizations over the years. Ringer Corporation's first product was the "Killer Kane", a dandelion spot weedkiller. Later, Judd's handsome face was on the company's brochures as they moved toward natural fertilizers and composting boosters, but D was the one who created those products.

My Aunt Donna's husband, engineer Paul Bredow also worked for the company, developing mechanical products like fine mist sprayers for insecticides in the 1960s. In 1973 D was granted a patent for a poison-filled ant trap and five years later for a soil supplement for potted plants - demonstrating his range of abilities. By the 1980s, Ringer's main product was called "Restore", a fertilizer D had developed that contained natural ingredients like steam-treated poultry feathers, bone meal, wheat bran and ash from burned sunflower seeds. Microorganisms and enzymes were added to release the materials into the soil.

Ringer Corp was at the leading edge of an organic movement away from chemical fertilizers and weed killers, and in 1988 an Upper Midwest drought killed so many lawns that homeowners, landscapers and golf course managers were all looking for a better way. At the time Ringer was doing $5 million in business, and tripled that within two years. Judd had sold a majority interest to investors in 1985, and with an infusion of capital new managers changed the format from a mail-order catalog company to a staple in 5,000 hardware and garden stores.

Another change was to go all-out in advertising. A high-profile Minneapolis agency created four clever 30-second TV spots featuring John Cleese (of Monty Python fame), who used his deadpan humor to demonstrate (in a chef's hat) how to make humus, and while holding a block of sod explaining how "Restore" feeds both the blades and the grass roots - claiming that unlike competitors, Restore was safe: "Nothing goes into it that could hurt anything it eventually goes into."

That statement brought complaints from chemical competitors like Chemlawn and Scotts, and the dust-up made business news in the *Wall Street Journal*. The EPA even got involved, pointed out that Chemlawn itself had been chastised for gimmick advertising with "feel good assurances and misleading claims."

That tempest in a teapot subsided and by the early '90s the product line included hundreds of products. As D prepared to retire he was awarded the 1991 G.B. Gunlogson Award from the American Horticultural Society for "Pioneering research into the life of the soil." The award was well-deserved, but an ironic honor for the man Wes Peters had once called "Silent Spring Lovness."

True to form, D supplied Taliesin with Restore for indoor plants, lawns and fruit trees, along with compost starter and other garden helpers. Several letters of appreciation from the Fellowship indicate that the fertilizers worked, both in Wisconsin and Arizona. The products were popular with gardeners all over, riding a trend away from harmful chemicals, although in the late 1990s the company acquired some traditional herbicide manufacturers and became more diversified. D was a board member for several years but his involvement diminished as he and Mother began traveling and collecting Oriental art in earnest. As a sort of exclamation mark to retirement they even bought a motorhome!

At top left, in 1985 a modest 20-page, 2-color, mail-order catalog was the primary sales tool for Ringer products. A sale of the company to investors soon expanded the line's visibility with TV ads featuring John Cleese, splashier catalogs (with a toll-free number for ordering) and expansion into retail outlets like hardware and garden stores.

At left, D and Judd Ringer confer during a trade show in Europe, another market expansion made by new investor owners.

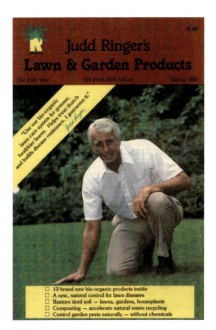

Storing and freezing

Over the years when the parents would take a road trip to Mexico or visit Taliesin, they would stash their daughters at the grandparents' houses. Mother would also stash her ever-growing wardrobe at Gladys' house in the basement on a seasonal basis. October and April were transfer months, and I always disliked going into the dank confines of Grandma's downstairs storage area. It wasn't an optimal solution but there was no place at home for extra clothing or other seasonal stuff. D had a shed where he could work on projects, store his chemicals and use his tools, and I think Mother was annoyed that she didn't have easy access to a spot for her things.

The south end of the carport was an 8' x 8' room that Mr. Wright designated a "tool room". We did store rakes, shovels and other implements there, but much of the space was taken by a chest freezer. In addition to the usual contents, that freezer held boxes of frozen mice from the University of Minnesota. Our pet screech owl named Hoot lived in a cage in the parents' bedroom and he would have a meal each day of half a mouse. D had an arrangement with researchers at the U: they would save dissected mice for him and he would pick them up frozen in bulk. This was certainly preferable to buying them at a pet store as he had done for Leda the Boa.

That freezer was also put to use during one winter when several puppies from a litter died. The ground was frozen so they would have to wait for spring to be buried, and D figured the freezer was as good a place as any to store them. Another unusual frozen item was part of a bear's head; the jaws were given to Mother so she could use the teeth in jewelry. One other time the freezer was packed with bull testicles. Mother, in her unending quest to find interesting meals thought she would try to make what she had heard called "Rocky Mountain Oysters". She went to an old-fashioned butcher shop in Minneapolis with sawdust on the floor and told the butcher what she wanted. He explained that they didn't stock them but he would order some for her, and asked how much she wanted. Having no idea, she said, "Three pounds?"

When the call came a few days later she went to pick them up. She gave the butcher her name and with a flash of recognition he smiled, turned over his shoulder and yelled, "The little lady's here for her testicles!" The butcher must have misunderstood her original order as there were in fact about 30 pounds worth, but Mother was so embarrassed she quickly paid, took her huge package and ran out the door. Some of the first "Oyster' meals were served to Taliesin apprentices. Apprentice Bill Calvert remembers coming to the Twin Cities to pick up a load of 3M products and of course, he stayed the night at the studio. On returning to Taliesin Mrs. Wright asked about what Virginia had served (perhaps sensing it was something out-of-the-ordinary) but he diligently avoided telling her the truth. Wes Peters became a big fan of them, sliced thin and sauteed. He would raid the freezer as soon as he arrived at the Lovness house to visit, to make sure it was on the menu.

Hoot the screech owl was rescued by Mother as a baby and she nursed it to adulthood. He was well fed with little mice carcasses every day and lived for decades. He had friends outside the parents' bedroom and they would often hoot to each other at night.

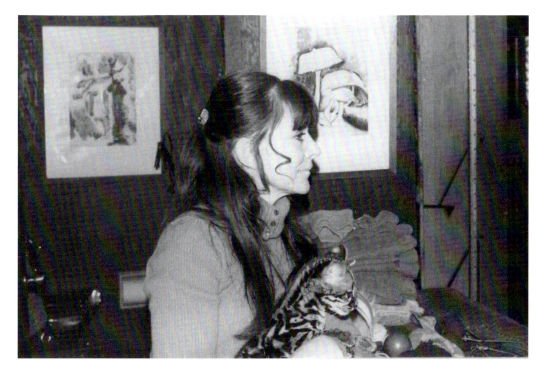

The margay lived in a cage in the parents' bedroom. She was gentle with those of us she knew but would explode in a ball of hissing, growling fur at strangers. The bedroom closet doors and the bathroom were the only places in the house mother had space to display any paintings!

Ten little piggies - or at least they seemed so at feeding time. This litter of Dobermans came to the rescue when cash was needed to continue building the cottage.

The menagerie

The constant parade of animals never let up. Peter and Rolf Ljungkull's son Gus remembers how Mother and D acquired Cindy the Margay, a South American wildcat. They were having dinner at a restaurant when in casual conversation the waiter mentioned he had a Margay, and explained that there was a problem. It would hide in the closet and surprise people by jumping out onto their heads. They told the young man they would take it, and it came to live at our house.

Dobermans were pretty much the standard for dogs, and there were several males and females over the years. Mother became something of an expert in the breeding world and the females were pampered. Others, however, lived outside in a doghouse.

A beautiful green parrot who lived for many years was named Chester. He was very good at imitating Mother's voice, although his vocabulary was limited to a few phrases. He would love to say, "Here, Bunny, Bunny". The cat named Bunny would come tearing around the corner, expecting to be fed by Mother. The poor cat never could figure out if it the voice was real, and probably suffered some psychological damage from the confusion. A blue and gold macaw later lived at the cottage for years. There were burmese cats, a baby squirrel named E.T. (who met his end when a guest flushed him down the toilet), more dogs and a constant parade of wild animals Mother would feed. The deer were ever present, and a lone male wild turkey would come to the cottage front steps for a handout most mornings for two years. One fall day he appeared with three females in tow. "Our boy has done well," Mother proudly said.

Bibles and baloney

Mother and D had each been given the opportunity to become practicing Christians as children. He just wasn't interested, and I think Mother was still embarrassed and angered by being baptised at age twelve along with some babies. Church wasn't a part of our lives, and in a way, that made it difficult for me at school. There was never any overt pressure or prejudice but I always felt a need to fit in. For many activities there were forms to fill out and often it would ask your religion. Hardly anybody would write "none", so I just put "Catholic" like some of the kids I knew. Since there were two Catholic churches in Stillwater, one for the Irish and one for the Germans just blocks apart, I could always claim to be from whatever the other church was, if asked. Thus, one problem was solved but another popped up; it was hard to remember that on Fridays I couldn't bring my favorite—a baloney sandwich—for lunch.

D was much loved by his friends and they enjoyed his jokes, but his sense of humor was often at other's expense. When Ty was still pretty little she found a beautiful wooly caterpillar and waited all day for D to arrive home from work so she could show him. She was so proud, and when she gave it to him he picked it up and said, "Is this for me?" When Ty said yes he popped it in his mouth, swallowed and with a wide grin exclaimed, "Yum!"

Chester the parrot would drive the cat crazy, imitating Mother's voice.

Multiple dogs was the norm for many years at our house. We also had Burmese cats (and kittens). The Doberman puppies were carefully groomed for new homes, their tails and ears cropped and propped to stand up properly.

A blue and gold parrot was a later member of the Lovness zoo, living in the cottage.

These were just two of my proms in 1968 and '69; Mother was busy for weeks making dresses for me. My dates made it through the Doberman gauntlet on these occasions, and we posed for D's camera.

A worse example is when one winter night he changed the time on my alarm clock. I was always a dutiful, hard working student and a member of the National Honor Society. I would never be late for school. One night he changed the 6:30 alarm to go off even though it was only about 3 a.m. I got up, was dressed and was ready to go out the door with my books in the usual amount of time. As I was about to leave, Mother came out from the bedroom and explained his prank.

When boys started coming around to see me he would make sure to say in a loud voice, "Get 'em, Rocky!" The dogs weren't actually trained to sic but just hearing that command was enough to send a boyfriend scurrying. After a while it was easier to just sneak out at night to see my beaus - and I had a lot of them. I got to go to two proms each year; one in Stillwater and one in North St. Paul where the Mahtomedi kids went to school. I had job at the Viking drive-in near there and as a waitress got to met lots of boys. The job was also a way to make money which I was putting away for college.

The collectors

As part of a growing interest in Wright's architecture, they began to collect related items like stained glass and decorative pieces from other buildings including Louis Sullivan's. On a trip to the East Coast where a Sullivan building was being demolished, D sent Ty and me inside to get a broken decorative teller grate while he waited for us in the car.

They also loved estate sales and would never miss a sale held by Tommy Kahn, where they would buy art items. Ty remembers that we would arrive in the middle of the night to get a number to be in line. The parents had the whole thing planned; each of us had an assignment, a particular item or items they saw at the preview, and when the sale opened we would each make a beeline for that particular piece.

They later began to attend auctions, especially at Rose Galleries in Minneapolis where Mother would bid on jewelry, her number card bouncing up and down during the whole sale. D never bid on anything, but Mother amassed quite a collection, certainly influenced by Mrs. Wright.

Mexican misadventure

Mother and D had been collectors since they were married, albeit on a small scale. They made occasional trips to Mexico and became interested in pre-Columbian figurines, which in the 1950s and '60s were available if you knew who to ask. Locals would sometimes dig them up in the hills and offer them for sale to Americans. Over time, however, border agents began to ask more questions about these stone and ceramic bowls, figures and animals, so Mother would put removable paint on them in gaudy colors to make them look like cheap souvenirs. Mexico was a place they loved, and had even considered moving there and opening a hotel when they were first married. They didn't think of it as particularly dangerous, and never had

Dressed in my Viking Drive-in waitress uniform, I admire some roses from an admirer.

No matter how crazy my clothes, I always looked like a wallflower next to my mother, shown here at Taliesin West.

Our extended family wasn't big, but we did the normal things on holidays. At Christmas 1966 Grandma Gladys and Aunt Mabel were in attendance with D's sister Donna and my cousins Leslie and David. Donna's husband Paul Bredow took the photo. D, as usual, looks uninterested in a family gathering.

Our friends in Mexico knew many locals who could procure pre-Columbian art, and my parents became experts at identifying the pieces. D did some carbon dating on them.

David and I had my parents' approval as a couple, not least because he was handy to have around when D needed some help.

any safety issues until a few years later when I came along on a trip to Mazatlan.

I had just finished a college year in Spain as a student at the University of Madrid (through Macalester College) and my Spanish was pretty good. The family drove down in our 1969 bright orange Dodge Charger, not exactly the lowest-profile car you could imagine. We visited old friend Dewey Albinson, a well-known painter from Minnesota who at the time lived in Mexico most of the year. In Mazatlan, we met up with his friend who supplied us with a nice selection of pre-Columbian pieces and shortly thereafter, we were stopped by the Federales. Guns drawn, they arrested us, took our car, our documents and our money and put us in their car. For the rest of the day they drove us around at gunpoint while I tried to explain we weren't the drug smugglers they were looking for. My father was smoking a cigar and making jokes, as usual. Finally arriving at an empty warehouse, we entered and saw a Mexican man chained to a bed-frame. Apparently they had found their man, and they acknowledged we were not guilty of any drug crimes. They didn't have any interest in the historic art pieces in the trunk, and returned the car and our documents (but not our money). By way of apology and to celebrate our freedom they produced a bottle of warm champagne and we all drank it from styrofoam cups. It was a strange end to a pretty bizarre day.

David

One of Ty's school friends was Mary Uppgren, who came to a birthday party at our house. Her mother brought Mary's older brother, David when she came to pick her up. He was fascinated with the house, something he'd never before seen. Several years later David, who was in my high school class, became fascinated with me as well. Thoughtful gifts and his intelligence won me over; we shared the pursuit of knowledge and culture, at least in a high-school sort of way. We were both part of honors contract, a program for A students, and of course, I was a striver when it came to studying. We dated in high school, beginning with the movie "2001, A Space Odyssey", which was a pretty big deal since we had to drive across town to the Cinerama theater to see it.

David and I both went to Macalester College in St. Paul, where I lived in a dorm for the first semester before moving home and commuting the rest of the school year. In my second year of college I spent the winter/spring semester in Spain, living with a family in Madrid and attending classes in Spanish, a language I was only just learning. The experience was life-changing and I am so grateful to have had the chance.

My parents did not pay for my college or my lodging - or my study abroad in Spain, so I became quite aware of monetary limitations in my late teens and early twenties. In my junior year I transferred to the University of Minnesota, as I could no longer afford private college tuition, even though it was only a few thousand dollars. Because my liberal arts prerequisites were mostly met, I could spend most of my time at the Studio Art department on the West Bank in Minneapolis. The old industrial building had high ceilings, concrete floors and lots of studios with opportunities to make art and meet interesting - and sometimes weird people.

My approach to living spaces took many twists and turns during my college years! Never satisfied with the ordinary, I seemed to always seek out 'different' types of dwellings. I was always on a budget, so perhaps those decisions were financial necessity. My first "place of my own" to live was in a building near the U that was cheap, but ended up being temporary - when it was condemned after my Stillwater friend Gee Gee and I had only lived there a few months. David was involved at the time helping my father with the latest project, a cottage on our property in Stillwater, so he and I ended up moving in together in a place near Dinkytown, a village of shops adjacent to campus. He had helped out around our house previously, and my father liked the idea of an enthusiastic, hard worker who didn't ask a lot. I doubt David was ever paid much for all the labor he put into the cottage and other projects, but being around my parents and up to his elbows in Frank Lloyd Wright designs set him on a course that would lead to his career as an architect, and a portfolio of stunning designs.

After a year or so David and I thought a studio for me would be a good idea, so we looked for space that fit our budget, which was about zero. A semi-abandoned building on North Washington Avenue in Minneapolis' Warehouse District seemed promising. All we had to do was clean out the old mattresses and trash accumulated during years as a flop house, stepping over the drunks who had passed out in the doorway. There was no heat or running water, so I'd have to clean up at the hotel where I worked as a waitress. After a few months of this, when winter came it was time to find another spot, and we moved to relative luxury on the fourth floor of the Textile Building a few blocks away. We now had space; open, raw and unadorned but it was warm. The adjacent rooms were piled high with car fenders, but at least these neighbors were quiet.

My first apartment, condemned!

Below, on our 1971 trip to Mexico, we drove our orange Charger, visiting painter Dewey Albinson and his wife Myra.

Ty and I went along on several trips to Mexico, although she missed the Federales adventure.

There was a freight elevator and bathrooms (but no shower) down the hall. The roof was our penthouse patio. Our friend Barry moved in to share rent and we got a cat named Earl Grey, who would perch on the window ledge and peer down four stories. He loved it, we loved it. I had boxes covered with colorful cloth as end tables, a Wright-inspired coffee table and a few bookshelves. My huge paintings were the room dividers and David's Altec Lansing "Voice of the Theater" speakers were the only furnishing really worth any money. Later I moved to another warehouse a few blocks away when David and I split up, but he ended up spending more time with my parents than I did over the years.

David was intelligent and well read, and unafraid to take on technical challenges. When he started work on the cottage with D he had little building experience. "Don knew how do a lot of things," he recalled, "and I knew how to do some things. It was a learning opportunity, I was eighteen, I didn't know shit from shinola." But he learned from my father, he taught himself and later, studied at the U of M Architecture School. He went on to know most of my parents' Taliesin friends, to work for Tom Monaghan, and to create some wonderful structures in the Wright style.

Gordon

In my last year of college I was full time at the Studio Art department, stretching canvasses that were taller than I was, throwing colors at them in abstract form—something my mother had done years before—and painting angels and biblical characters in colorful tableaus. Who knows where that came from? By spring I had a new Bachelor of Fine Arts degree and a new job at a new hotel downtown Minneapolis, the Marquette Inn in the new 52-story IDS building. On the third floor was the Gallery, a balcony restaurant that hung over the Crystal Court, the glass-enclosed atrium of the full-square-block building. I served the diners in a tight blue and white Swiss-miss outfit, with knee-high stockings and a frilly white blouse. We had to supply our own white waitress shoes but I didn't have any, so I painted my clunky platform shoes with gesso, the white base paint used as canvas primer.

The kitchen was shared with an adjacent restaurant, the Marquis Room, where tuxedoed waiters did tableside service, filleting and flaming up a storm as high rollers watched. In the restaurant biz at the time, waiters were fairly rare and as a rule of thumb, they were either foreign or gay. And that's what I assumed about the cute dark-haired young man named Gordon I saw ladling consommé onto his service cart; he wasn't foreign, so... But as I found out after a little test flirting, he wasn't gay after all. We would ride the elevators to the unfinished floors of the hotel to make out while our tables waited for their salad. We went out after work to a beer and pool joint on the West Bank; clearly he knew how to treat a lady. He drove me home that night and on subsequent dates in his Mercedes - a 15 year old roadster with rust holes and a patched canvas top. But his cars were like my living quarters: bohemian. Maybe we had something in common.

The roof of the Textile building was our penthouse sunbathing spa, cocktail hour venue, and where I posed with one of my paintings for David's Hasselblad camera on a sunny day in 1974.

My relationship with Gordie (he dislikes that name, but I'm grandfathered in) was tumultuous at times and it took a few years before it was solid enough to be called, well, solid. But by 1975 he and I had been dating long enough that a "meet the parents" moment was due. By that time he had worked hard to restore his 1957 Mercedes 190SL roadster with some engine work, a new top, extensive bodywork and fresh paint. Like the other men in my life, he had learned by doing. We put the top down on a lovely summer day and headed for Woodpile Lake. Being a car guy, he was proud of his rare model, and the fact that it now looked pretty good. But when we pulled in the driveway he didn't even acknowledge the two Wright structures, as his eyes were on the 1955 Mercedes 300SL Gullwing that my parents were selling for Wes Peters, a car that made his look as common as a VW. Adding insult to injury, when they walked over to greet us, Mother was as charming as ever, but D didn't offer a handshake or even say hello. He just looked at Gordie's front fender and said, "You've a got a few runs in the paint there."

It was an inauspicious start to the relationship between Gordie and me as a couple and my parents. We were never really part of their inner circle, most likely because they thought David Uppgren and I should have stayed together. David did end up very much involved with them and their friends for years, while Gordie and I visited and socialized only occasionally. And that was OK; after almost 40 years of marriage we've had a pretty good run together.

As an art student, I made friends among other painters, printmakers and photographers, like Debbie Bell, who took this fun portrait of Gordie and me.

In a studio of my own in the Warehouse District I could devote the entire space to painting, but in 1976 I moved to the St. Croix valley and never looked back at city life.

A 190SL (top) is cool, but nothing like Wes Peters' 300SL Gullwing!

8

The cottage

In the fall of 1958 Mr. Wright was pleased that my parents had finished their home on time, under budget and—from the photos they showed him—to a high standard. They had also cemented the relationship with Taliesin by supplying adhesives, recording tape, sealants and other 3M products gratis. He wanted to give them a bonus: more designs for additional houses on their property. As they spoke with him in the drafting room at Taliesin he pointed to plans on a table. "Why don't you build this one? He'll never build it."

The drawings were of an 880 square foot, three-room cottage with an angular, cantilevered roof. The project was underway for a young man who had commissioned Wright to design a small home. His name was Seth Peterson and he had been an admirer of Wright's work since an early age. Growing up near Spring Green, after high school he applied for an apprenticeship position at Taliesin but was refused, not having the "tuition' amount. He became a computer operator for the State of Wisconsin, then joined the Army. After two years in the service he returned to his job with the State in the new field of computers. Undiscouraged by missing an opportunity to join the Fellowship, and now with a reliable income he asked Mr. Wright to design his dream house. After being rebuffed (Mother had related that Wright didn't like Peterson) he cleverly took a step that would ensure his request was accepted: he sent a retainer. Naturally, money in hand was a motivator to the ever-strapped Wright, who, after cashing the check was now obligated to create a plan.

Clearly, from his comments to my parents, Mr. Wright had little respect for or faith that Seth Peterson would bring the project to fruition, but Wright and architects at Taliesin drew plans in the summer of 1958 based on topo maps and photos (just as he had with my parents home). Mother's notes had an interesting entry:

It turned out that Michael Sutton had just arrived at Taliesin—a new young apprentice —and someone handed him a sketch of Mr. Wright's to do a cottage for a young man named Seth Peterson. So with little knowledge of the workings of architecture he went ahead with a drawing. Everyone else was working on the Marin County project and didn't have time to bother with such a small commission. Michael said he never got any supervision, so when it was built, it never really functioned. The bedroom and kitchen were too small.

The following spring, work began on the cottage at a lovely site Peterson owned above Mirror Lake, some 40 miles from Spring Green near the Wisconsin Dells. Mr. Wright never visited the property, and did not live to see the finished product, passing away in April of 1959. Peterson hired a contractor but in order to save money, put much of his own time into construction as well. Like my parents, he had a vision and was doing all he could to see it through.

Sandstone came from a quarry some 20 miles away. Masons and carpenters had the structure essentially complete by late fall 1959, although several shortcuts had been taken in the quality of materials and processes. Peterson and his fiancé spent weekends at the nearly complete home in November, but sometime later the planned marriage was called off. He and his

The restored Peterson cottage in 2017.

At the Peterson cottage, sandstone with a red tinge came from a quarry nearby. Much of the trim in the original structure was plywood and other inexpensive woods, replicated in the restoration in the early 1990s.

Far left, a simple folding door separates the living room and bedroom. The small bathroom has a minimalist shower.

Below, the tiny kitchen with doors to the mechanical area - within which is the upper room reached by ladder. In our Lovness cottage the kitchen is larger and an upper room is accessible by stairs. Note that the space here is so limited the only kitchen countertop area intrudes into the entrance window area.

parents had taken out a building loan that summer but by the following spring cost overruns caused subcontractors to file liens.

Unfortunately, the 23-year-old took his own life in April, 1960, never having lived in the almost-complete cottage.

New owners

The construction was halted for some time but the cottage was finally finished when the property was sold to Lillian Pritchard in April, 1962 for $15,000 - significantly less than the construction cost. Mrs. Pritchard's son Owen took up residence and added outbuildings and a chain link fence. Photos from the period show that he had pedestrian taste in furniture, and probably considered the house too small. He commissioned the Taliesin architects to design an addition. The plan presented to him included two additional bedrooms, a gallery, a large studio with a "Birdwalk" style lookout and an expansive terrace with pool. Huge retaining walls, stairs and paved areas increased the size of the original project four-fold or more. It's not surprising that Pritchard was unable to finance the plan. The property was offered for sale soon thereafter and in 1966, after protracted negotiations, sold to the State of Wisconsin. Mirror Lake State Park had been in the planning stages since 1962 and was opened in August, 1966. The Peterson cottage became part of the new park.

The cottage was a mile from the park headquarters and there was no consensus about how to use it. The State of Wisconsin boarded it up after 1966 and it was a sort of albatross for the park administration. They didn't really know what to do with it and no maintenance or efforts to slow nature's attack had been made. Their only focus was on keeping people out and preventing injuries. There was no plan for rehab and at that time it appeared that the cottage's fate would be razing. In fact, it would be almost 25 years before the structure was rebuilt, and during that time it would decline even further at the hands of both nature and vandalism.

Around 1970 Mother and D visited the Peterson cottage, taking many photos and inspecting every corner. It had been closed up for four years and even though it was only a decade old was showing distinct signs of decay, as the original building process had involved some shortcuts with materials and it was clear the waterproofing was substandard.

Looking around the damaged structure my parents tried to imagine a similar cottage on Woodpile Lake. In reality, anything built by them would be a copy but it seemed probable that if built, their cottage would be the *only* cottage; at the time Seth Peterson's original appeared not long for this world. I'm sure they felt some kind of obligation to preserve the design, which even in its ramshackle state exuded an energy and solidity even though it was tiny. Wes Peters once described the Peterson cottage as having "More architecture per square foot than any building Wright ever built," and Mother and D probably felt as much during that summer visit.

In 1970 the Peterson cottage was closed but had not yet deteriorated significantly. Mother and D inspected the building and D took many photos. Opposite: the flat roofs and shingled sloped roof were still intact. A seven-foot addition to the chimney can be seen as lighter-colored stone. Twenty years later almost all of the structural wood, all mechanical systems and most of the glass were replaced in a restoration that cost over ten times the original amount to build the cottage.

The other three designs from 1958 had not been built on our property, maybe because their practical use was in question. Did we really need three tiny guest houses? Perhaps one compelling reason the Peterson design was attractive had to do with the potential for a basement. The seasonal movement of our clothes from Grandma Gladys' house and back again was tiresome, and the amount of storage space available for other "stuff" was severely limited in the studio. A basement, that most Midwestern of housing design attributes, was sorely needed.

Frank Lloyd Wright had no use for basements, however. He had criticized the common central plains home, once writing, "Invariably the damp, sticky clay of the prairie was dug out for a basement under the whole house and the rubble-stone walls of this dank basement always stuck up above the ground a foot or so - and blinked through half-windows." But in reality, what would prevent putting another level—inconspicuous from the outside—under the main floor if the cottage design was built? In Mother's notes she wrote:

Wes and Mrs. Wright, Don and I were sitting in the living room at Taliesin talking about the cottage plans. Mrs. Wright asked why we would want to build another of Mr. Wright's designs when we had a beautiful home already. I answered, "They should be built."

Mrs. Wright then said, "You'll be very wealthy someday. You know how much Mr. Wright's houses are worth nowadays."

I remember answering, "It will cost a lot to build. Then we'll have upkeep and taxes. So instead of being wealthy we'll be even poorer!" And so it is.

The problem then was which cottage should we build? The Seth Peterson cottage was going to be demolished. Reminiscing about how Mr. Wright had suggested we build that one before he designed the other two smaller versions of our main studio, both Wes and Mrs. Wright said that was the answer. Go ahead and build the Peterson design with the necessary changes: room somewhere for the furnace and water heater; not in the tiny kitchen! Not just a rope to climb up to the balcony. And cabinets low enough that the lady of the house could reach the knob.

Wes Peters got right to work, pulling out the original plans, and with John Rattenbury, making corrections to make it more livable. He also did the engineering and brought the design up to code. One of the key differences between the Peterson and the Lovness designs was an outgrowth of having a basement. At Mirror Lake, the utilities were awkwardly placed in a room adjacent to the small kitchen. The cupboards were too high for Mother to reach. At Woodpile Lake the well pressure tank, water heater and key plumbing components were downstairs, as well as the washer, dryer and hydronic boiler, mirroring what would be found in a typical basement.

In our cottage, access to the lower level was through a 27 inch door in the kitchen (narrow by necessity and to avoid it being obtrusive) and a steep stairway going down. As in most houses where stairways were "stacked", in this case another set of treads went up at the same angle to a small loft above the kitchen. The loft was not very practical except maybe as a meditation

Following the letter of the law, D applied for a building permit which was issued in July of 1971. The Township of Grant had about 2000 residents at the time, and administrative work was done by part-time "consultants".

The work was described as a "summer patio addition" and the permit fee was $11.25. It's doubtful the job was ever formally inspected.

D and helpers laying block for the south side basement wall of the cottage. Friends and acquaintances were enlisted to work when extra hands were needed. The base for the fireplace is seen at center. The area in the foreground became a secure storage area with an old safe door later installed.

Below, Mother's work shoes were flip flops.

Below left, the fireplace takes shape with firebrick forming the back wall.

space, but a skylight gave it and the kitchen space below a nice glow. The circuitous way you got to that stairway was through the bathroom, which was off the bedroom. It didn't get used much.

Our kitchen was truly tiny (although larger than the Peterson kitchen), but because the ceiling was 12 feet it didn't feel claustrophobic. Red countertops made the space cheerful and Mother usually had a row of red goblets on the open shelves.

Another marathon

Fifteen years after beginning construction of the studio, Mother and D again committed to a huge undertaking which promised to absorb their time for at least three years. The difference of course, was that this time they didn't have to live in a trailer, their financial circumstances were better, and their two little girls weren't little anymore. Ty was still at home but I was going to college, living in Minneapolis. The bank loan for the studio was almost paid off, a loan that had been hard won by pleading with the bankers that the unusual home was a good risk. Mother recalled, "Ironically, over the years those same bankers brought lots of prospective clients out to see the kind of inspired investing their bank did!"

The limestone from the St. Thomas project was similar in color and texture to the studio rock although it came from 100 miles away. The real difference was that it was flat, top and bottom and after being split, ready to lay.

In planning for construction, some of D's true character came to the fore. He was a pragmatist and always willing to look for a way to save a buck. He also recognized that some of the best building material didn't necessarily come from a lumber yard. On Minneapolis' north side near the river were the scrap iron yards and companies that dealt in used equipment and construction materials. D and David Uppgren hauled truck loads of long rough dimensional lumber home and spent days pulling nails, many of which—being a hundred years old—broke off. David recalls they went through a lot of saw blades cutting and ripping them to size. These large pieces would form the cantilevered roof framing.

In another act of inspired scrounging, D picked up the clear redwood of huge water tanks from the Grain Belt Brewery in Northeast Minneapolis. The large boards were ripped and cut to make the interior and window trim.

The cottage would be placed on a rise 100 feet south of the studio, slightly higher and overlooking the lake to the southwest. It was a siting arrangement similar to the Peterson cottage but much closer to the water. Construction began in spring, 1972 when a neighboring farmer excavated a hole and a foundation perimeter was poured. A central slab would hold the base for the fireplace, a huge hearth like that in the studio and the central element in the home. Blocks were laid to create the basement and 2x10 joists with plywood flooring completed the base - all pretty standard stuff. For the exposed walls and the fireplace, stone came from a quarry near Mankato, Minnesota; it was slightly softer Kasota limestone that came with a dual bonus. It was already cut and finished six sides, but was in large sawn slabs, and had to be split by hand into long 4-inch wide pieces to be used. Best of all, it was cheap, being left over from a huge project in St. Paul. In 1971 St. Thomas College (now the University of St. Thomas) built

Looking northwest, a plank walkway leads to what will be the entrance to the cottage. The wall at left was faced with stone but most of the area in the foreground was filled and topped with huge boulders. D was careful to not damage the large oaks that provided a grand entryway to the home.

David Uppgren laying blocks. The metal ties between courses make a connection between the inner blocks and the outer stone.

the O'Shaughnessy Educational Center at its Summit Avenue campus. Limestone made up the exterior on that building and the surplus was perfect raw material for the cottage.

Unlike the first time around with the studio fireplace and some walls, this structure was built with concrete blocks, then faced with limestone. Very little of the blockwork was carefully finished, with no attempt to tool the joints; it would be covered anyway. It only had to be level in both planes, and some of it was stepped back as a base for the courses of stone. The limestone finishing was another matter. The patterning was a little more uniform than on the studio, but they managed to make it interesting. Even though the stone was pre-cut, there were at least three thicknesses in height, and some variations in color - which D used to attractive advantage in places like the bedroom. Lengths were random and protrusions were made with different sized pieces for a nice variety.

The original cottage in Wisconsin had a random slate stone floor and D created a facsimile of that using Kasota stone similar to the walls, but already flat cut in one inch slabs. The stone was easy to work with, cutting and fitting to size. When the grout was dry it was sealed. The sloped roof was finished in cedar shingles. The exterior was treated with creosote, as on the studio.

David Uppgren works on the top layer of stone. Behind him the window framing is in place and the old timbers are ready to be set in their positions.

The first stones laid for the project, Mother is raking the joints near the corner of the bedroom entrance; that section was stone from floor to ceiling. Keeping her company is Rocky the Doberman.

The back wall of the living room had built-in benches, so no stone was needed on the lower part. Two horizontal strips of wood were set in the wall to anchor shelves.

Roof framing starts with support beams where the flat roof changes to the cantilevered area.

The project ended up taking about four years, mainly, as my mother said, "Because we were living comfortably and there was no hurry." There were some snags, however. Mother wrote about a recurring theme:

Then the money obstacles again! Armed with photos of our completed studio and the cottage —as far as it was built—plus photos of the land, we again hit the bank, very confident this time. Construction of a complete house under our belt and paid for, and land that we owned. Plus another wonderful Frank Lloyd Wright plan partially completed. But the banks had the same response as before. We couldn't get a loan anywhere.

At this time we had a beautiful pedigree show German Doberman. Stocky, broad chest, dark colored, intelligent; a real beauty that we had bred with a top German Doberman from Canada. We were working with an avid show breeder who flew in for the birth event. There were special vitamins and immediate socializing for the newborn puppies. It was a really big deal with special training for the whole litter. We had the best vet to do the tails and later the ears, and then the labor-intensive job of getting the ears to stand perfectly.

The time came to find homes for our pampered family so we put an ad in the paper for $140 each, as the going rate was $130. There was no response at all! When we put another ad in and no response, panic began to set in. The gorgeous pups were growing rapidly; what to do, we couldn't keep them all!

Then Don commented that nobody knows they're special. Raise the price! And we did. At $500 the prospective puppy owners came immediately. It would take a visit or two or three to determine if the hopeful owners were worthy of owning one of these jewels! Surprisingly, all were young men, not families hoping for a guard dog. The young men came, admired our architecture and then loved their chosen puppy, armed with five crisp $100 bills straight from the bank. After each puppy left, with strict orders on diet, training, socializing, etc., we'd throw the bills in the air and jump up and down as they fell, to celebrate the next phase of building which we were now able to accomplish.

One puppy went to George Foreman, heavyweight champion of the world. He was going to take his Doberman with him as a running companion in his training. Another puppy won a top award in India. But the best thing was that we could keep on building - without the damn bank! Later a local bank finally came through when the cottage was almost completed. Thanks a lot!

Mother's role in construction was similar to the studio: she was the cook, the go-fer and the joint raker. In that role, she had to wait until the cement was partly set up, which was sometimes near midnight. Don might be hungry and tired, but his supper often had to wait. She didn't like the job but Mother wouldn't let him rake the joints because, as she said, "He was far too sloppy."

The first guest in the new cottage was to be Mrs. Wright herself. As they were finishing building there was a mad dash to get the chairs done so that she'd have something to sit on. Mrs. Wright called to ask if there was room for her entourage. Mother assured her there was, but then she asked if any "strange things" had happened lately. She may have been remem-

Corteena von Alarich, (we knew her as "Tina") the pedigreed Doberman that bankrolled construction when funds ran out in 1973.

Finished stone work wasn't wasted on areas that would be below grade. By the time snow came in the late fall of 1974 the house was covered and mostly closed in. Rough excavating was finished, although a low limestone wall would be added to the entry area later, and landscaping would include huge boulders.

Note that with a low sun angle in December, the cottage windows are filled with light. In the summer midday sun they would be shaded by the roof.

In the following spring and summer the ceiling, soffit and decorative panels were added before the windows were installed.

The chairs and table were originally designed for the Hollyhock (Barnsdall) house in Los Angeles in 1921. The original drawings were dusted off by Wes Peters and provided to D, who built a variation on the theme. The square blocks were weights tied to the cushion tassel ends in the back of the chair. These chairs weren't particularly easy to move but they certainly looked "regal". In 2018 a pair was offered at a premier auction house with an estimate of $20-$30,000

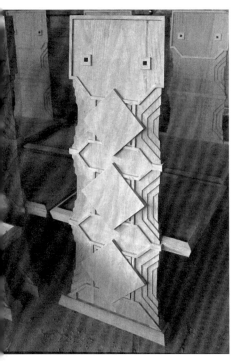

A loft above the kitchen was lit by a skylight with a leaded glass Little house window.

By the summer of 1975 the interior was nearing completion. Gordie and I visited and took photos of the progress. At left, looking from the bedroom into the living room you can see the built-in shelving above the bed area. Below, the cabinets at the opposite end of the bedroom, with decorative square holes that double as "pulls" were originals from the Little house in Minneapolis (the original location in the Little house at right below). The shelf at left would hold the TV, which D and Mother would watch from bed, as in the studio. These built-ins were a departure from—and an improvement over—the Peterson cottage design.

bering Katie, the neighbor who broke the studio windows in 1957.

Either Mrs. Wright was clairvoyant or news traveled fast through the Taliesin grapevine, because there had indeed been some "strange things" going on. Mother's notes recall:

Mark, one of the young men who had bought a Doberman called to ask if I could help correct a mistake he made on a pedigree paper; the AKC need my signature. "Of course," I said. And could he bring a friend? "Of course." When they came on a Saturday we stopped working long enough to give them a short tour.

The following Saturday Mark called, asking if Don was there. I was confused but he explained, "No, my friend Don." I hadn't gotten the name, I only remembered a tall, handsome blonde young man. Mark asked if we'd let him know because Don's parents—and the police— were looking for him. No sooner had I hung up but I heard a car honking all the way from the road and down our long driveway, into the car port and up to the loggia. And there he was - the tall, handsome blonde "Don".

"I've come to stay!" he said, and his car was packed with everything he thought he needed to move in with us. He kept looking behind him saying, "They're after me!" so it wasn't difficult to imagine he was a bit paranoid. I assured him he was safe here and suggested he lie down on the hammock while I finished on the phone.

I called the police and asked them to help, telling them to please come quietly so the young man would not be frightened. Meanwhile Don had been working at the cottage, heard all the honking and came in asking, "What are you doing now, bartering again? The guy out here says he has some stuff for you." When I explained what was happening, Don got his gun, put it in a paper bag and went out to talk to "Don". The young man took everything out of his pockets and wallet to show Don, then took off all his clothes and lay down on our sidewalk. He had painted his private parts blue!

Meanwhile the police arrived, three squad cars with sirens screaming. When they saw the size of our visitor, they took their time. The confrontation lasted hours - so long that I made coffee and brought it out with cake. The police asked if I would try to talk "Blue Boy" into getting his clothes on to go to the hospital - he wouldn't talk with them. Eventually the police did take him to the hospital - nude.

His parents arrived after the festivities were over and had coffee and cake, with a tour of the studio and cottage. They were grateful to find that their son was with us, in a safe and beautiful place. Mrs. Wright called that afternoon, wanting to finalize her plans to be our first guest in the new cottage. Her first question was, "How far is it from the cottage to the studio?" Then, "You haven't had any more strange visitors, have you?" After a I gave her a synopsis of the day's events there was a long pause, while I waited for some deep philosophical comment.

"Well," she said, "if it had to happen wasn't it lucky he was young and handsome?"

Mrs. Wright postponed that visit at the last minute, after D, Mother and Al Drap worked well into the night before her scheduled arrival. But over the years Mrs. Wright always enjoyed telling people the story of "Blue Boy", even embellishing it to the point where a naked blue boy was standing at the foot of Mother's bed at night.

Mother and D moved to the cottage as their principal residence, and in spite of its small

D salvaged a few items from the Little house, including an intricate window, which was used in the cottage as a skylight above the kitchen. It's ironic that no one wanted the Little house when it was torn down in 1972, but in recent years, single windows like this have sold for $100,000 or more.

D had only a small workshed some distance from the cottage, so after it was enclosed the living room became his wood shop for building furniture, cabinets and a light totem. Cabinets under the windows held radiant heat elements, powered by a boiler. No cabinets were used there in the Peterson plan.

Unlike when they began construction of the studio, D was now equipped with the best power tools: a unisaw (table saw) a jointer and a complete selection of specialty hand tools.

By the summer of 1974 the rock and landscaping were in place and the approach stairs and low wall were under construction. The boulders had a coarse surface and grew interesting moss and lichen as they aged in place.

size she always thought of it as perfect for the two of them. The basement became a storage area for her expanding wardrobe, there were tables for working and sewing (with an industrial sewing machine) and the washer and dryer were there, out of the way. The only snag was the steep and narrow stairway from the main floor, which over the years caused her to fall more than once. Thankfully, no serious injuries ever ocurred.

As careful as D was with details in the woodwork, he was a contrarian when it came to the septic system. In keeping with his aversion to building inspectors, he kept it simple. The sewer pipe that exited the basement under the front steps went directly to a tank, then a drainfield downhill to the south. That gently sloping bowl was just a few feet above lake water level and after a few years, when the lake level rose, Mother complained the floor drain was backing up in the basement. Eventually, professionals had to be called in and a new set of tanks was put in place, with pumps pushing the effluent uphill to the only place where a drainfield could legally be placed. It annoyed him no end, as he hated to spend money on what he considered non-essentials!

Pat Kluempke tells about a time when D bought a water heater for the cottage, wholesale of course, from a Twin Cities supplier. When it turned out to be too tall for the space he jury-rigged a vent that went down, then up. The building inspector was not amused and made him replace the unit. No way would the vendor take it back, and D's cheapness cost him double.

The fireplace grate is stylized, a Wes Peters design, unlike the straight grill in the Peterson cottage.

The folding screen to the bedroom with gold leaf was also designed by Wes Peters; it reflects the shape of the shadows cast by the clerestory windows.

Unlike the Peterson cottage, ceilings were nicely grained fir in angled patterns that complemented the flow of the space. Above, the west patio doors have not been installed but the clerestory glass and patterned covers are in place.

The careful ceiling pattern extended out to the soffits. Small slots allowed venting.

In a departure from the Peterson design, the cottage patio was a lovely, private spot that overlooked the lake and offered great sunset viewing. Mother loved geraniums and small potted plants as well as her exotic tropicals.

After a couple of decades the cottage looked more like it belonged. The trees and shrubs had grown, walls were built and my father's sprites graced the entry. Similar to Taliesin, chimes and Soleri bells hung from the trees. Here my mother and I share a laugh on the steps during a summer afternoon.

This 1986 shot shows the furniture and lamp stands that D built.

Built-in shelving was custom-fitted to the rock walls. At this point in 1976 a table was built but the sofa and chairs were not yet finished.

Below, the small desk at right was suggested by Jack Howe while the cottage was already under construction; there was a joint in the stone at just the right height. And as usual, Mother filled the house with plants.

Growing Up Wright **179**

The cottage kitchen was suited to a single cook at a time, but because the ceiling was way up there, it didn't seem claustrophobic. This 1976 photo shows the original countertops and sink.

At a Christmas get-together in the 1980s the Lovness girls tried working together in the space but it wasn't successful. The door at right leads downstairs.

Later, in the 1990s, the counter was changed to red tiles, and a black sink was installed. Mother was only 5' 2" (and shrinking by then) but she had an effective means of getting to the shelves that were higher than her reach.

Just as in the studio, the parents' bed was up against the wall with no headboard.

In the main room, a dining chair back is shown with the cord and block that kept the cushions upright.

A sofa and chairs were built from white oak, based on designs from the Little house, like the ones in the studio. Mother sewed bright red cushions but later they were replaced with beige ones.

9

Arcola idyll

My parents were friends with the Van Meiers from Stillwater and had seriously considered building the Wright home on their river property. Henry Van Meier was the resident doctor in town, known for his unusual and experimental treatments. A believer in hypnosis, Dr. Van Meier used this practice on his patients to solve many conditions. He and his lovely wife Katherine owned a home and office, a narrow brick Victorian a half block off Main Street on Myrtle in the heart of downtown Stillwater. The lower level was Henry's medical practice with a waiting room, two exam rooms and an office. Upstairs was their living quarters where they spent the winter months.

In the 1930s they had purchased 60 acres along the St. Croix river, six miles north, with a home built in 1847 in a grand Greek Revival style. The third oldest and largest timber frame house in Minnesota, it was originally built by brothers John and Martin Mower, and a small but prosperous village had grown at the site, where spring-fed streams drove a 34-foot diameter waterwheel sawmill. Arcola, as it was called, included a general store, blacksmith shop, a small school and other services for the mill workers whose homes were built along the sloping hillside. Their lumber company lasted only into the 1870s, however, and by the time Henry and Katherine purchased the property, much of it was in decay.

The young couple discovered Arcola by accident - while searching for ferns, it's been told - and we can assume that the attraction for Katherine was the grand home with its majestic view of the river. A true Southern Belle at heart, she had grown up Katherine Copenhaver at Rosemont, an old estate in Marion, Virginia. Her mother Laura Lu Scherer and father Bascom were leading citizens of the town. A biography notes that "...the Copenhavers were able to provide for their several children the great advantages of education and culture." Katherine's older sister Eleanor was a national leader of the early YWCA and married writer and poet Sherwood Anderson, who came to Marion as its newspaper editor. He also came to Arcola as a visitor. Interestingly, Anderson had written promotional brochure copy for Wright's American System-Built Homes in 1916. Anderson had stated that Wright was "the greatest architect America has known," and felt that his own efforts to create a distinct American style of fiction paralleled Wright's drive to provide Americans with inexpensive, quality housing - an idea that came to fruition with his Usonian homes a few decades later. Katherine told stories of other art world notables who spent time at Arcola, from Gertrude Stein to Minnesota painter Jo Lutz Rollins. Rollins had started the Stillwater Art Colony which brought art students to the valley for working seminars during a decade in the 1940s.

It was a concept akin to this that motivated the Van Meiers to build - and in some cases drag or roll - structures onto the property to create their own colony for creative types. Although most of the original village buildings were long gone, the huge 40 foot stone mill chimney still stood and to it they attached a rustic three-season cabin, sided in tree bark. Other structures appeared over the years in the mossy shade like mushrooms. Just to the north of the Mill, another small house was set back from the bluff, which at that point rose to ten feet above the

Katherine and Henry were photographed on the main floor of his Stillwater office in the 1940s. Up the stairs were their winter living quarters. Henry is likely relating a fishing tale; they were both avid outdoor sportsmen, in skiing, hunting, fishing and horseback riding, along with hiking and gardening.

Above, Henry in the 1950s, about the time my parents were looking for property for their Wright home.

The Mower house had been modified and added to over the years and in the 1970s it was still an impressive sight - but the gracefulness was slowly giving way to dilapidation. Deferred maintenance was taking a toll from roof to basement, where every rain storm would bring more silt.

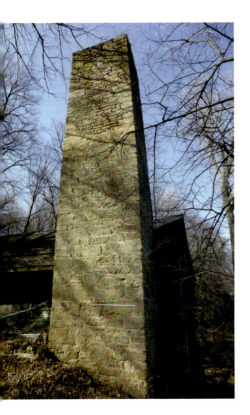

water. Further on as the bluff got even higher, an ancient forty foot long houseboat was perched on a wooden pedestal framework just feet from the edge. How the Van Meiers actually got it there is a matter of conjecture, but just the fact it is there is a source of amazement for anyone who sees it from the river. Further north was the "Gypsy Wagon" a more or less derelict caravan that wasn't going anywhere ever again. The North Star was a tiny cabin at the end of a track that started as a narrow road and ended as a rocky foot path through the trees well back and up the hill from the water. What they all had in common was uneven floors, faded paint and a comfortable mustiness, thanks to heavy shade and several streams criss-crossing the property. In 1955 my parents had considered building their Wright home on the property, before they found the site on Woodpile Lake.

In the 1970s the cabins were populated with an assortment of outdoors-type men, mostly single. They weren't artists but they thoroughly appreciated the simplicity of life and ease of communing with nature there. In the early summer of 1976 I was ready for a change from living in a warehouse in the Minneapolis North Loop. At that time that section of town was still a gritty warehouse district and gentrification was a long way from anyone's mind. I drove my 1962 Ford Falcon to Arcola and with an introduction from my mother, met with Katherine. She was taken with the fact I was a painter and she probably felt I was a kindred soul in the makeup department. She seemed to like me immediately and appreciated my vision and my spunk. She agreed to let me have a cabin for the summer. Rent was $100. We never discussed whether that was for the month or the season but she never asked for another payment.

The cabin in question was called "Ernie's Place", nothing more than a two-room concrete bunker built into a shallow hill across the lawn from the "big house". It had a flat roof, cracked concrete floor, an old ceramic sink and not much else. Perfect. I brought my paints, some large colorful scarves (which when used to cover an old packing crate made a lovely bohemian side table), and a few old chairs, rugs and cushions. I immediately felt at home there, perhaps because the place was in tune with Wright's dictum that a building should be "of the hill" rather than "on the hill", as Taliesin was. Of course, it was no Taliesin, but it was mine - at least for the summer.

Arcola was the Van Meiers' summer residence; they would move there in May and decamp in October, Henry making the drive into Stillwater and his practice each day.

It wasn't long before my on-again, off-again boyfriend Gordie decided he, too could use some country air and his social calls turned into a move-in situation. He wasted no time ingratiating himself with Katherine by replacing the radiator in her Mercury Bobcat (an upscale version of the Ford Pinto). She had bashed it on a driveway rock after one of the rut-gouging rains that regularly turned the steep dirt driveway into an obstacle course. Henry drove a Cadillac Eldorado and had for years suffered the same frustration in trying to get up and down the hill. "I can have a rich man's car or a poor man's driveway, but not both," he said. His solution soon afterward was to buy a VW.

The mill had been powered by an adjacent stream which in 2018 was still full of watercress, sort of a salad bar for our dinners when we lived next door. Just upstream was the houseboat - a real one that was perched on the edge of the bluff.

Top right: "The big house" had survived a century of storms and fallen trees, and the one at upper right came down over the pool in 1978. Residents Gary Kent and Jerry Cullen worked to remove debris from the water.

We were only a few weeks into the summer when Gordie and I had a frightening experience. A huge midnight thunderstorm was pounding rain on the flat roof over our heads, when in between booms we heard another noise. There was a loud snap, then an agonizingly slow craaaaaack that seemed to go on and on. It only took a few seconds to recognize the sound of a large tree falling, and before we could do anything it hit the roof directly above the bed. Wide-eyed in shock, we could only stare at the ceiling for several minutes but there was no sign of leaking, so eventually we drifted off to sleep. The next morning as we were inspecting the roof Henry joined us and noted our electrical wires were down. This was nothing new to him, as the property was full of old trees that, like everything else at Arcola, were long past needing maintenance. He clicked his gold-capped teeth a few times, as he was wont to do when thinking, and went to fetch some tools.

He returned with a knife, some black tape and a Pepsi bottle. Trimming the wire ends, he wrapped them haphazardly in tape and inserted the ends in the bottle, which he then threw back up on the roof. Out of sight, out of mind and back in service!

Henry Van Meier in 1979

I found out later that my cabin's namesake Ernie had been a caretaker of sorts, living on the property and doing yard work and maintenance in exchange for a place to hang his hat, modest as it was. He had been gone a few years by then and the responsibilities for maintenance were taken over by the other renters who spent their summers in the cabins. It soon became clear that it was a group effort to hold the place together and we now understood why they didn't ask Henry to fix anything.

Maintenance was undertaken by the renters. If it broke, they fixed it. Bruce and Ed lived in the Mill, mostly on weekends and Jerry was more of a full-time resident in his cabin a bit further upstream. They were all outdoorsmen and not afraid to get their hands dirty. When a storm would knock down the power lines to the cabins—which were strung through trees from an old fuse box at the big house—they would climb through the tangles of limbs to see where the break was. With a pliers and some black tape, they were usually back in business pretty quickly. There was no thought of calling the power company and not only because of the expense. There was a real fear that the whole property would be red-tagged for having substandard electrical wiring.

Other utilities were provided by Mother Nature. A hillside spring furnished excellent water through a makeshift piping system and toilets were plumbed to a sunken 55-gallon drum in the great outdoors. We figured the fact that it never smelled meant that natural composting was under way. We didn't really want to know any more.

Adjacent to Ernie's was a collection of attached sort-of buildings with corrugated steel walls and yawning holes in the roof, all overtaken with vines and trees. It was a storage area for old furniture, farm machinery and a lot of unrecognizable items - all of which were in some state of decay. We called it the "Heirloom shed". From time to time Katherine would ask about this item or that; she expected it could be retrieved and put immediately back into use. However,

between rot, mold and mud, few of these heirlooms were ever going to see any use again. The same was true of old cans of weed killer, turpentine and other unknown chemicals and even the contents of an old freezer that stood in a cramped and creaky vestibule between the big house and Mary's attached quarters.

Some years before, Katherine had put a fine Smithfield ham in this freezer and one summer she asked Jerry to take it out and trim a bit of the skin off so she could make a ham dinner. Considering that the power went on and off regularly during the summer and who knows how many times when no one was around in the winter, this ham had a less-than-optimal storage life. Jerry tried to explain just that, but Katherine was adamant that a preserved ham should still be good. Acquiescing, he took it well out into the yard and cut it up on a picnic table. It was the color of a carp's belly and the smell was something between kerosene and a wet dog. He was finally able to convince her to make something else for dinner. The ham then got a decent burial well off into the woods.

A conversation with Katherine was usually an epic event; a simple question would take 15 minutes or more. She would normally insist that you join her for tea or at least take a seat while you discuss the matter. Once your comment or question was made, she took the bit and ran with it. There was no subject so arcane that she could not find a related topic to comment on, and going further afield by the minute, she would go off on tangents that could give you whiplash. Incredibly, she always somehow managed to make an entire circumnavigation of thought and return to the original subject, all the while ignoring your attempts to interrupt. It was an amazing thing to experience and of course, we gave it a name: "doing a Katherine".

We also gave her a name: "Old Smudge". Her proclivity for wearing heavy makeup was at odds with what we can assume was failing eyesight. The rouge was heavy and the eyeshadow

The sub-par electrical work is evident in this photo of Ernie's place in 1976. It was a homey spot in an English country cottage sort of way, and was "of the hill" as Wright had preached. Gordie's photographer friend John Posl took some images that summer.

By 2017 Ernie's place was on its way to being "of the Earth" and soon, it was gone.

Looking over the prospects for our "new" cabin in the spring of 1977.

Big birds, big problems. The Tom turkeys didn't take kindly to interlopers on their turf. We gave them a wide berth.

was usually several layers thick, along with mascara that streaked the insides of her cat-eye reading glasses and flaked off into her lap. And then there was her wig...

Henry was thin, not too tall and a gentleman through and through. He called her "My Bride" and it was clear even after decades of marriage he still felt that way and was always tender with her. There was an intuitive side to Henry, a feeling that he was an old soul and had sensibilities about human nature that perhaps escaped many of us. He was in his mid-seventies when I got to know him and was developing some of the "old man" traits that are easy to laugh at, but his culture and intelligence always shown through. He was at ease with strangers and could make them feel the same.

One July weekend Bruce was having his annual hog roast at the Mill and Henry stopped his car to say hello. After a few words with some of the party-goers, the hum of conversation seemed to change and turning around, I realized Henry was leading the group in singing "La Marseillaise". It was Bastille Day. They couldn't follow the words as Henry sang in French but gave him an enthusiastic accompaniment with "Da da da, da da, DAH da da." Henry had a way with people.

In late October we moved to a tiny apartment in Stillwater, enjoying warmth at night for the first time in weeks. Over the next six or seven years we would continue this pattern, moving in autumn to a place in Stillwater, often to "home-sit" while the elderly residents went south.

In the spring of 1977 Gordie and I (we were now a couple, but living in sin as far as his parents were concerned) moved back to Arcola but this time to new digs. Just north of the "big house" between the main stream and the mill was a small 10 x 15' wooden cabin built on stilts. It had a screened porch and was close enough to the river that during high water its "front yard" was gone and water lapped at the base. "The Little Red Houseboat Run Aground" (a non-literal name given by a former tenant) was an upgrade from Ernie's Place but on our first inspection we noted the ceiling was six feet from the floor. For me it was no problem but Gordie was brushing the roof joists with his then-ample hair. There was only one thing to do: build up.

With Katherine and Henry's blessing we added a new roof, eighteen inches higher. The three small existing windows in the cabin gave it a cave-like feel, and light was something I had grown used to in my parents' home. To get some needed light we decided to add clerestory windows, which could be done without disturbing the existing walls. Since we had no money, my parents made a connection with the owner of Cardinal Glass, the commercial glass supplier that had custom-made the beveled insulated corner glass for both the studio and cottage. At the time, that feat was technologically new ground and it gave Cardinal bragging rights to have their glass as part of a well-known Wright house. It gave my parents, as usual, a chance to get something on the cheap. It was a win-win for both parties.

Our cabin needs were more modest, but the flat quarter-inch panes of glass we used would still have been expensive without Cardinal's generosity. The rest of the new roof was comprised of 2x4 window framing and 12-foot-long 2x6 rafters, 4 feet on center with only a slight pitch. Plywood and roll roofing completed the job. If you stood back and squinted it almost looked Usonian.

Mechanical engineers reading this will have noted that 2x6 boards spanning ten feet above single 2x4s at four-foot spacing is a recipe for disaster. Snow loads on a 1/12 pitch are akin to parking a small car on the roof - for six months at a time. Add to that inevitable water damage and aging materials, and you would expect the whole thing to last a few years at best. Incredibly, that roof remained mostly intact for four decades.

In 1977 our new home was an exciting, albeit tiny place to live. There was hardly enough space for a table in the "main" room, where we re-used an old ceramic-on-metal sink and an ancient Crosley refrigerator that I painted chrome yellow. Another room had a toilet, shower and a metal cabinet for my clothes. A small stairway went to a sleeping loft, just two feet under the roof. There, the river and the sky were the last things we saw before drifting off as the stream made lullaby sounds a few feet away.

With bright scarves and towels thrown over packing crates, I once again made a foreign place home. We had adopted two kittens who by now were grown and adventurous. We left a lower glass panel out of the nine-light entry door, allowing them to come and go as they pleased. Gumbo became an accomplished night hunter, catching bats and bringing them inside where he made great sport out of chasing them around and up the walls just as we were dozing off. We kept a broom handy for bat chasing.

Wild animals created other problems as well. While moving our modest belongings to the new place in May, Gordie was confronted with a wild turkey. These had only just been re-introduced to parts of Minnesota and few locals had ever seen or dealt with one before. This big Tom must have considered Arcola his turf and after charging several times, sent Gordie retreating to our VW van, where one of the boxes held a canister vacuum. He grabbed the vac hose and spinning it around over his head, was finally able to back down Mr. Turkey. The bird, for his part, flew to a tree above the path, where he perched, aimed and took a dump. Sore loser.

By mid-summer we were settled in and my ever-expanding collection of funky clothing was tucked into boxes, on shelves and in the old metal cabinet. One afternoon I pulled open the rusty door (which never did close completely) and reached for a sweater on the bottom shelf. The sweater was red but what was on it was not. I jumped back when I realized a huge gray bull snake was coiled on my clothes. Unlike my father, snakes creep me out and this was a big one. The fact that he was asleep and that bull snakes are harmless (beneficial, in fact, as rodent eaters) made little difference. Poor Gordie (no fan of snakes, either) had to get rid of this guy who, now awake and hissing, had us both wondering whether rattlesnakes lived this far north.

At night it was either owls, racoons, coyotes or, from time to time, a guttural but unidentified growl that would wake us. Thankfully, the stream was the one constant, an ambient source of pleasant white noise. In spite of the wildlife, between the river and the streams—some of

Yet another photo of me with a cat. I filled the cabin with books, plants and art.

Our cabin, still standing in 2020, but about to be razed.

Below, in 1978. In addition to a new roof and clerestory windows we planted hosta, my first attempt at gardening in what would develop into a lifelong love of flowers and foliage. Gordie and I enjoyed the bohemian life; filling the cabin with books and exotic plants - something I picked up from Mother. There was no TV, just nature to watch.

which produced a bounty of watercress each spring—living at Arcola cemented my desire to always live on water. We spent four summers at Arcola and sometimes visited in winter, when it was an entirely different, cold and quiet world.

David Uppgren then moved into the Little Red Houseboat for about four years, and commuted to the U of M where he studied architecture. After Katherine died in 1991, there were a few years of uncertainty about the status of the renters, and word finally came as plans were being made to renovate the Mower house. Katherine's last wishes were that it would be a retreat center although she left no money toward that end. The cabins were vacated and have since fallen deeply into disrepair. The main house was rebuilt in the early 2000s and is now open occasionally as a river interpretive center and for art and naturalist activities. The "poor man's driveway" as Henry called it, remains today however, and limits the number of open houses that can be hosted by the Arcola Mills Foundation. The organization is continuing to work to preserve the site's history and carry on Katherine and Henry's vision for this beautiful property.

Real life and real estate

We had been playing house at Arcola, enjoying the woods and river but in 1980 we decided it was time to own a place of our own. Having little money our choices were limited, especially since we wanted to live on water. Just like my parents, we found a walk-out basement that could be had with little down and a contract for deed. It was well-built on a small hill with pillars of local blue-tinged trap rock and modern casement windows, ready for a second floor that would have a great view over a lake in Wisconsin. There were five acres and lovely pines. It seemed like a great idea at the time and when we moved in that fall we had big—although

unfocused—plans. Gordie took a job a few miles away but my connections were all in the Twin Cities and Stillwater, which was now some 20 miles distant, over the bridge across the St. Croix river. It felt like light years.

The old joke goes, "What's the difference between Wisconsin and Yogurt? Yogurt has active culture." No offense to the locals who would attend meat raffles at the bar and dirt track racing at the nearby speedway, or even the ones who would shoot target practice in the woods behind our place, but I needed art and theater. I needed to talk about architecture, to be challenged and creative. What I didn't need was to commute for an hour or more to my job as an administrator at the State Arts Board in St. Paul.

We stayed in rural Wisconsin for two years and never did build anything above our walkout basement. When our son Dana was born and I had just taken a new position as Managing Director of Theatre de la Jeune Lune in Minneapolis, the combo of new mom and new job was just too much. We moved to a rental house in White Bear Lake where we developed some new skills sailing racing scows with our landlord, Larry the Lawyer. We were back on the water and loving it. It was in a lawn chair in our front yard there where I first began to string beads in interesting patterns and thought to myself, I could sell these! As it turned out, I could - and did for the next 32 years. Lonnie Lovness Accessories became the way of expressing my artistic self, and making a living at the same time.

Living at Arcola was only a few steps above camping, but it ingrained an appreciation of nature and the St. Croix River in both of us, and we have spent the last 30 years living just upstream from Arcola on that wild and scenic waterway, in a prairie-school inspired house. Every day Gordie and I ask ourselves a rhetorical but important question, "How lucky are we?"

The "big house" at Arcola, the original Mower home, has been nicely renovated.

At left, we lived simply at Arcola but we always had cool cars. The Porsche ended up as a down payment on our Wisconsin walk-out, which would have been great, had it been closer to civilization.

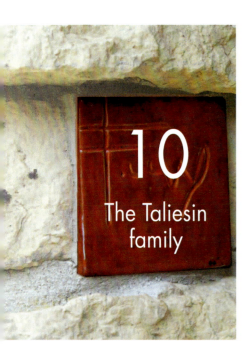

10

The Taliesin
family

Frank Lloyd Wright was a genius and a visionary. He was also a charlatan and a scoundrel. It just depended on who you talked to. He was famously difficult, according to some clients. In an example close to home, S.P. Elam and his wife built a large Wright Usonian design in 1950 and '51 in Austin, Minnesota. Before the project was finished there was so much friction between architect and client over a small window that the Elams parted ways with Wright, finishing the kitchen to their own design and cutting ties with Taliesin.

My parents were just the opposite. They were very pleased with Mr. Wright's design and although D questioned a few of the processes, they had every faith in the architect's decisions and worked hard to build their home according to his vision. During construction they made a number of trips to Spring Green to consult with Mr. Wright, Wes Peters and others. Gene Masselink was their main contact through correspondence and many times a phone call was made to clarify something on the plans or ask about rock patterning or framing details. Over many months they got to know Mr. and Mrs. Wright very well.

I think Mr. Wright recognized their sincerity in wanting to build the house properly, respected their work ethic and overall, simply grew to like them. "He would always joke with me," my mother would say. "He knew we were rubbing nickels together to make this all happen but when he answered the phone it wasn't 'Hello', it was 'How much money do we have to spend today?'" He referred to the Lovness project as "The Love Nest" and developed a real paternal concern for their success.

For their part, Mother and D were enthralled with the man. The impressions from that first meeting in 1955 never faded and as time passed, they began to embrace not only his ideas about architecture but about life itself (and he had some strong opinions there). They followed in his footsteps by collecting oriental art. Although they only knew him for a few years, his wife Olgivanna carried on his legacy after his death in 1959, and they became very close to her. My parents became unofficial members of the fellowship, attending most of the Taliesin "high holidays" including Mr. Wright's birthday and Easter each year. Summer visits to Spring Green were regular outings for our family, where Mother was often Mrs. Wright's right-hand woman at social events, helping her entertain and keep things lively. D became a consultant to them on things like sound systems, water treatment, duplicating and printing, weatherproofing, office machines and more. He was also a supply conduit for things like tape and adhesives. The deep friendship between my parents and Mrs. Wright lasted until she passed away in 1985. For another 15 years they remained close to the Taliesin group and an extended family of former apprentices who went on to successful careers. My father passed away suddenly on Memorial Day weekend in 2001 at 76. Mother still visited Taliesin from time to time after that but so many of her friends there were gone as well, and she was less inclined to travel.

Wright's work attracted people of all stripes, from wealthy industrialists to middle-class workingmen and women. Although disparate in their circumstances and in the kind of Wright structure they wanted, there was one thing they all had in common. As Wright clients they

Dear Virginia and Don Lovness: Thank you for thinking
of us this Christmas. Corn-husking was once my favorite
pastime.

Faithfully,
Frank Lloyd Wright

January 21st, 1957

The friendships that developed between Mr. Wright and my parents, and between them and so many of the people at Taliesin began with a business arrangement - a contract to design a house, but became so much more.

Mother was a thoughtful correspondent and always sent thank-you notes and gifts, like a bunch of colorful Indian corn at Christmas in 1956. However modest the gift, her thoughtfulness was appreciated. Mr. Wright's response may seem a little tongue-in-cheek, but in fact corn-husking at Taliesin was a well-loved tradition among apprentices.

In this 1955 photo, taken just about the time my parents first visited Taliesin, are the three men whose friendship brought D and Mother into the fold. Wes Peters, at left, was Taliesin's chief engineer and the Wright's son-in-law. Gene Masselink, at right, was Mr. Wright's secretary, did the billing and receiving, bookkeeping (such as it was), early archives and in his little free time was a painter and muralist. Both were "lifers" in the Fellowship.

August 3rd, 1959

Dear Don,

Arnold and Joe tell me that any of the following would be most welcome . . .

    3 x 24 belts, sanding fine, med, coarse
    3/4" masking tape
    #33¾" electrical tape
    Scotch #102, 7" reels
    3M Clear Windshield Sealer, 1 gal.
    8½" sanding discs, box ea. fine, med, coarse
    contact cement

Looking forward to seeing you this weekend.

Gene Masselink

D was a pragmatist and had access to useful 3M items that Taliesin could use, so why not help them out? In 1959 it was sandpaper and tape, but over the years he supplied much more, including professional advice and useful contacts.

were, by definition, interesting people. Imagination, creativity, a sense of adventure and an appreciation for beautiful things were attributes of my parents, and I believe these were shared by the Fellowship, by Taliesin's clients and by Wright's wide circle of admirers. Mother and D were fortunate to become a part of the inner group and know so many of these kindred souls.

It all began as the house was under construction. Mother wrote many years later:

Taliesin in Wisconsin seemed formidable at first. But everyone was helpful and friendly and we soon felt at home. It's a complicated place and we still don't know how they accomplish so much, so smoothly. We were always greeted on arrival; someone would take our bag and take us to our room or apartment. Wes always left special bottles of liquor and arrived with presents. There were always flowers everywhere - several bouquets in your bedroom.

The philosophy was that all would work hard during the week on design and engineering and doing repairs, maintenance, gardening, cooking, cleaning, whatever was necessary, and rotate duties. Everyone seemed proficient at everything. Such talented people, not only at architecture and everyday functioning but sculpture - like Heloise Crista whose work is sold worldwide. And their entertainment could fill a book. Always music of their orchestra and choir.

For a well-rounded lifestyle, weekends were formal. Women looked elegant in long formal dresses and men would wear dressy attire. Cocktails were served, then dinner with decorated tables. Then music in the theater with their talented musicians and choir. Afterwards there would be a film that the Wrights admired, often a foreign film.

Sundays, after a special breakfast together with the Wrights, Mr. Wright would talk about a wide range of subjects. Everything he said was profound and provocative; he was so quotable. We were always captivated in Mr. Wright's presence.

Their relationship took a tragic turn in April of 1959. Mother's notes recall:

Mr. Wright was so vital and alert, for us there was never a thought about him in terms of age. Once when we had shown him photos of our latest work he was holding a photo upside down and we gently turned it around. He never wore his glasses when we were with him, although we had seen him in the drafting room wearing glasses.

Mr. Wright had invited us to Taliesin West for Easter, 1959. Our bags were packed and in the car; our daughters were stashed with relatives. Just as we were leaving we heard the phone ring through the door so we went back in. Our friend from a local TV station was calling to tell us that news of Frank Lloyd Wright's death had just come in.

We didn't believe it. We had talked to him just a few days before; he was hale and hearty and seemed excited about our first visit to Taliesin West. So we started the drive west and as we listened to the radio the same sad news came through that on this day, April 9th, Mr. Wright was dead. Finally, after several hours of denial, we had to accept the fact. There was nothing to do but turn around and go home.

Mrs. Wright celebrated his life on his birthday, June 8, 1959 at Taliesin North. It was a belated Easter

As Mr. Wright's secretary, Gene Masselink wrote something like 100,000 pieces of correspondence, many of them on this typewriter. He became a dear friend and confidant to my parents.

breakfast and was full of sadness, mixed with joy - a fitting tribute. On returning to Spring Green she seemed overwhelmed by the sadness of being in their Wisconsin home without him. On our visit she hugged us and cried, remembering our frequent trips from Stillwater to visit Mr. Wright and ask questions about his design for us.

The Iron Lady

At the center of the group and as head of the organization, Olgivanna Lloyd Wright shepherded the Taliesin Fellowship through dark days after Mr. Wright's death and onward for another quarter century. A dancer in her younger days, she appreciated theater and music, and saw to it that both were incorporated into the lives and education of the apprentices, the architects and the families who lived and worked at Taliesin. Formal dinners and extravagant pageants, recitals, plays and performances in each person's talent area were regular parts of life at both Spring Green and Scottsdale. Once when Ty and I were still very young (I was 10 or so) we were invited to a gala at Spring Green. There would be a special dance, and although it was partly in our honor we were not enthusiastic about taking part. The last thing we wanted was to be the center of attention, and we let Mother know. While chatting during cocktails in the garden court, Mother told Mrs. Wright that we were apprehensive since we didn't know how to dance. She smiled and replied, "Oh, that's all right. Then we'll give them an experience."

And that was how she viewed life. Much like her husband, she had specific viewpoints, writing in her 1963 book *The Roots of Life*, "Man understands only that which he has experienced." Maybe that Taliesin dance was a catalyst. I'm not sure I ever came to understand dance,

A well-known early formal portrait of Mrs. Wright was mounted to illustration board signed "with love" and presented to my parents in 1976.

Dance was a regular part of Taliesin activities. This performance, on the lakeshore in about 1962 featured members of the fellowship, probably choreographed by Iovanna Wright.

Note that the dishes and chairs are all "Cherokee red".

but I came to love the experience of dancing. Years later as an adult I took ballroom lessons and the instructor told me with a smile, "You don't know how to dance but you certainly know how to have fun!" Thank you, Mrs. Wright.

There was a rigidity in her thinking that would grate on some people, and a certain domineering attitude in running the fellowship, but my mother and father loved her and took to heart many of her teachings. About entertaining, Mother wrote:

She gave us so many memories and ingrained this into us: Make your dinners so memorable they will never be forgotten. The atmosphere, the presentation of the food, the conversation, the music. Everything should be special, nothing common.

Toward that end, when they were preparing to leave after a visit to Taliesin, apprentices loaded a box in their car. Mother said there was some mistake but was told, "Mrs. Wright's orders." When opened, she found the box was full of dishes: Imperial Hotel designs, the same as those she had admired at Taliesin dinners. Mother cried at having this "happy design", and Mrs. Wright told them, "You deserve them. Use them every day and enjoy!"

D couldn't resist getting in a little of his twisted humor when he replied to Mrs. Wright, "It's a mistake. Virginia serves everything on paper plates." She always thought his jokes at Mother's expense were very funny. But in spite of his twisted humor, my father took his connection with the Wrights very seriously. It's a little surprising that a man who was highly educated and accomplished would eschew higher learning, but Taliesin changed his mind, he said. In a 1990 interview he stated:

I learned more in the first six months with Mr. and Mrs. Wright and the Fellowship than I learned in five years in college. What it taught me also was to forget everything I learned in college, because it had no bearing on what we were doing. Anything you learn in college you can look up in a book. Everything that you learn at Taliesin you cannot look up in a book - it's part of your soul. I think that if architecture wasn't even taught here at Taliesin, and you taught people to be obsessive about what they're doing, like Bruce (Pfeiffer) is about the drawings, or Chinese art or something, they'd automatically become architects, you wouldn't have to teach them to become architects.

(Virginia) has a degree in art - an art major, and I'm an engineer, so we're quite a ways apart on this thing. As an engineer though, I was absolutely amazed at some of the stuff that went on in that house - I mean it's got engineering that would just defy mathematics, almost.

Mrs. Wright's strong opinions were based somewhat on the teachings of George Gurdjieff, an Armenian-born mystic and philosopher. She felt that all men should strive to better themselves and according to Mother, Mrs. Wright made continuing efforts to "improve" her and D. She mentioned one instance in a Taliesin interview:

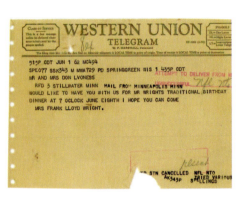

Easter at Taliesin West, and Mr. Wright's birthday at Taliesin North were the two important dates on the calendar. From the early 1960s my parents were invited to each of these and pretty much every other event, including reunions of apprentices in the 1980s and '90s.

Spaces like the living room at Taliesin and the theater at Hillside would make an impression on anyone; they certainly did on my parents. The curtain in the theater was finished on June 8, 1955, about the time my parents first visited.

Many of Wright's designs have proven to be timeless, like the Tokyo Imperial Hotel dinnerware from 1922.

A stainless steel cuff, with a chain attached to a ring was designed by my mother and crafted by my father early in their marriage. She wore it often, for the rest of her life.

Later as her jewelry collection expanded with eclectic pieces, she favored unusual things like articulated silver rings, which she wore two or three at a time.

Mrs. Wright would try with us, to make us into better people, but I think she finally gave up. She never really could handle Don - he was hopeless. She felt I should look feminine and soft, but I just don't feel right in a soft, sweet dress. Once when she and Iovanna were talking about me she said, "Virginia, you always look like an artist."

Then they were going to cut my hair, style it in some way, and I was just horrified. Don must have sensed that I didn't want them to take me to a beauty shop so we excused ourselves, and went out and bought a wig. It was a nice wig, something like a page boy. When we came to dinner they were both very happy that they had influenced me for the better.

During the first formal weekend we were invited to at Taliesin North, at the dinner-dance on Saturday evening Mrs. Wright took one look at me and said, "Virginia, our Saturday nights are always formal. Where is your gold?" Gold! I didn't even have silver! I had designed jewelry and Don had made it out of stainless steel; a wide bracelet attached to a stainless ring with a chain. We were proud of it because stainless is so much harder to work with than silver or gold. And we had an unwritten agreement that earrings should be at least 4 inches long; we made a pair from stainless with colored glass inserts. However, as much as we loved these pieces, they weren't gold!

When I told Mrs. Wright I didn't have any gold she ran out of the room and returned with a 22K gold necklace Mr. Wright had given her, and a gold ring so that I would be presentable.

In her later years, Mother was a jewelry hound. She would wear rings on several fingers, huge necklaces, and she loved her Persian gauntlet cuffs with inset stones. Each one of those covered most of her forearm and weighed over a pound. We always joked that she kept fit by "pumping jewelry". She also amassed a collection of gold that she found at auctions and estate sales. Mrs. Wright had set her on a course and there was no turning back!

Suitably swathed in jewelry, Mother became a helper at Taliesin social functions. Her notes recall the beginnings, where she was learning the ropes:

Mrs. Wright would ask us to be here for a reunion or a dinner, to help host and hostess. Then she would scold me because I was having too good a time and I wasn't circulating enough.

With the guests who frequented Saturday night festivities, conversations were always lively and worldly, about art, literature, music and creativity. Mrs. Wright asked us to entertain just as the fellowship did. She treated us with the same respect she did all the famous and wealthy. Often the guests stayed for the week-end so we'd get to visit more on Sunday without the large Saturday crowds. I remember Mrs. Wright, Helen Wrigley and I sitting around on the floor, looking at and trying on Mrs. Wright's jewelry. When she ran out of the room to get yet another piece to show us, Helen leaned over to me and whispered, "I wish I could afford all this!"

In fact, Mrs. Wright did have a lot of jewelry, mostly gifts, but the Wrigleys were one of the wealthiest families in the country!

By the early 1960s my parents were accepted into the inner circle and became involved with most activities at Taliesin. Kitchen and dining room duty was shared among apprentices but Mother and D, or Wes Peters were never obligated to help cook or serve. His involvement here must mean this was a special occasion. Even Mrs. Wright was wearing an apron.

Mrs. Wright would visit us at the studio but generally stayed at a hotel until the cottage was built.

Wright home owners like Katherine Lewis and my mother were regular companions to Mrs. Wright at gatherings.

Kamal Amin was a successful architect who had become an apprentice in 1951, coming from Egypt to join the Taliesin group. He was a friend and occasional visitor to our home. In his book *Reflections from the Shining Brow*, he wrote, "Oligvanna designed the organizational structure upon which the Fellowship operated. She had unfettered control over all that went on at all times." She took an interest in each person, he explains, "Always manipulating someone to take a course that would be of some use to her purpose."

"Besides the personal qualities that qualified a member of the Fellowship to become close to Olgivanna," he continues, "it did not hurt that he or she had had an absentee mother or a traumatized maternal experience."

I think he was describing my mother.

Mrs. Wright would strive to know everything about everyone in the Fellowship, and was not shy about inquiring on personal matters, even one's sex life. Mother explained in her notes that soon after becoming frequent guests, Mrs. Wright asked about their personal life, and she was reluctant to divulge anything. But she was very persuasive, and Mother told her story:

Kamal Amin and Effi Casey at a Taliesin West Easter celebration.

At a Taliesin North soirée Mother and Mrs Wright share a laugh with the local newspaper editor. Wes Peters is in formal attire. Like my father, his height sometimes posed problems when navigating the low ceilings of a Wright home. Mr. Wright loved him like a son but was known to yell, "Sit down Wes, you're spoiling the scale!"

At Taliesin, Mrs. Wright presided over formal evenings for adults where Mother made the rounds meeting many interesting people, like Mrs. Lloyd Lewis, whose husband published the Chicago Daily news. They had an early Usonian house in Libertyville, Illinois. Mother, however, was probably the only woman in the room who had sewn her own dress!

There were also exotic costumed celebrations for the children. Ty and I (third and fourth from left, in matching outfits made by Grandma Gladys, as usual) were enthralled along with the rest of the group as a sorcerer and a magician entertained.

Summer events at Taliesin in Spring Green included extravagant pageants that focused on the children. A pirate ship was created and apprentices swam below huge swans on the lake - which in those days was quite free of weeds due to my father's chemical potions. Ty and I watched with the others from the grass beside the lake while Mother and Mrs. Wright observed from a central table. Iovanna (right, center) was dressed in a huge hoopskirt and apprentices wore outrageous costumes.

My father was a crook. I remember running through an Indiana jail looking through the bars for Daddy. He was an alcoholic and a womanizer, and I loved him. My mother was a much younger school teacher but couldn't find a job. She took up cosmetology and palm reading, making prints and encouraging customers to come back after she'd analyzed them. She had to send me off to her sister when I was only six.

Mrs. Wright listened and when my story was finished she said, "You could have gone either way; been on the streets or worked your way up."

Maybe the latter wasn't inevitable, but it's hard for me to imagine my mother being anything but the driven, determined, hard working and yet sweet woman who was now rubbing shoulders with high society. Of course, there was always still a glimmer of her father in her character that would surface from time to time, but it was offset by an authentic charm that was not lost on Mrs. Wright. Her notes continue:

After that Mrs. Wright seemed almost like a mother. Each time we visited she recalled, "Mr. Wright always said he really liked that young couple."

The gifts from the Lovnesses that had begun on such a small scale now became specific and more grand. Mrs. Wright was accustomed to nice things and like any woman, clothing was important. Mother's fashion style, eye for a bargain and sewing skills allowed her to find lovely pieces that she would send to Taliesin. In spite of her protestations, Mrs. Wright was usually thrilled with the gifts that came from Minnesota.

D was supplying the usual items from 3M, and as technology changed, he kept the Fellowship up to date on things like thermofax paper for copying. This chemical-coated, heat sen-

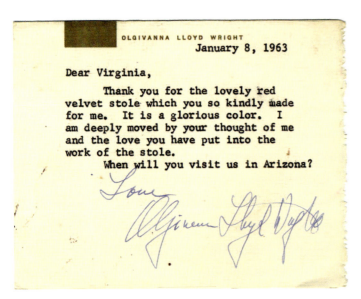

OLGIVANNA LLOYD WRIGHT
January 8, 1963

Dear Virginia,

Thank you for the lovely red velvet stole which you so kindly made for me. It is a glorious color. I am deeply moved by your thought of me and the love you have put into the work of the stole.

When will you visit us in Arizona?

Love
Olgivanna Lloyd Wright

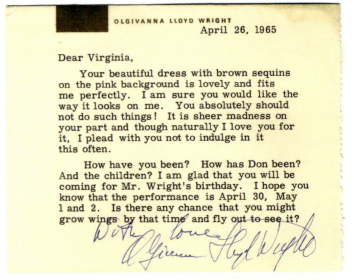

OLGIVANNA LLOYD WRIGHT
April 26, 1965

Dear Virginia,

Your beautiful dress with brown sequins on the pink background is lovely and fits me perfectly. I am sure you would like the way it looks on me. You absolutely should not do such things! It is sheer madness on your part and though naturally I love you for it, I plead with you not to indulge in it this often.

How have you been? How has Don been? And the children? I am glad that you will be coming for Mr. Wright's birthday. I hope you know that the performance is April 30, May 1 and 2. Is there any chance that you might grow wings by that time and fly out to see it?

With love
Olgivanna Lloyd Wright

Olgivanna Lloyd wright's correspondence folder, which was well used for decades.

kitchen very soon so that we can place the priceless gift of extraordinary equipment you gave us.

We are eagerly looking forward to your visit here. I could also accomodate the girls if they would stay in a tent, otherwise there is no room. Tell them I would like to have them but it is up to you to decide.

Love to you
and yours
Olgivanna Lloyd Wright

In this second page of a note of thanks for the kitchen equipment, Mrs. Wright demonstrates that children were more or less a liability at Taliesin. Ty and I were welcome, but only if it was convenient.

sitive paper was pretty high tech for 1960, and of course, expensive. With the "Lovness discount", however, it was manageable. Other items included a 3M bow-tying machine. The "Sasheen" S-71 was capable of creating elaborate, multi-row bows, made with 3M's own brand of "soft and satiny" ribbon; a little out of the ordinary but apparently the women at Spring Green loved it. D even managed to acquire an entire "de-acquisitioned' stainless kitchen for Taliesin and had it shipped to Wisconsin from St. Paul. Mrs. Wright was overwhelmed with gratitude and asked Don who she could write to at 3M to thank. He immediately responded, "Don't do that. I've already thanked the appropriate people." What he meant was, don't do that as they might notice that it's gone! He always had his eyes wide open for bargains and freebies.

Mrs. Wright was no slouch either, when it came to digging for discounts. She would visit Minneapolis often and whenever possible, joined Mother and D to go shopping at Banks. Banks was a "liquidator", a place where you could find damaged, discontinued and heavily discounted merchandise of all kinds. The big building just off Hennepin Avenue in the near Northeast part of town would hold sales a few days a week, with Wednesday and Thursday devoted to stocking one or two floors with fresh merchandise followed by the sale opening on Friday, when customers would line up to get in first for the best deals. One week it would feature auto parts and hardware, the next week formals and prom dresses, followed by electronics and TVs. Usually there was an eclectic group of new, used and damaged stuff each week and what didn't sell immediately was marked down further. There was something for everyone if you were willing to elbow your way through the crowds to find it.

My parents became good customers and after a while, insiders, having become friends with owner Marvin Banks. When Banks received high fashion dresses with slight damage, Mother would take them home and do repairs. With her industrial sewing machines in the cottage basement she could work on heavy furs and became an expert at minks and all kinds of exotic skins. More than a few of these made their way into her wardrobe over the years.

D would repair electronic equipment, effectively giving new life to items that were worthless because they didn't work. It was a win-win for both sides and although they worked for free, Banks in turn gave them and Taliesin great deals on the already-marked-down products. Mother recalled one shopping trip:

Mrs. Wright, Eve and I were shopping. Mrs. W. was feeling tired and wanted a chair (non- existent in a plain, pipe-rack place like this) but somehow, one appeared. Eve was meanwhile rapidly filling a cart with boutique clothes. Mrs. W. decided she wanted to go back to her suite at the Marquette Inn, but Eve and I wondered what to do about the pile of gorgeous clothes she hadn't yet had time to try on. We asked the manager and he said, "Take it all. $50!"

The same with air conditioners and TVs. Taliesin would send a truck up and we'd load as many goodies as the truck could hold.

OLGIVANNA LLOYD WRIGHT

January 8, 1966

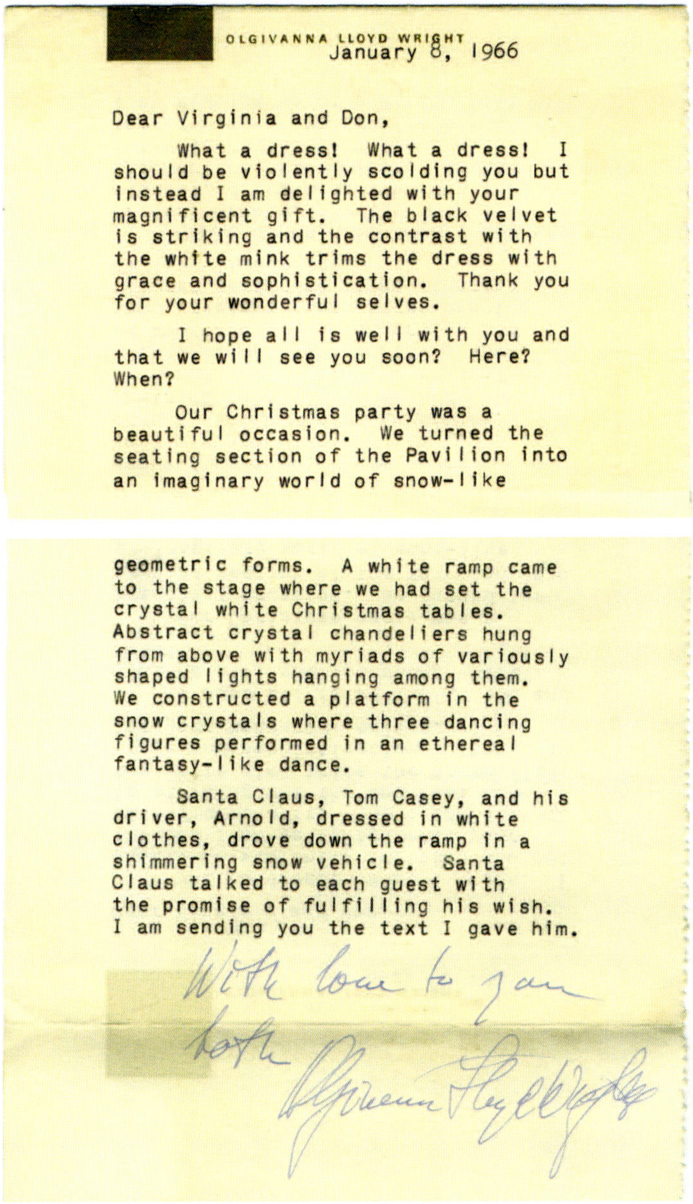

Dear Virginia and Don,

What a dress! What a dress! I should be violently scolding you but instead I am delighted with your magnificent gift. The black velvet is striking and the contrast with the white mink trims the dress with grace and sophistication. Thank you for your wonderful selves.

I hope all is well with you and that we will see you soon? Here? When?

Our Christmas party was a beautiful occasion. We turned the seating section of the Pavilion into an imaginary world of snow-like geometric forms. A white ramp came to the stage where we had set the crystal white Christmas tables. Abstract crystal chandeliers hung from above with myriads of variously shaped lights hanging among them. We constructed a platform in the snow crystals where three dancing figures performed in an ethereal fantasy-like dance.

Santa Claus, Tom Casey, and his driver, Arnold, dressed in white clothes, drove down the ramp in a shimmering snow vehicle. Santa Claus talked to each guest with the promise of fulfilling his wish. I am sending you the text I gave him.

With love to you both

Olgivanna Lloyd Wright

OLGIVANNA LLOYD WRIGHT

April 11, 1967

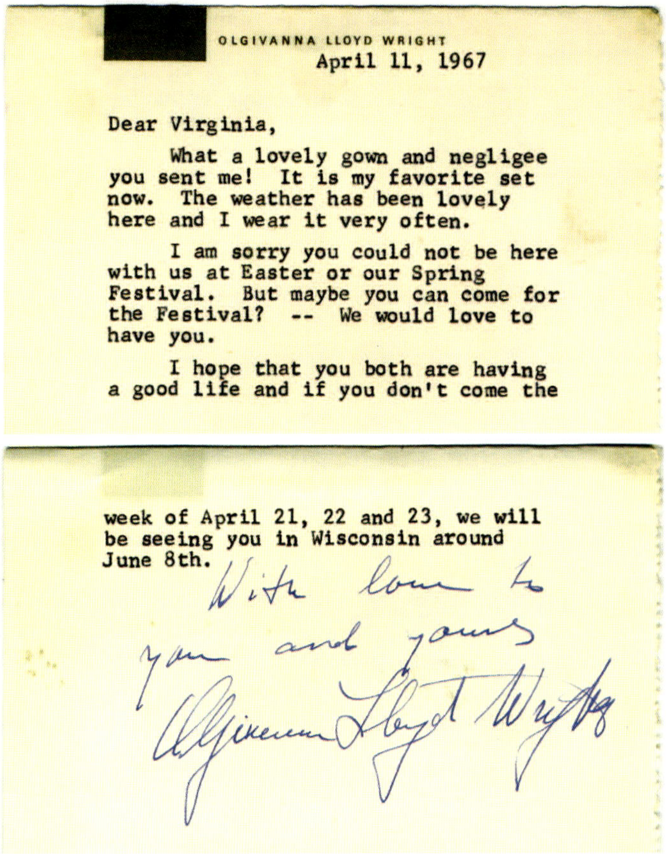

Dear Virginia,

What a lovely gown and negligee you sent me! It is my favorite set now. The weather has been lovely here and I wear it very often.

I am sorry you could not be here with us at Easter or our Spring Festival. But maybe you can come for the Festival? -- We would love to have you.

I hope that you both are having a good life and if you don't come the week of April 21, 22 and 23, we will be seeing you in Wisconsin around June 8th.

With love to you and yours

Olgivanna Lloyd Wright

Mother described the long black velvet "sheath" with white mink trim as her favorite gift to Mrs. Wright. It was another Banks purchase.

The description of the 1965 Christmas pageant at Taliesin West is a typical Olgivanna production with dance, elaborate sets and a script she wrote for Santa, who appears in an "exotic space vehicle" and was granting wishes to many of the guests, including *Time* and *Life* publisher Henry Luce and Senator Bill Benton, publisher of the *Encyclopedia Britannica*. Mother was not in attendance but "Santa" said, "And Virginia! To satisfy your zoological interests I am raising over on Mars sixteen cats of a special breed the likes of which you have never seen. But it is going to take a little more time so you will have to be patient. As soon as they are ready I will bring them right along for you."

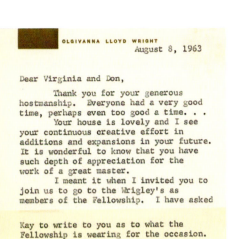

OLGIVANNA LLOYD WRIGHT

August 8, 1963

Dear Virginia and Don,

    Thank you for your generous
hostmanship. Everyone had a very good
time, perhaps even too good a time. . .
    Your house is lovely and I see
your continuous creative effort in
additions and expansions in your future.
It is wonderful to know that you have
such depth of appreciation for the
work of a great master.
    I meant it when I invited you to
join us to go to the Wrigley's as
members of the Fellowship. I have asked

Kay to write to you as to what the
Fellowship is wearing for the occasion.

With my love
and gratitude
Olgivanna Lloyd Wright

Mrs. Wright sent a thank you note after staying at our house in 1963. The "additions" she mentioned would be eight years away, when cottage construction started, but she knew my parents were dedicated to the idea of more Wright structures.

Mother did receive a note the next day from Kay at Taliesin, suggesting that she should wear a cotton shirt waist dress to the Wrigley's party. Mrs. Wright dictated much about Fellowship life, but Mother was not about to wear something so country club conservative.

This cozy relationship once went a little too far. Mother got a phone call from Mrs. Wright who asked, "What were you thinking? These dresses are hideous." A huge box of old-fashioned long dresses—the kind worn by sister wives in a compound—had been received from Banks. Mother and D were unaware that the manager had taken it upon himself to send these directly to Spring Green, as they had once bought a number of formal gowns. Proving that Mother's fashion eye was still an important link in this chain, the manager didn't repeat that mistake.

Once Mother sent a large quantity of graduation gowns to Spring Green, thinking they could be used as robes or costumes. When Mrs. Wright called, Mother thought maybe another scolding was coming, but instead she asked if they could get more!

Visiting Stillwater

Frank Lloyd Wright tried to visit Woodpile Lake several times. Once during construction of the studio he said he was bringing the whole Fellowship and planned to stay with us. Mother was excited but concerned:

With no place but our tiny trailer, I was confused about how we would feed so many with no running water and no place to store food. Unfortunately he caught a cold and there were worries about pneumonia so the visit had to be postponed. I called Mrs. Wright and asked if Mr. Wright might be able to visit later. She said no, and hung up abruptly. But a few years after Mr. Wright died she came for a long weekend and brought the entire Fellowship! Iovanna slept in the girls' room but Mrs. W. insisted on sleeping outside. Most of the apprentices slept on the ground in sleeping bags, but they set up a tent for Mrs. Wright. The interior was fit for royalty with an oriental carpet on the ground and an oriental vase filled with flowers next to her cot.

Food for so many mouths took a little planning. There was not enough refrigerator room so friends of ours helped; they cooked Swedish meatballs and brought steaks. Everyone pitched in on the cooking and it worked. Afterwards we asked Mrs. Wright if everyone had a good time. Her response was, "Too good a time." Some of the apprentices had gotten into the liquor cabinet.

Mrs. Wright usually traveled with a group, too large to stay at the studio. She was famously fussy about food, refusing to eat airline fare. Once she asked Mother to make her some meals for a plane trip, and the prepared food was presented carefully wrapped in Saran Wrap. Mrs. Wright threw it in the trash, stating that she wouldn't eat anything in plastic. At hotels, even the best suites weren't good enough, as at the Plaza in New York where she and Mr. Wright had remodeled their entire group of rooms over a period of a few years there. Mother described a typical stay in Minneapolis:

Once when Mrs. Wright and Cheetah (her Great Dane) came to town with her entourage—which changed but often included Kay Rattenbury, Bruce, Minerva and Dr. Rorke—they stayed at the Marquette Inn downtown in the new IDS Center. They changed the furniture around and set up cooking in the bath-

room, where the toaster kept setting off the fire alarm. The manager called me and asked if I could request that they move the toaster, as it was costing the hotel $500 each time the alarm went off.

The manager became a friend since we often spoke on the phone, and he would call to say Mrs. Wright wanted to make some changes in her room and asked if it was alright.

Cheetah

Mrs. Wright always had a dog; her preference was a large one. When her black Great Dane Fiera died she asked Mother if she could find another to replace it. Since Mr. Wright had died, she told mother, she had been so alone. Even surrounded by people, she needed a companion - another dog. Mother recalled:

She was specific, she wanted another Great Dane and she and a group had rented a motorhome to check out kennels in the East, unsuccessfully. She wanted a beautiful two-year-old blue female, loving and intelligent. (Joe Rorke did a good funny imitation of a stupid Great Dane.) I remember telling her that if there was one out there with those qualities, the owner wouldn't part with it! I called all the dog people I knew but there were no dogs like that. The only option seemed to be to buy a pup, keep it myself, train it and then present it to Mrs. Wright. At the same time, calls were coming in from Taliesin, "Please don't get a puppy!"

Taliesin West was not much of a tourist attraction in 1960 when my parents first visited, and was not that easy to find.

After an initial visit in 1960, when D took a photo of the rustic entrance, my parents became regular guests at Taliesin West near Scottsdale. In the early 1960s Mother is shown with Joe Rorke, Mrs. Wright and "Bueno", and Mrs. William Benton, whose husband was a senator from Connecticut and publisher of the Encyclopedia Britannica.

A Minneapolis breeder had a handsome litter but they were all black. We thought we would take the best black female, train it and see if it was bright enough and beautiful enough for Mrs. Wright. The breeder, however, was due to give birth herself and the immediate problem was where to keep the dogs while she was in the hospital. Knowing how difficult it would be to find someone who knew how to cope, I offered, "Just bring them over to our studio."

Don was furious; we were having company and a large litter of puppies was disrupting. But here's where fate stepped in again. The puppies' location was to be kept private but the breeder's mother gave an eager young couple the address. I was surprised to see them at the door but showed them the puppies. They wanted the same female I had earmarked for Mrs. W. and I had to explain that we had to keep that one since a two-year-old blue female was not available.

"Is that all you want?" they answered. "There's a beautiful one at the St. Croix Animal Shelter." And they were right. I called Mrs. Wright, described the dog and she peppered me with questions. She was a blue harlequin and I had to tell Mrs. W. just where the spots were - not large and asymmetrical but smaller and scattered.

"Did she seem intelligent?" Very.

"Was she friendly?" No. And my heart sank. Surely Mrs. Wright wanted one I could at least pet. But she said, "That's good. I want her just for myself, not everybody's dog here at Taliesin." She asked me what I thought and I told her I loved the dog; I would buy her and bring her to Taliesin and if it didn't work out I would keep her myself.

"How soon can you bring her?" Mrs. Wright asked. I told her Wes Peters was coming to town and he could bring her back but she said, "No, I want you to bring her."

Don was working in a trench laying electrical cable, so he quickly showered and we went to pick up the Great Dane. We put her in the back seat with trepidation and drove as fast as we could. Stopping at a fast food place we shared a sandwich with the still not-too-friendly dog. When we arrived at Taliesin there was no one around. Don hunted and found Mrs. Wright sitting alone, waiting for us. There was no hug, no kisses, just, "Do you have my dog?"

Don fetched us both from the car and the dog jumped up on Mrs. Wright, almost knocking her down. Don caught her just in time. She took the dog by its chain and retreated to her room - for hours. Joe Rorke came and made cocktails, and we waited and waited. We didn't know if we should leave, but just in case it didn't work out we thought we should take the dog home with us.

Finally she appeared, with hugs and kisses all around, and she was leading a well-mannered canine companion with a stone-studded collar, looking very elegant. We were invited to dinner and as usual, Mrs. Wright insisted we stay the night. The next morning we realized we weren't out of the woods yet, as Johnny Hill and an apprentice were seen carrying a large oriental carpet out of Mrs. Wright's bedroom. When she came to meet us with "Cheetah" - named because of the harlequin spots - the two were already inseparable. She said to me, "Virginia, after this you can do no wrong!" What a relief.

For a week or two we'd get phone calls, "How many yummies should I give Cheetah, her stool is loose." But what a wonderful home for Cheetah. There were velvet curtains surrounded her bed so she wouldn't be in a draft. And a soul mate for both a lost beautiful intelligent animal and a lonely intelligent

Cheetah was a fairly rare blue Great Dane, with "harlequin" spots. She and Olgivanna were constant companions.

human being. Cheetah died just a few months after Mrs. Wright in 1985.

Selling the Fellowship

In 1970 Mrs. Wright was lecturing in South Africa and as usual, a small group of Taliesin people were with her. Mother's notes have an amusing story about something Mrs. Wright had been working on for years - getting the parents to join the Fellowship:

On the long way back to Spring Green Mrs. Wright wanted to see us but there was no time to drive to Stillwater so we went to the airport while she waited for her flight to Madison. It had been a difficult trip. Her assistant Kay was a small woman, and taking care of Mrs. Wright and Davey Davison, who was in a wheelchair, was exhausting. Kay had fallen during the trip and had a black and blue eye, and had not had time to have her hair done; her dark roots showed in her straight blonde hair. She looked awful, slouched in a chair, sleeping.

Mrs. Wright was once again extolling the virtues of my joining the Fellowship, but I already knew. I had cried the first time I saw Taliesin, it was so beautiful, then cried every time after when I had to leave. As an only child, abandoned by my parents, no brothers or sisters, it felt to me like everyone there was my family.

Then it was time for the plane to leave and Mrs. Wright summed up her arguments. Pointing at the sleeping figure she said, "Take a look at Kay. I could do that for you!"

Mother and D, having their own home, a career and two daughters, never really considered joining the group formally but they were "honorary" members for years.

Mrs. Wright, Wes Peters and Cheetah at a Taliesin West Easter Celebration.

Mother is shown at the doorway to the Lovness Suite circa 1980s. My sister Ty and I inspected the rooms in 2017 at which time they had been gutted in preparation for refurbishment.

The Lovness Suite

Mother and D had become such regulars that a permanent place was needed for their visits to Spring Green. In the late 1970s a lower level suite of rooms was refinished and renamed "The Lovness Suite". It was a cozy spot for the two of them, and it became a "get away" for many of the Fellowship members and apprentices. Because it was on the north side, opposite Mrs. Wright's quarters, there was some privacy from the all-knowing, all-seeing matriarch. D got to be known among the apprentices and architects as a good storyteller with a repertoire of some ribald tales. On occasion these got back to Mrs. Wright, although there was an unspoken rule about that. Perhaps out of fear that D would be seen as a bad influence on the young men learning architecture, it was, "what happens in the Lovness Suite stays in the Lovness Suite."

The Lovness Suite was not only an apartment for my parents, but when they visited it was a gathering spot for people, a place to socialize informally, watch TV, have a drink and gossip. Opposite, Bruce Pfeiffer, an apprentice, Mother, Dick Carney and David Uppgren enjoy a beer and TV. Right, no watering hole would be complete without custom napkins and Taliesin made sure there were plenty available for "patrons" at the Lovness Suite bar.

On the occasion of my parents' 40th anniversary in 1988 Wes and the others couldn't pass up an opportunity to poke fun at them with this "Daily News" headline page full of silly stories that was distributed around Taliesin and to friends far and wide.

EXTRA! *The Daily News* **EXTRA!**

LOVNESS SUITE ANNIVERSARY GALA

VOL. MXMCIIV No. 264   FINAL EDITION

LOVNESS ARCHIVES GROW
Spring Green, WI

The Lovness archives acquired a rare set of Le Corbusier drawings last week, which are being mounted on the Official Dart Board for the delectation and enjoyment of their guests. The Rembrandt dart-board was finally so riddled with pieces that the once-famous Night Watch painting was sold by Lovness to the Metropolitan for a sales-breaking price of thirteen million last month. The director of the Met was overheard to say, "The Rembrandt is so covered with delightful tiny little holes, that we are lighting it from within, featuring backlighting which enhances the stately characters no end." Thomas Hoving remarked, "The more paintings that come from the Lovness Dart Board, the greater the collections grow in fine museums. We are through buying fakes with the word "Merde" written across them and turning to Mr. and Mrs. Lovness' original way of enhancing original works by great masters. The director of the Louvre was asked his comment, and he said, quite simply, "Moi, je prefere Merde." French are so chauvinistic, however, and his remarks carry little weight in the great art markets across the world.

NEW PRODUCT STUMBLED UPON
Following his purchase of 3-M, Lovness reveals his venture into German Manure. A companion product to Restore, it is called, modestly, GALORE.

FUTURE PLANS FOR LOVNESS WOODS
The Lovness have announced their plans to build a third home on their lovely woodland property. No architect has been chosen, but a world wide competition with prizes and awards has been set up. Designs are pouring in from all parts of the globe, and Don Lovness said he might just have to use all of them, combined into one Grand Edifice. Mrs. Lovness is down in the quarry getting stone, we think. Mr. Lovness is up in the manor getting stoned, we are certain.

FURS ADVANCE IN STYLE
La Casa Virginia has announced its fall line of furs, with one great innovation: a white polar bear. Live. It simply walks along with you, and when you feel a chill, you command "Wrap me, honey!" and there you are, all wrapped up and warm and cozy.

Her skunk scarves, of the same ilk, have been a smash hit at outrageous parties, opening sessions of the Supreme Court, joint sessions of the House and Senate. Church weddings, with skunk scarves, are as Mrs. Lovness remarked, "A definite no-no, what with all that incense and such, the true grit is less appreciated." Mrs. Lovness is world famous for her furs and her fur designs. She has created the only mink-lined memory typewriter, a genuine Chinchilla drafting instrument set (for rather cold and wishy washy architects, she admits), and the Phillip Johnson Chippendale Mugwump Coat.

RENOWNED JEWELRY ON DISPLAY
J-Y Jewelry Corporation was established, this week, under the presidency of Mrs. Don Lovness. She has purchased nineteen junk-yards around the country and is slowly assembling them into various fabulous pieces. Wrought iron, steel, and old cars are the best ingredients, and the side effects are staggering: it has proven better than mace, tear gas, etc. etc., as a protection against muggers. You simply swing your arm and several pounds of impounded steel and rusted iron clobber the assailant, and you are left scot free and unharmed. For a more elite audience, many of the pieces are covered with epoxy and strawberry jam.

3-M + LOVNESS = 4M
Don Lovness announced, yesterday evening, the final purchase of 3-M Corporation on his steady climb to out-bech the BechTel Corp. The newly formed conglomerate will be called 4-M so as not to confuse the public, and Scotch brand he will change to Bourbon brand, the only corn whiskey-scented masking tape. Mr. Lovness is confident that the new products will catch hold quickly, and he has branched out into cosmetics and the like. One special product is a new deodorant spray made, actually, of black (for blacks) and, white (for honkies) lacquer. One spray guarantees* lasting protection for weeks at a time, and it is to be called PIT-PLUG.

CIRCUS TRAVELS
The Lovness Menagerie is on its way again, with animals, birds, fish, insects and infectious diseases on display across the country. A three legged alligator named Alphonso is the hit, this year. There is also a crockigator, but porno laws prohibit...

Wes Peters

William Wesley Peters was the first apprentice to join the Taliesin Fellowship, in 1932 . In addition to teaching architecture the goal was, "from the beginning to be a community, everyone participating in and contributing to all the activities required of daily living." 20-year-old Wes had already graduated from MIT and over the years became the main engineer supporting Wright's designs. In 1935 he married Mrs. Wright's daughter Svetlana who was a teenager at the time. They had two sons, but Svetlana and Daniel, age 2, died tragically in a Jeep accident near Taliesin in 1946. An older son, Brandoch, survived and was raised by the Wrights while Wes often traveled on business. Losing her daughter, Mrs. Wright was grief stricken for years, and Wes always said that if Svetlana had lived, the history of Taliesin would have been completely different.

Wes had an important part in such projects as Fallingwater, the Johnson Wax buildings, the Guggenheim Museum, and when Frank Lloyd Wright died, he became head of the Taliesin organization. He was loyal to the Fellowship and Mrs. Wright all his life, sometimes to a fault. He became a dear friend of my parents and with a tremendous sense of humor, was the source of many stories Mother and D would tell for years. Mother's notes about him exude warmth and love, and always, a smile:

Taliesin weekend activities would include a Saturday dinner, and afterwards, recitals, readings, dance, music, performances and skits. We can only guess what was going on in this photo with Mother but it's entirely in character for Wes, who loved outrageous costumes and even in his daily dress was rarely conservative.

Wes was a large man. He'd eat two banana cream pies at a sitting. When we'd have clients for dinner at the studio we'd have to make sure to pass the dessert cookies the other way around the table so they'd reach Wes last - as he'd finish the plateful.

Wes was a great guest, everyone loved his stories, but sometimes he'd get carried away, especially when driving. Traffic cops were a taboo subject, as he'd get so agitated he'd take his hands off the wheel. He told about taking Brandoch to the Mayo clinic in the Gullwing Mercedes at a pretty good clip when a police siren sounded. He put the pedal to the metal, losing the cop quickly. When they later stopped to smell some flowers in a field, the police car pulled up and proceeded to escort them to a judge in a nearby small town. The policeman was red in the face and agitated as he told the judge Wes had been doing 130 mph.

For his part, the judge was more interested in the exotic car, and told the officer to be quiet, he wanted to hear about the 300 SL. Wes invited the judge to go for a ride and the whole speeding case was dropped.

Wes was a collector like Mr. and Mrs. Wright and he enjoyed giving gifts to friends. He was also gracious when receiving a gift, as this letter shows. In his relations with my parents, however, he could rarely pass up an opportunity for a clever joke. In this case D had sent a female figurine, probably some fertility symbol from their latest Mexico trip. In this same spirit he was always willing to do something for my parents, and if they made a request he delivered and then some. Mother, in her letters to Taliesin had always asked for more designs and one of the items they felt was needed was a well-designed poker for the huge hearth. Their Wright house was a work of art and some simple wrought iron rod just wouldn't do. Anyway, the size of the

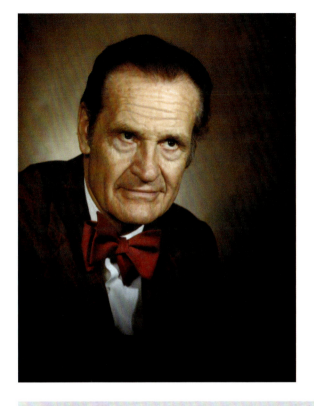

January 22, 1966

Dear Don and Virginia,

I was overwhelmed by the magnificent although ancient girl friend you sent me for Christmas.

How lovely and delicate she is! Do you think she is too old for me? I am presently writing a rather learned treatise based on this beautiful maiden under the title "Sex and the Teen-Century Girl" or "How Love Came to Montezuma".

There are some rather vile and miserably uninformed scoundrels around here -- notably John deKoven Hill and Kenneth Underwood Lockhart, who maintain that Don Lovness is the secret owner of a modern Mexico-based plant for manufacturing pre-Colombian objet d'art, and these same malfeasants claim to see that the present charming damsel was sculptured from life and bears a striking resemblance to Virginia. I have naturally dismissed these base canards for the twaddle they are!

All jocularity aside -- I appreciate and am grateful for the handsome gift; the fruit, I presume, of your archeological expedition last year. Thank you.

We missed you here at Christmas and the Holidays. We had hoped you had initiated a practice of coming to Arizona around that time.

Mrs. Wright enjoyed here stay in Minneapolis and was certainly appreciative of your hospitality and help.

We are returning to Wisconsin this summer (around May) for Mr. Wright's birthday celebration. Perhaps we will see you before that.

Regards and best wishes,

TALIESIN ASSOCIATED ARCHITECTS
OF THE
FRANK LLOYD WRIGHT FOUNDATION

TALIESIN WEST
SCOTTSDALE, ARIZONA
948-6400

In 1955 when Wright designed a Manhattan auto showroom and a home on Long Island for importer Max Hoffman, part of the deal was that two new Mercedes Benz would join the Taliesin stable at a steep discount. Mr. Wright would ride in the top-of-the-line 300D sedan and Wes would drive the tube-frame, fuel-injected 300 Sports Light (SL) with gullwing doors. Both in Cherokee red, of course.

logs D used to build a fire required something much more hefty than you could buy in a store. Wes' cleverness and humor came through when he sent three pages of designs along with a choice of pokers for different situations.

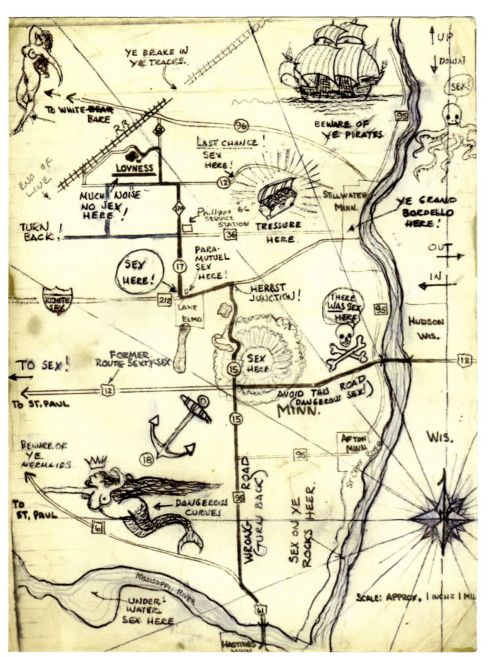

As the Lovness house became better known, the visitors kept coming. One saving grace was that our place was out of the way and hard to find, so the casual tourists were kept at bay. Even the ones who made it to the end of our driveway would often just keep going, as the house wasn't usually visible from the road, especially after the pines grew up. For those they did want to have visit, the parents made a simple map for use by Taliesin apprentices and other friends who were becoming regulars. At some point, the map was "adjusted" to resemble a pirates map, with warnings not about "Here there be monsters", but "Here there be sex!" We don't know if it was Wes or Jack Howe who actually "adjusted" the map, but our money is on Wes.

Wes, as chairman of Taliesin Associated Architects, and later, Chairman of the Frank Lloyd Wright Foundation, oversaw the entire operation (under the watchful eye of Mrs. Wright, of course). Mother and D were helpful in supplying small items for the organization, but they also functioned as a sort of welcoming committee for prospective clients, who would sometimes visit our house to get a feel for what it would be like to have a Wright home. Wes would also depend on my father for advice and suggestions about 3M products that

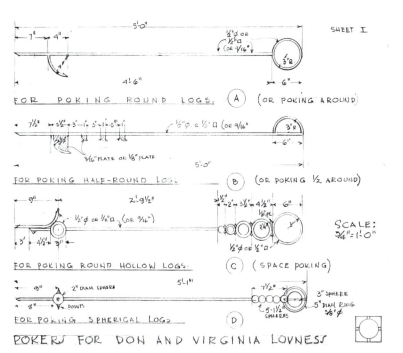

POKERS FOR DON AND VIRGINIA LOVNESS

Wes designed a custom fireplace grate for the cottage, and a poker to deal with the huge logs D loved to use.

His designs for all other types of logs covered pretty much any situation.

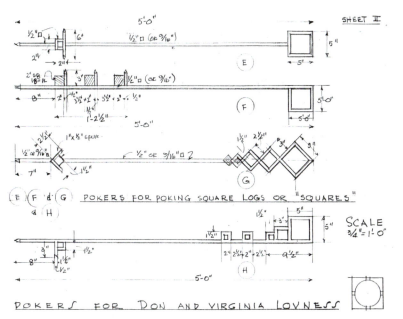

POKERS FOR DON AND VIRGINIA LOVNESS

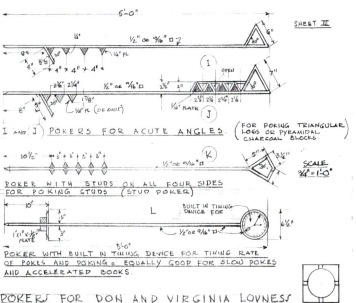

POKERS FOR DON AND VIRGINIA LOVNESS

Wes and D corresponded about business opportunities for 3M products (opposite), and mixed in some cultural observations, gossip and friendly ribbing. His comment about Easter eggs was perfectly serious, however. At Taliesin Easter was taken seriously and no small effort was put into painting eggs such as these by Wes (top left), Heloise (top right) and others.

Below, touring Gamage Auditorium, with Aaron Green.

could be used on Taliesin building projects. D would confer with his associates, using reference material that included photos, drawings and specs sent from Spring Green or Scottsdale. It was a mutually beneficial arrangement and helped deepen the friendship that lasted until Wes passed away in 1991.

Wes had worked closely with Frank Lloyd Wright and when the latter died in 1959 there were several projects still unfinished on the drawing boards. One of these was the Grady Gammage Auditorium the campus of Arizona State University in Tempe. It was based on an unbuilt Baghdad plan for King Faisal II of Iraq, incorporating circles and spheres, much like the Marin County Civic Center also under construction in the late 1950s, and the later Pearl Palace for the Shan of Iran's sister. In 1963 Mother and D got a guided tour of the auditorium under construction from Wes and a few years later, our family visited again to see the finished building. On that 1971 visit, Wes was kind enough to show us around the auditorium, whose construction he had overseen, and the Music Building he had designed nearby, which came to be known as the "birthday cake building" based on its shape. In leaving, however, I somehow got left behind. D must have let his enthusiasm for the buildings get the best of him because he didn't bother to do a nose count as he drove away. I wasn't in the back seat; I was standing on the sidewalk wondering if this was another one of D's cruel jokes. As usual, I didn't think it was very funny, but after a few minutes the family returned to pick me up.

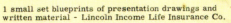

Mr. Don Lovness
3-M Company
400 Bush Ave
St. Paul 6, Minnesota

January 4, 1963
TW 63-128

RE: Proposed 3-M building materials

We ARE ENCLOSING HEREWITH: *

WE ARE SENDING UNDER SEPARATE COVER:

REMARKS:

    *1 set small blueprints of presentation drawings and
written material - Keystone Towers
1 - 8 x 10 glossy "   "

    1 small set blueprints of presentation drawings - Kentuckianna

    1 small set blueprints of presentation drawings and
written material - Lincoln Income Life Insurance Co.

    1 set small plans and elevations, Court of the Seven Seas
1 brochure International Village

    Sarkisian Snow Flake Motel - Working Drawing Sheets 12
and X-11, one each. 1 small print perspective

YOURS VERY TRULY,

William Wesley Peters

TALIESIN ASSOCIATED ARCHITECTS
WWP;sjw

April 3, 1967

Mr. Donald Lovness
Minnesota Mining & Manufacturing Company
900 Bush Avenue
St. Paul 6, Minnesota

Dear Don:

Thank you for your letter of March 17 and the enclosed
clipping.

Mr. Grim's comment was very interesting, although I
would take issue with him about the brass or timpani
being "jumbled into a clangor".

What is the name of your sales representative in Alma--
the one on the Building Committee?

We missed you on Easter--particularly after I had painted
a number of nude Easter eggs for your delectation and
special approbation.

We are looking forward to seeing you in June, if not before.
Why don't you come out for the Festival (April 21, 22, and
23)?

Regards and best wishes to you and Virginia.

William Wesley Peters

WWP:pas

Patinating the bust

Mother wrote an amusing story about the bust of Frank Lloyd Wright they had. Boris Blai was a world-renowned sculptor and educator at Temple University, and a friend of the Wrights who had been instrumental in connecting the architect with Rabbi Cohen for the Beth Shalom synagogue commission. Mrs. Wright asked him if he would create a bust of Mr. Wright in bronze and he came to Taliesin to do the work. Mother described it:

"Mr. Wright would sit reluctantly while Mr. Blai worked the clay into a likeness. When he quit for the day he would carefully cover the bust with a wet cloth to keep it pliable for the next day. Mr. Wright would get up in the middle of the night to see how it was progressing. He would think that his nose didn't look like that, so he'd change it. And the same the next night. Boris Blai left without finishing the bust.

"Later Mrs. Wright asked Heloise Crista, a very talented dancer and member of the Fellowship—who had not previously done any sculpting—to do Mr. Wright in clay. She produced an excellent likeness and Mrs. Wright had three cast in bronze - one for each Taliesin and she later gave one to us!

"It was shiny brass and a striking likeness. Don suggested that it would look better when it aged and patinated a bit, and he mixed up some chemicals to tarnish it while waiting for nature to do the trick. He filled a pail with copper sulfate and gave me the head to dip. It was scary. I asked Mr. Wright for forgiveness and dipped his head upside down. He's now a softer version, and hopefully he approves."

Mother and D joined a star-studded group during a tour of the yet-to-be-completed Marin County Civic Center in 1959. Here some of them pose on the roof. From left, project supervisor Aaron Green, Maria Stone, Edward Durrell Stone, three unidentified, Ben Raeburn and Wes Peters.

Wes was busy with many projects and traveled extensively, but often stopped in the Twin Cities on his way here or there, and visited our house when he could. Wes had sophisticated taste and enjoyed buying lovely things as gifts (even when he couldn't afford it) but he also got into the swing of it at Banks. Mother wrote about him:

Wes Peters was quite a shopper. He loved to come with us to Banks and would stand in line waiting in the cold for the 8:30 a.m. opening. He would run over to a restaurant a few blocks away for bacon and egg sandwiches with coffee to eat while we were waiting. (One of us had to stay in line to keep our place.) Wes loved to buy long dresses for everyone at Taliesin, or jewelry, or anything!

Wes wrote to Don from Karaj, Iran in 1971 asking for advice about how to keep the water clear at the planned lakes around the "Pearl" palace, sending an aerial photo with notes about the position of each water body.

He later sent photos of the finished palace, built for the Shah of Iran's sister, Shams Pahlavi. When the Shah was deposed in 1979 the palace complex began a long slide into neglect; it is now occupied by a paramilitary militia and in need of massive repairs.

The distinctive mailbox was a landmark for many years, guiding wandering guests to the inconspicuous driveway they were seeking. It has been retired from the road but still exists.

There were details that my father felt were missing at our Wright "compound", and Wes came though with some designs to fill the voids. One of these was a mailbox, "For the Love Nest" as he wrote on his plans. In addition to specific dimensions on the drawing, he added a slightly exaggerated drawing of Mother and D showing their difference in height. And of course, Virginia was wearing heavy jewelry. He just couldn't resist a chance to poke fun at his friends. D built the mailbox with his wire-feed welder (he was now much better equipped than when they began the studio in 1955) and it stood opposite the driveway as a marker for visitors, withstanding the elements, snow plows and the occasional vandal for years.

Wes also was a source of archival plans for furniture, lights, planters and all kinds of items that D would re-create or adapt for our use.

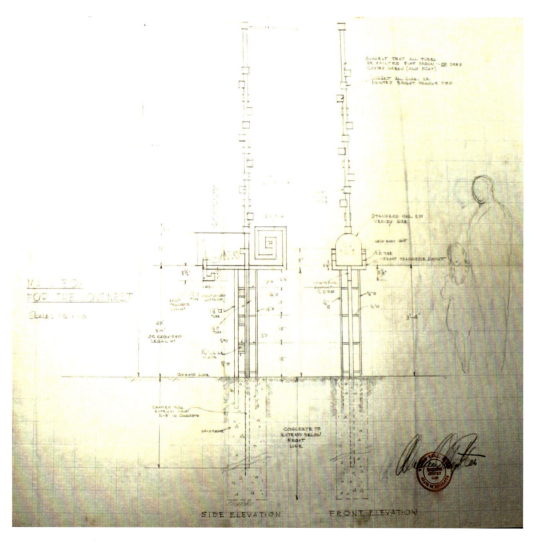

SIDE ELEVATION   FRONT ELEVATION

Wes' sister Margadant was married to S.I. Hayakawa, a linguist, writer and professor who had lectured in Madison and Chicago. He was later president of San Francisco State College and a senator from California. In the late 1980s Wes, Aaron Green, and my parents visited the Hayakawas in California. S. I. was a big jazz fan; I'm sure he and D had some good discussions.

In the early '60s Wes adapted an old Wright square design for metal gates to rectangular and D had a welding shop build them. The first gate walls had been built crudely from what was left of the studio rock pile, with little in the way of footings. In the late 1980s D and Ty's husband Pat built an new gate and walls with cut stone left over from the cottage, now with solid footings. The new gate design was adapted by Aaron Green to more closely reflect Wright's original "square" theme.

Stalin's daughter

In April, 1967 newspaper headlines were filled with news of Svetlana Alliluyeva, the daughter of Joseph Stalin, who had defected to the United States from Russia. Well after her arrival in this country she remained quite newsworthy after writing a book, *Twenty letters to a friend*, and making a considerable sum from its publication. During the next few years she received several calls from Olgivanna Lloyd Wright, who invited her to visit Taliesin. Mrs. Wright told Svetlana that she had lost a daughter of the same name, and Svetlana thought perhaps Mrs. Wright would remind her of her own mother, who had killed herself when Svetlana was young. In March, 1970 she arrived in Phoenix and went to Taliesin, where she was seated at dinner next to Wes.

It's pretty well documented that Mrs. Wright carefully arranged that meeting, a whirlwind courtship and the marriage of Svetlana and Wes just three weeks later. Wes and his new wife—with the same name as his first wife who had died in 1946—settled down at his apartment at Taliesin West. She was happy at first, both there and at their summer quarters at Taliesin in Spring Green, but it took only months for her to realize Mrs. Wright's dominance over the group would minimize her own role. For his part, Wes refused to change his allegiance to the Fellowship, the only life he had known as an adult. Complicating the situation was an expectation that Svetlana would pay for Wes and his considerable debts, and help fund the Fellowship. She was in love but angry and exasperated. There was no one to talk to at Taliesin, but she did have a friend on the "outside" - my mother.

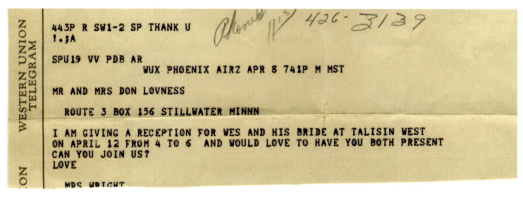

Wes and his bride on their wedding day at Taliesin.

Since Wes was a good friend it was natural Mother and D would get to know his new wife, and they met her that spring. The marriage started out as a happy one and Svetlana, who had been married twice before, desperately wanted to have that American ideal of a loving mate and a simple home for them both. What she got was a few rooms in the desert compound where "the kitchen and bathroom were in the wrong place," as she complained. With relations between her and Mrs. Wright quickly deteriorating, she came to see my mother, especially, as an ally and a confidant. Her letters to my parents were initially upbeat but after only a few months there was discontent in what she wrote:

July 1, 1970.

Dearest Virginia,

It was so nice to see you and talk to you at Taliesin. Those days were very difficult and peace was restored very slowly. Now, when everybody left, life seems to be more quiet and relaxed here, but I'm trembling with fear about the future. Indeed, it seems to me that I am facing the most hopeless time in my life. I love Wes, I would not be able to exist without him, and at the mean time I cannot imagine how would I be able to find any modus vivendi here, under the two ladies. Iovanna now seems to turn against me with full strength. These changes, these controversial passions from adoration to hatred - ala dostoyevski - make me feel sick.

But the most important thing is not me, but Wes. He will be the target of shooting, he will be the subject of all charges, shocks and opposite trends. I do not know what to do (thinking about the fall and winter) and I cannot say that I am very much encouraged with his behaviour and attitude. He really believes, that if he brings another nice dress or something from the shop, that can make me absolutely happy. But I never cared about all these material possessions - feelings are the only important things to me. I do not know how long it will take for us both to meet somewhere in the middle - for the time being we are on opposite poles in many respects, concerning the way of life at Taliesin, where I guess I have to live a long life.

Please, my dear, do not worry to answer this letter. It gives me great consolation just to write it to you. Our talks were very helpful to me, I learned many good things. I know all you would tell me again. I hope we shall see you on our way to Wisconsin - somewhere in the middle of July. Much love to both of you.

Yours, Svetlana.

The daughter of one of the world's most brutal dictators made news from the time she defected from Russia to the USA while in India. Her marriage to Wes Peters sparked another round of sensational headlines and their daughter's birth and their separation the following year did the same. One headline read, "Peace of mind and heart at last for Svetlana". Unfortunately, that peace was short-lived.

On January 14, 1971 she wrote a breezy letter to Mother talking about jewelry shops in Scottsdale, and how Wes's sister Margadant had hosted them in California for a New Year's Eve party, which she enjoyed tremendously. She ended the letter by mentioning her skepticism about something Wes had discussed: Wright's mile-high city. "Who on earth could live in such a thing?" she wrote, adding, "But I kept my mouth shut. If I only could manage to do that more often - we would be a very happy couple."

That, however was not in her nature. A few weeks later she was sounding desperate. She was pregnant, Wes was traveling constantly—often as far away as Iran—and "the two ladies", Olgivanna and her daughter Iovanna, were openly hostile. On January 25, 1971 Svetlana sent a four-page single-space typed letter to my father asking for confidential advice about the couple's financial situation. They had been married nine months and she had already emptied $400,000 of her bank account to pay off his debts and, she had discovered, to pay Taliesin bills as well.

Mother responded that she and D were "appalled, but not surprised." She continued, "Don and I have had so many years to understand, but you've been thrown into it all so suddenly. But by now you must realize that something must be done and soon - before all is lost." A handwritten postscript said, "Don't worry! This isn't an insoluble situation - everything can be worked out."

That May a daughter was born in San Rafael, California. With little enthusiasm for a new baby at Taliesin, she and Wes were staying with Margadant in Marin County. Wes was in a San Francisco meeting when the time came, so Margadant's husband S.I. Hayakawa drove Svetlana to the hospital. She was happy to be a mother at 44 and her daughter was named Olga, after her grandmother - not after Olgivanna as Mrs. Wright initially thought. The icy standoff between the women reached something of a climax when a baptism date was set for September at the Milwaukee Greek Orthodox church, a Wright design that was celebrating its tenth anniversary. The two events seemed like they should be a happy confluence, but afterwards Mrs. Wright was incensed, as "Stalin's daughter" (and granddaughter) were more newsworthy and the baby had upstaged the architect of the church in the celebrations. Mother and D were at Spring Green after the baptism and Svetlana was very upset. In a Taliesin interview they recalled the day:

Mother: (The baby) was small, and she said she didn't have a friend here, Taliesin was evil and sinister and she hated it. She couldn't stay with Wes any longer but she couldn't take care of the baby. Would I go with her back East?

D: We'd made arrangements with Ling Po to bring him to Minneapolis. He was waiting down by the main gate with his suitcase. This is at ten in the morning. Virginia went into the bedroom with Svetlana. Wes and I went down to (his farm at) Aldebaran and looked at cows or something. And this went on for hours up there.

Mother: She was so upset I thought she was going to - I don't know. She was so ill I didn't think she

Svetlana kisses Olga during the baptism ceremony in Milwaukee. This AP wirephoto was widely distributed to newspapers.

could take care of the baby. And she was saying irrational things. One of the worst was, "Someone tried to burn Taliesin before, and they didn't do a good job. But I'm going to burn it down and I'll do a good job!"

And this terrified me because you could see she wasn't in her right mind. But she kept asking if I would help her and go East with her, where she felt she had some friends. And of course I said I would; I mean, you'd do anything for someone this upset.

I didn't tell Mrs. Wright (at the time) because I didn't know what to do.

D and Wes returned and they all went to lunch in Spring Green. Then, dropping Wes and Svetlana at their apartment, they picked up Ling Po (who had waited almost all day) and headed home. Alarmed but not quite sure how to proceed, the three discussed it while driving. Arriving back in Stillwater, Mother called Mrs. Wright, (who was expecting a call) telling her how upset Svetlana was and that she was concerned. Along with Wes, Mrs. Wright decided to post a guard and the next day, had a family practice doctor see Svetlana. In the course of this meeting Svetlana asked the doctor questions about who had reported on the previous day's episode. The doctor, not fully realizing the relationship between her and Mother, said, matter-of-factly, that it was Virginia. Svetlana, of course, felt betrayed by the one friend she thought she had.

In November 1970 the parents stayed at Taliesin North with Wes and Svetlana. Mother recalls that Svetlana cooked: the coffee was thick like oatmeal and the oatmeal was thin like water. In this photo everyone is smiling but things would change quickly in the next year.

49-year old Mother was wearing wild pants, a Mexican rebozo scarf, pony tails and a monkey coat, part of her ever-growing collection of furs.

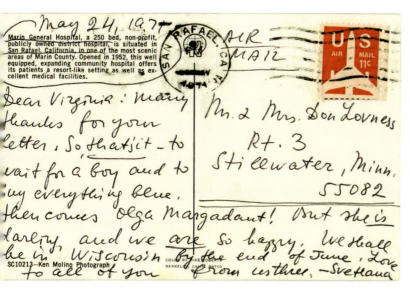

A happy moment was when Olga was born. She was supposed to be a boy, but as these things go, parents adapt pretty quickly. Olga was named after Svetlana's grandmother and Wes's sister Margadant.

At one of the annual Easter celebrations at Taliesin, Wes and Mother, both outrageous dressers, have a smooch.

In 1990 at Taliesin West the three friends share a moment.

A week later Mrs. Wright called and ordered Mother and D to be at Taliesin at 7 a.m. She held what could be called an inquisition ("This was a Gurdjieff thing," D later commented), quizzing both Mother and Svetlana about the encounter they had had. After hours of tears, accusations and recriminations, Mrs. Wright put her arms around Mother and said, "I've known Virginia for over thirty years and I believe what she said. She doesn't lie." Svetlana, D recalls, "just exploded." At a tense dinner that night he said it was the last time Svetlana talked in a civil manner to them. Even so, Mother was tearful and concerned, saying, "She was hurting so, and frightful and hateful, and vengeful..." Adding to the drama, when Iovanna heard about the encounter she said of Svetlana, "I'll kill her!"

Returning to Arizona that fall, the couple made plans to relocate from Taliesin to an apartment a short distance away, something Svetlana was adamant about, hoping to save the marriage. When the move was made, Wes announced to Svetlana he would be staying at Taliesin after all. His allegiance remained with Mrs. Wright, as did my parents' in the end. Svetlana had been left to work it out on her own.

That winter Wes was visiting my parents. He called Svetlana to discuss something and then he put Mother on the phone to say hello. They had a nice conversation and "everything seemed like old times," D recalled. A last letter came soon thereafter:

January 31, 1972
Dear Don & Virginia,
It was an embarrassing surprise two days ago to hear you on the telephone; all I could do at the moment was to be polite. Yet after a terrible experience I had last summer I do NOT believe any word of yours and do not trust the declarations of friendship. True friends of Wes should have done something long ago to free him from a terrible prison he is living and working in. Yet you always do more for Mrs. Wright keeping him there - for HER - adding more work, etc.
What Wes really needs is a free life of a grown-up man - he is 60 now - a life of an independent and talented architect.
Once I heard something like truth from you, but apparently it was one of your hypocrisies. Strange enough, you do not see, being double faced is your behavior. You always bring only trouble for Wes and me.
Please - do not call me, do not write to me. It would be much better for us. I am not able to (be) friendly with people when I do not know what to think about (them).
Sorry for all this, Svetlana

Lana Peters (as she was later known) was divorced from Wes in 1973 and against her lawyers' advice, never asked for financial compensation from Wes or Taliesin. She moved to the East Coast, to England, then Russia in 1984, and back to the USA in 1986. She was never really out of the public spotlight and newspapers reported on her moves, especially her renunciation of the USA and her later return. She passed away in November, 2011 while living near Spring Green, Wisconsin.

After Svetlana left with Olga, Wes remained at Taliesin, as busy as ever. The struggle to deal with financial setbacks continued, however. Even though the infusion of cash from his wife's account had helped, he was still in debt. Investments in cattle at Aldebaran, the farm adjacent to Taliesin, had been a bust. His penchant for buying expensive things to keep and as gifts was coming back to haunt. The only solution was to liquidate some of the things he had collected, many of which had become quite valuable.

Whether it was to keep it all out of Mrs. Wright's sight or that my parents were seasoned wheeler-dealers and the best people for the job—or both—I can't say, but they helped Wes sell stuff for years. D acted as an intermediary, dealing with auction houses in Chicago and New York, keeping exhaustive inventories of Wes's possessions in both Wisconsin and Arizona, and running interference with lawyers who represented both Wes' interests and those of his creditors. In itemized lists from 1974 there were rare books, jewelry, antiques, watches, Japanese prints, and hundreds of eclectic items, from a set of civil war lead soldiers to an Apache chief's wool blanket. Some notable items on the list are 13 custom made suits (remember, Wes was 6' 4"), 7 tuxedoes, 7 silk rain coats, 170 four-in-hand ties along with 28 bow ties, a Russian-

In this letter from 1969, Mrs. Wright wrote to my parents with a "Day in the life" of Taliesin. D's suggestion may have been a catalyst for a Taliesin newsletter. An exclamation mark after Kay Rattenbury's name probably reflected that Kay, her personal assistant, had already been married to or involved with three other Taliesin men; Mrs. Wright was famous for "arranging" liaisons. It's interesting to read her description of the apprentices being "wild with joy" about working to finish her new quarters. I'm sure had anyone asked them they would have had a different view. She mentions all the players by first name, as Mother and D knew almost everyone at Taliesin. In closing she inquires about D's "industry", meaning his new venture as a partner with Judd Ringer in a plant nutrient company - that had not yet proven "prosperous".

OLGIVANNA LLOYD WRIGHT

November 26, 1969

Dear Don and Virginia,

You spoke to me once that you hoped to receive a bulletin issued from Taliesin to keep you informed about its various activities. I have asked Bruce to tell you of the exciting happenings at Taliesin.

You probably know about the work on my new room, born in the minds of a John Rattenbury and Kay, his wife -- I have now lived in the Cottage for five weeks hoping that my palatial mansion will actually be finished one day. . .

During these five weeks 20 people have been engaged daily in working on that room. They all seem to be wild with joy the way it is shaping up, and they take every tiny facet of it very seriously. For instance, Minerva was terribly upset one day because somebody did not clean out her concrete mixer. Jay Jay, our new Japanese girl, when speaking on philosophy, uses comparisons such as, "We need something like the spark that is used in welding," or, "It takes time to set concrete, the same as with the human being." And so on and so forth. Another new Japanese student, Itoh, drives the electric surrey-truck the way a Roman warrior would drive his chariot. Shizuo seems to be always welding when I go by, and Charles wields the wheelbarrow up to the roof on a precarious narrow board as an acrobat on the tight rope.

John R is the captain, the marechal, the dictator, the benevolent teacher, giving directions in the midst of sawing, hammering, grinding, scraping, buzzing of the power saws, and the rock 'n roll blasting at top volume. Lath, with a heavenly expression on his face, shovels concrete to the mad rhythm of the music. Linda, the new girl, has a carpenter's apron on, doing all the odd jobs while inaudibly humming and swaying to rock 'n roll themes.

In the afternoon the drafting room fills to capacity and everything appears as calm as the unruffled surface of the quiet ocean.

How are you -- what are you doing? I certainly hope that you, Virginia, are not getting too much out of hand in your art work. Remember that you did not fare too well the last time when you overdid it. And I wish that you, Don, remain strong and healthy and prosperous. I wish and hope you one day will be. How is the industry going? With love to you both

Olgivanna Lloyd Wright

Wes' 300SL became Mother's grocery-getter for a one summer.

Below, at a summer event in Lake Geneva, Wisconsin, Ben Raeburn (left) joins Mother and Wes.

made camel-hair coat and an elephant skin jacket. And that was just Arizona items. Wes had good taste in books and of course, had over the years been in a position to acquire the best. He had some original German "Ausgeführte Bauten" portfolios, one signed by Mr. Wright to him, and many other of Wright's books with Wright's signature.

One unusual item that wasn't among the many stored in my parents' cottage vault: the Mercedes 300SL coupe Wes had been driving since 1955. When it was new, it was the fastest production sports car you could buy; a "halo" car for Mercedes that touted the company's domination in endurance and Grand Prix racing. With fuel injection, a space-frame chassis, aluminum panels and "gull-wing" doors it had been an instant sensation.

During the summer of 1975 it was at Woodpile Lake, while D and Mother advertised it for sale. She used it for grocery shopping and errands, although its trunk was tiny. Even when it was in our driveway that summer, it was still considered an icon, one of the most celebrated sports car ever built. Rolf Ljungkull wanted it but his wife Peter wouldn't allow it. After several months it was sold to a collector for $5000, the going price at the time. Recent sales at auction have seen the cars sell for over 1.5 million dollars.

Ben Raeburn

One of the "peripheral" but extremely important members of the Taliesin circle was the owner of Horizon Press, Ben Raeburn. He was known for publishing authors who had not yet found a mass audience but would become successful. His books were recognized in the industry as being exquisitely designed, and he had a hand in all aspects of production. Mother wrote about him:

Ben was Mr. and Mrs. Wright's publisher for most of their lives. He was dedicated to them both, a sensitive and loyal friend. He had a photographic memory and would reminisce for hours about his visits to Taliesin and their visits to New York, where he lived. Once when he flew to Minneapolis to stay with us a few days before we all drove to Taliesin, he made the only complaint I ever heard from him: he said the birds' singing had awakened him in the morning!

Mother and D would visit New York regularly, often seeing Ben there, where he lived and worked. They would also cross paths with him at one or the other Taliesin, where Mrs. Wright would summon him, sometimes on a moment's notice, to discuss one of the books she was writing (Horizon Press published five of hers and seventeen of Mr. Wright's works). Ben and my parents corresponded regularly and he often sent copies of new titles to them, anxious for their opinion. They were both avid readers, D for technical information and Mother for pleasure but they always enjoyed Ben's books, as well as his company.

Buckminster Fuller

Like Wright, Bucky Fuller was a visionary but without credentials. His only degrees were honorary ones given long after he had proven to be one of the greatest minds of our times, and not just in architecture. A friend and mutual admirer of Wright, Bucky sometimes visited both Taliesins when he traveled on a lecture circuit. He was a friend of a sculptor my parents knew in the Twin Cities, and Mother remembered a talk he gave in Minneapolis and another meeting at Taliesin West:

We heard him at a lecture that got so convoluted. It was the usual about geodesic domes, his three-wheeled cars and tensegrity. We couldn't follow and Wes fell asleep, so we crept out, hoping he didn't recognize us.

At the time (1968) he was obsessed with his diet. He was eating only steak, fruit and tea, and chewing each bite to minute pieces, to help digestion. His enthusiasm for it was interesting, quite a departure from what he normally talked about. At a cocktail party around the pool at Taliesin West Bucky asked me if I'd join him around the other side of the pool so he could talk to me alone. That seemed like a novel proposition! It turned out he wanted to talk to one person only, as his hearing aid was picking up too many sounds in the crowd.

Below left, outside Trader Vic's restaurant, Scottsdale, June 1968. (Trader Vic's was Wes Peters' favorite in town.) On this occasion Mother wrote, "Bucky excused himself and made a phone call. 15 Minutes later a lady friend arrived." The lady in question seemed to take a shine to Ben Raeburn, however. At right is Taliesin architect Vernon Swaback.

Edgar Tafel

Along with Wes Peters, Edgar was one of the first apprentices to join the new Fellowship in 1932, at age 20. He was involved in key projects during the 1930s including Fallingwater and the Johnson Wax buildings. He lived in Racine for two years overseeing much of the construction and "client relationships"- a challenging task. He left Taliesin in October 1941 and in 1943 served with army photo intelligence in Calcutta during WWII, then post-war started his own practice in New York City.

Both his work in design and as a member of several boards centered on churches and religious groups, museums and colleges. He wrote two books about Wright: *Apprentice to Genius, Years with Frank Lloyd Wright*, and *About Wright*, the latter a collection of essays by those close to the architect. Aside from his own architecture work he became a circuit lecturer on Wright, and made a decent living giving talks and slide shows, sometimes showing a home movie from 1930s Taliesin. He consulted and contributed to several films and books about Wright.

In spite of his going off on his own, he was a great promoter of Taliesin over the years, mostly because telling stories about it allowed him an income. He was also critical of the Fellowship many times. In a letter to D he described what he heard from a friend who had spoken to Mr. Wright:

Mr. W told him, 'I regret that Edgar left the fold.' I looked up the word "fold" and my dictionary says, "an enclosure for domesticated animals." !! So, we apprentices were domesticated...

In the 1980s and early '90s Edgar wrote often to my parents, and forwarded some of the letters he received from others. Most of the notes have a breezy gossip theme, with Edgar confiding his opinions about a wide range of people and projects. One letter described how, while at Taliesin for nine years, he had taken the Broadacre City model to New York, tended it for a month and brought it back. He had also been at Fallingwater for "a couple of winter months" while checking the woodwork at the mill, and noted (with apparent regret) that he didn't get to go to Arizona for two winters. He continued:

And I was virtually the general contractor for the Schwartz and (Lloyd) Lewis houses — Whilst on Johnson Building it was Tafel who went to the mills: Corning, International Door, Streater Brick Co. And after the war I brought Horizon Press to Taliesin, found the right contractor for the Guggenheim, without whom it wouldn't have been built for it was so far over the budget. And I brought the job from England, and Atlantic City tho they fell through due to economics only.

It was a rant that he felt he had "never received appreciation," and ended with, "That's off my chest for the moment." Edgar was dedicated to showcasing Wright's work in his own books and talks, and he took an interest in everything else that was being produced about the architect including magazine articles, both his own and from others, and events. In a letter to D of June, 1987 he noted that Taliesin was announcing an anniversary celebration and wondered "what they were trying to accomplish." Going on, he wrote:

Every time I visit, Cornelia says, "Edgar, you and Wes tell the apprentices what it was like the first two years - all the pranks and fun you had." But for us all to talk out a weekend and to end with no accomplishment, what does that do for anyone? Last week I spent a day with (early apprentice) Yen Liang - he has written a piece for my book - and we went through taped remembrances of the early days... Yen has a great awareness of history, and that led to an idea: That a film be made on Mr. W by those of us who were there, to describe what life was like at the beginning... The film must be made by a real film pro... At any rate, something should be done whilst we are still around, for posterity. Bits could be taken out for a film for PBS or such. But this can't be done honestly by Taliesin, they would have some droning voices affording monotony.

In 1995 Edgar followed through, producing a 55-minute film called *The Frank Lloyd Wright Way.* Maybe this was a catalyst for Ken Burns' documentary in the late 1990s (which was also fodder for much discussion between Edgar and my parents). Just as Edgar had envisioned,

At his house in Florida there seemed to be constant construction, and Edgar's notes to D lament that contractors were generally clueless. He loved to complain about people.

Burns and Lynn Novick interviewed many people, including Edgar, in producing the movie. He appears in it, as does *New Yorker* writer Brendan Gill, author of *Many Masks*, a somewhat contentious 1987 biography of Wright. Gill was another subject of many letters between the parents and Edgar.

In addition to regular correspondence, Mother and D would visit Edgar and his companion Jean Gollay (an accomplished author and editor under the name Jean Libman Block) in New York and at their home in Florida. Edgar was a visitor to Woodpile Lake many times as well.

In 1982 Norman McGrath spent several days at the studio to photograph an article for *Architectural Digest*. The 8-page feature was written by Edgar, who sent the manuscript to my parents for edits. Ironically, the final version had many small factual errors.

The Little house

Edgar also was active in efforts to save Wright structures, which were falling like dominos in the 1970s and '80s. In 1982 he wrote, "Having worked on four of the twelve Wright houses now in public domain, I have kept them under constant surveillance and acted when the existence was in jeopardy." The first of those actions was in 1971, when the Francis Little House "Northome" on the shore of Lake Minnetonka was faced with demolition. My father and Edgar worked together to salvage something, anything from the 1914 Wright structure that was headed for the wrecking ball. D knew the Little's daughter Eleanor and her husband Raymond Stevenson. They had lived in the huge, drafty house since the 1950s, after Eleanor's mother Mary Little moved to a small cottage on the property in the 1940s. As they aged, the need for a smaller

Edgar visited Minnesota in the 1990s and my parents brought him to one of my semi-annual jewelry sample sales at Lonnie Lovness Accessories. We ducked into the hallway for a group photo.

Like many old Minnesota buildings, the Stevensons took whatever means necessary to keep the drafty Little house warm in winter.

This bed was typical of the built-in furniture designed for the house. D copied some of the designs for the studio and cottage furniture.

house became clear and the Stevensons tried to sell the house for several years, but the city of Deephaven would not allow them to build the new home they wanted on the same property. D was involved in dialogues with local museums and organizations to find a place for the structure, but there were no takers. By 1971, when demolition became inevitable, D and Jack Howe contacted Edgar in New York, who in turn wrote to Thomas Hoving, Director of the Metropolitan Museum of Art.

That winter the Met sent Hoving and Morrie Heckscher, curator of American Decorative Arts in the new "American Wing" there, to negotiate purchase of the home. D, the Stevensons and a small group of others met at the house and worked out a plan by which the Met would dismantle the huge living room for display in New York. The library would be saved and put on display in Pennsylvania at the Allentown Art Museum, which Edgar was helping to expand and remodel at the time. Over the next several years bits and pieces of the house were sold; 13 of the 300 windows in the house went to the Dallas Museum of Art (and one of them came home with D to be used in the cottage skylight). Although D made an effort to get the Minneapolis museum to purchase the entire master bedroom (Jack Howe also wrote to them), they ended up only with a hallway, including 10 more windows.

It took ten years for the Met to install the "living room" (which was actually a recital space for Mary Little, who was an accomplished pianist) and Edgar's original vision was that it would be a meeting or performance space for the Met. It remains a static display, unfortunately, as does the library in Allentown. The hallway at the Institute in Minneapolis is a little more accessible, but always seemed to enthusiasts to be a disappointment since they could have had the bedroom. That room was sold to Tom Monaghan in the early 1980s for the Dominos collection, but has never been installed. Other items from the house are scattered in private collections, many of them having been sold "garage-sale style" before the house was torn down. Windows that appear at auction have recently sold for six figures. Wright furniture of all kinds is also quite valuable these days, and D acquired some of the drawings from the Stevensons. Architect Al Drap worked with D on the cottage in 1975 and visited occasionally thereafter. Regarding furniture from the Little house, he recalls:

Top left, at the winter, 1972 meeting Morrison Heckscher, Eleanor Stevenson, Thomas Hoving and Raymond Stevenson share a laugh.

Above, D smiles with a pocketful of cigars on hand for the celebration of consummating the deal.

Below, Raymond Stevenson had complained for years that "there wasn't a stick of comfortable furniture in the house." Note that the furnishings in their main living area are definitely not Wrightian.

Entry doors, like all the glass in the house, were leaded art glass. The original Wright plans called for much colored glass but the Littles insisted on having more clear glass, to be able to enjoy views of Lake Minnetonka.

Growing Up Wright **233**

The furniture in the living room of the main (Lovness) house had two chairs and a matching couch and two pedestal end tables that were made from FLW designs for the Little house on Lake Minnetonka. I don't know where Don got these designs, but I suspect they came from the original drawings that he got from the Little's daughter. Don once showed me those drawings, they were in the flat file in the dining room. I also don't know when Don built this furniture or if John Howe was involved. They were not new when I first visited in 1975.

In the living room of the Little house at the Metropolitan Museum, most of the furniture is from the Little's earlier house in Peoria, Illinois. It is easy to tell the pieces from the Peoria house because they are stained dark and do not match the light color of the room trim. They are also of an earlier style. Don told me that the experts from the Metropolitan Museum were sitting in his living room discussing what furniture Wright would have wanted in the room. He said, "The idiots didn't realize they were sitting on the furniture Wright designed for the room."

The end result may not have been perfect—the Little house was gone—but some of its glory was saved for generations to appreciate in museum settings that were accessible. And it was all accomplished in an unorthodox way. As Edgar wrote in his book *Apprentice to Genius*, "Saving the Little house required no public meetings, committees, groups, politicians, preservationists, historians, planners or architects' societies - just a few of us with our hearts in the right place and with the financial ability to act."

D took photos in 1972 when the "living room", and especially the fireplace, showed some wear and use. The wall sconces were simple (D made replicas for the studio) but the stained glass windows were spectacular.

December 26, 1979

To Whom It May Concern:

In response to the petition circulated by Mr. Thompson in respect to the Little House (designed in 1912 by Frank Lloyd Wright), I wholeheartedly support the proposed acquisition of the master bedroom by the Minneapolis Art Institute. I believe it to be the most important room in the house, excepting the living room.

As an old friend of the Stevensons, I was involved with the sale of the house to the Metropolitan Museum in New York. The irony of this is the house was for sale for five years. The house was extensively advertised by realtors, plus publicity in local papers. I personally had many meetings with Tony Clark, then Director of the Minneapolis Art Institute, without any success. Just before the Met became involved to acquire the house, a decision was made by Mr. and Mrs. Stevenson at a cost of $30,000 to demolish the house and auction the windows and furniture through Parke Bernet. I personally made these arrangements with Parke Bernet. At the time, this decision by the Stevensons was completely justified.

These mistakes were made years ago. We now have a rare opportunity to rectify these previous mistakes. I know a great deal about this house and all the transactions that took place since the 50's, and will certainly volunteer my services where necessary.

I believe also that the other Wright houses in this area are all in a similar danger if more public awareness is not generated. This should be done through the Art Institute, publicity, tours, etc. If this is not done by us, it will certainly be done by people more aware of Wright's contribution to our midwest heritage.

Historians, through the Art Institute of Chicago, are continually searching in this area for stained glass, furniture, and drawings from the Prairie School, and they have been very successful. For example, tellers' wickets and many artifacts from the interior of Louis Sullivan's Owatonna Bank are in the possession of the Art Institute of Chicago.

I do sincerely hope that the Minneapolis Art Institute will at least consider Mr. Thompson's proposal.

Yours truly,

Donald E. Lovness

DEL:d

The Minneapolis Institute of Arts was in the middle of a huge addition in the early 1970s, and was not able to finance the purchase of the Little House at the time it was demolished. By 1979 the master bedroom was still available and D pleaded with the "home town" museum to make arrangements for its acquisition.

The Metropolitan Museum of Art

Fifth Avenue at 82nd Street, New York, N.Y. 10028   212-TR 9-5500

July 10, 1973

Mr. Don Lovness
Route 3
Stillwater, Minnesota   55082

Dear Don:

I remember that when you were last in New York City you kindly offered to send me xeroxes or photographs of the drawings for the Little House furniture. I would not have had the time to incorporate that material into the little brochure of the current Wright exhibition; nor, in fact, was my aim to be all-inclusive in that preliminary study.

Now, however, the situation is different. I am writing an article on the Little furniture and would be most remiss not to include everything that survives. Thus, I would very much appreciate getting photographs of all the furniture-related drawings in your possession. I will, of course, pay all photographic costs.

As you have all along expressed concern about the Wright-Little story being properly told, I know you will agree that all this material must be incorporated in ongoing scholarship.

Best wishes to Virginia,

Sincerely,

Morrison H. Heckscher
Curator, American Wing

mhh:jbl

This letter from Morrie Heckscher came a few months after the Met had launched a 1973 mini-exhibition of articles from the Little house—furniture, windows, drawings and correspondence — a preview of things to come when the entire room would be installed nine years later, in 1982. D's knowledge of Wright's other houses and their furniture was invaluable to researchers like Heckscher.

One disappointment in the whole process was D and Edgar's inability to convince Hoving that Jack Howe should be hired to measure, document, catalog and oversee the house's disassembly. He was arguably the best qualified person for the job - and a local, but the museum didn't take D's advice.

John Howe

John Howe was another of the early apprentices at Taliesin, joining in 1932 and over the next three decades honing his skills as a draftsman and illustrator for Mr. Wright, becoming known as his "right-hand man". He supervised the drafting room, overseeing such projects as Fallingwater and Wingspread. Architect Al Drap told a story that summed up Howe's close relationship with Wright, who called him, "The pencil in my hand":

Fay Jones told me that when he was working at Taliesin Mr. Wright came in one day and gathered the people in the drafting room around him to talk about a new house project. John Howe was behind him at the drafting board. As Mr. Wright talked, John drew, and when Mr. Wright finished talking, there was a house design. Fay was amazed by this. That story is why I wanted to come to Minneapolis to spend some time with John Howe.

Lu serves dinner at the Howe's home about 1971, before Jack designed and built Sankaku, on Horseshoe Lake in Burnsville.

He went out on his own in 1964 when he and his wife Lu moved to California, to work with Aaron Green. A few years later they moved to Minneapolis where his practice flourished and he built houses for wealthy clients with many of the same principles Wright espoused, but more in tune with both the local climate and the environment. His houses were carefully fitted to a property's topography and natural features. They also were acknowledged to have more light than a Wright house. When Jack moved his practice to Minnesota in 1967 he told the Minneapolis Star that good contractors were one of the main reason he wanted to work here. He mentioned the beauty of the area, especially around the lakes, of which there were many.

Jack, as he was known to my parents, and his wife Lu, became very good friends. They had corresponded with Jack at Taliesin from the days when the cabin plans were made in 1958. A decade later, unlike so many of the Taliesin people or other architect friends, they were living relatively close by and dinner at Woodpile Lake or at the Howe's place were regular affairs. There were also picnics and of course, parties with local architects or visitors from Spring Green. Jack had a thriving practice in the 1970s and '80s and built a glorious home for himself and Lu in Burnsville, south of Minneapolis.

Perhaps more a of a pragmatist than Wright, he made some suggestions to D for the cottage. According to Al Drap, Jack added the little built-in table under the light fixture between the kitchen and the living room; there just happened to be a horizontal joint in the stone at the right height. He also worked on the light cove over the living room windows, as the original soffit design didn't have very big openings and D thought it made the room too dark. Jack revised the pattern with bigger openings to let more light go down.

TALIESIN,
OCT. 16, 1961

DEAR VIRGINIA AND DON:

I WANT TO THANK YOU NOT ONLY FOR YOUR
MOST GENEROUS HOSPITALITY BUT ALSO
FOR THE IMMEASURABLE HELP YOU GAVE
IN GETTING THE WEARS OFF TO A GOOD
START AND ON THE RIGHT TRACK. I HOPE
THAT WE WILL HEAR SOON FROM MR. BREEDLOVE
AND THAT HE WILL BE BUILDING BOTH OUR
HOUSES. HE PARTICULARLY IMPRESSED ME
AS "OUR TYPE" OF MAN.
LU WAS VERY JEALOUS WHEN I TOLD HER
OF THE DELICIOUS MEALS AND DRINKS
WE HAD WITH YOU. WE ALL ATE SO
MUCH OF THE DELICIOUS BEEF AND MUSH-
ROOM STEW THAT WE DIDN'T EAT AGAIN
THAT DAY.
I HOPE THAT MY PICTURES OF YOUR HOUSE
COME OUT ALL RIGHT. I WILL WAIT TO
GET THEM DEVELOPED UNTIL WE GET TO
ARIZONA. IT WAS SO GRATIFYING TO SEE
WHAT A BEAUTIFUL JOB YOU DID WITH
A HOUSE THAT TRULY RANKS AMONG MR.
WRIGHT'S REAL MASTER PIECES. YOUR SITE
IS ONE OF THE LOVELIEST HOUSE SITES I
HAVE EVER SEEN.
I LOOK FORWARD TO SEEING YOU BOTH IN
THE SPRING, WITH LU.
AGAIN, MANY, MANY THANKS.
AFFECTIONATELY, Jack

At Christmas time in 1963 Jack sent a card with greetings and a photo of "the old folks at home" from Taliesin. Below is a sample of Jack's color illustration, this one of "Sankaku" (Japanese for "triangle"), the home he designed for himself and Lu, who ran the business end of his architectural practice.

Jack wrote to the parents after visiting Woodpile Lake with a group from Taliesin in 1961. There was already a well-established program of using the Lovness house as a staging area and promotion stop for prospective clients; Mother and D were becoming seasoned recruiters for new commissions.

In early December Jack wrote again, thanking D for his help not only with clients but in finding contractors - an underappreciated part of getting a Wright project off the ground.

HOUSE FOR MR. AND MRS. JOHN H. HOWE
WOODHOME, BURNSVILLE, MINNESOTA
JOHN H HOWE, ARCHITECT

Jack was a skilled draftsman and also a talented illustrator, rendering lovely color impressions of planned buildings. He also excelled as a graphic designer, and created logos for my father. I'm not sure why D would need a logo, but Jack's were impressive designs, although I don't remember ever seeing them in print or in use. Jack's own logo was very stylized and reflects the thoughtful intensity he put into all his work.

Jack was soft-spoken, a gentle man, while Lu was a strong, outgoing woman, but a sweetheart to those who knew her. Jack's health declined in the 1990s and he passed away in 1997. When my father died suddenly four years later, Lu wrote my mother many letters of love and support, and called regularly even though she lived in California. Mother visited Lu there just after 9/11. Ty remembers taking her to the airport, where the combined sadness of two widows was intensified by the gloom pervading our whole country at the time. The friends found solace in each others' company and remained close until Lu's death in 2013 at age 90.

Edgar Kaufmann jr.

My parents had been Wright fans for years before they met the architect, and had seen a few of his houses before building their own. Later, as Wright house owners, they accelerated the pace and visited many more, now with better credentials. They made a pilgrimage to Fallingwater, and later got to meet its owner. Edgar Kaufmann, jr. studied art in Europe and was an apprentice at Taliesin in 1936. It's said he was instrumental in steering his father to Mr. Wright for the commission to build a rural retreat on their property at Mill Run. Mother recalls her meetings with Edgar, jr. :

Fallingwater is everyone's favorite Wright house - mine too. And Edgar Kaufmann, jr. is one of my favorite people. He lectured so eloquently and was so brilliant. And his sense of humor was captivating also.

After we finished the cottage a problem became apparent; it was a lot of work but I loved both houses so much I couldn't think of anything but living in them both. We were sitting next to Edgar in a booth in a bar in Milwaukee and I told him about my problem and inquired if could ask him a personal question. He agreed and I said, "What a rift it must have been to your heart when you gave Fallingwater to the Pennsylvania Conservancy."

He said it was a relief, he was glad to be rid of it! I thought he was joking and said I couldn't believe it. He explained it was so difficult to get and keep a "house sitter". His friends were in New York, so he had to "import" them. When he'd arrive at Fallingwater his clothes were musty, his shoes mildewed. His books would be moldy. And at this same time he had a villa in the South of France that hung over his head, calling for his presence. I understood, but that was of no help to me and my dilemma.

Anytime we saw Edgar it was enjoyable. Once at dinner at Taliesin some stories were told about Don and me, so the pump was primed. Edgar's friend Paul Mayén sat to my left and Edgar to my right. Paul kept leaning over me to encourage Edgar to tell us about Fallingwater. He was reluctant but after much persuading, Edgar told his story.

Edgar Kaufmann, jr. was a delight as a storyteller.

Below, a painting of Fallingwater, a gift from Ling Po, the artist who first joined the Fellowship in 1946.

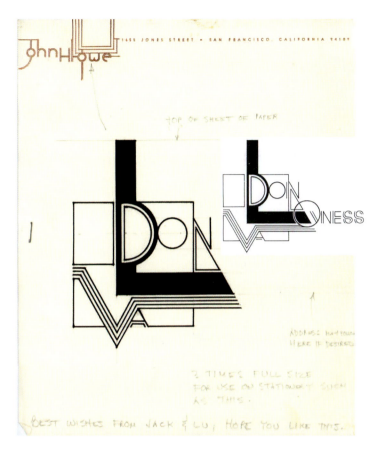

Above, Mother gives Jack a hug during a visit to the studio, as Lu looks on smiling.

Another good friend, Dick Carney, finished his career as CEO of Taliesin, but in 1967 he was registrar of the school of architecture and he wrote to my parents. With many young architecture students and enthusiasts touring the house, it was natural that Mother and D would be considered recruiters for the Taliesin program, and for Taliesin clients. Below, Dick Carney, Mother and Ling Po at Taliesin West in the 1970s.

September 10, 1967

Mr. and Mrs. Don Lovness
Route 3
Stillwater, Minnesota

Dear Don and Virginia:

We thought you would like to have the latest Taliesin brochure and related information for your own use, and to enable you to answer questions which many students who see your house undoubtedly ask.

We will be glad to assist anyone who would like further information regarding our school and architectural work.

Sincerely,

Richard Carney
Registrar

RC:sgc

Enclosures

His mother and father only stayed there in the summer, part time. The main problem was getting a caretaker for the winter. Finally they found the perfect person - it seemed. He was cultured, educated, personable. He was very responsible and kept the place immaculate! He loved classical music and was a gourmet cook. The Kaufmanns couldn't believe their good luck.

In fact, this caretaker would take reservations from men with their lady friends from all over the country, who would come to spend an evening or weekend. He would meet them at the door with Martinis or whatever they wished. Classical music would waft throughout the dimly lit house and he'd serve them an exquisite five-course dinner, then direct them to their respective bedrooms. He had a flourishing business and his fees were considerable.

One night, however, the Kaufmanns were traveling from California to New York and decided to drop in at Fallingwater. What they found was quite a surprise, and the caretaker's employment was immediately terminated.

Family travels

Being only six hours from Spring Green, we would often visit Taliesin in Wisconsin, where Ty and I would be left to our own devices, exploring the fields while the grownups mingled. We usually would sleep in quarters at the Midway barns, where the children of other Fellowship members stayed. Weekend events would include performances and later, large dinners at Hillside. We weren't at all in awe of being there; in fact, we felt perfectly at home because it all looked like our house. June 8th was Mr. Wright's birthday and the parents hardly ever missed that celebration.

Mrs. Wright always looked elegant and graceful (due in some part to the fact my mother sent her nice dresses) but we were always a little uncomfortable around her, as the parents were enamored of her and we knew she was famous. We would sit at her feet as she talked to Mother and D; they all assuming we were soaking up wisdom from her bottomless fount, but in fact much of what she said never made an impression on us as young girls.

We were never required to take part in the communal work, but we would keep our friends, Fellowship children, company as they worked in the kitchen. Sort of like summer camp, those connections were intense but short-lived; I don't remember continuing as pen pals with anyone. By the time we were teenagers we were no longer excited about going to Spring Green, as that was Mother and D's world, and we had our own new, independent world, centered around us. I hated to leave my social circle and my boyfriends, but then again, there were young male apprentices at Taliesin.

We would make family pilgrimages to Wright buildings like Unity Temple and the Robie House in Chicago, the Greek Orthodox church in Milwaukee, and as far afield as the Marin County Civic Center in California and the Guggenheim in New York.

Over the years the parents got to know almost everyone at Taliesin, and if Mother had kept a guest book with the names of everyone from the Fellowship who visited, it would be a long

Mother and D on a visit to Fallingwater in the early 1970s.
Below, during a visit to the Guggenheim, Ty and I look down from the top of the ramp. We all loved New York and would see plays, visit galleries and eat at D's favorite, Tad's Steakhouse.

list. They probably were the closest "not official members" of the group and in many ways had better access to the head of the organization—Mrs. Wright—than others who lived and worked at Spring Green and Scottsdale.

Ty and I visited the Taliesins often with the parents. In about 1967 little Eve Wright sat with us at Taliesin West while D took a snapshot. In 1981 Eve and I met again in Spring Green. Below left, like my mother I always tried to be fashion forward, but with my own style. Since Taliesin was filled with young men, I took advantage and made time to go canoeing and walking with an apprentice or two.

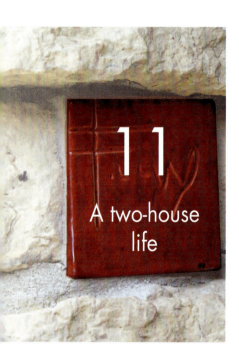

11

A two-house life

In my second year of college I went to Spain to study in Madrid. I had attended a meeting at Macalester about studying abroad and on impulse, just decided to do it. I had never been on an airplane and had never been to Europe. I didn't really even know what to expect; it just sounded like an adventure. As I had done to pay for Macalester College, I used money from my summer waitress job to pay for it.

In Spain, a friend from Macalester and I lived with a family in a modest apartment, arranged by the school; they took us in as a way to make some extra money. They spoke no English, and everything about their life was simple; the food was basic, amenities were minimal and their attitudes reflected the conservative culture in Spain under Francisco Franco. I met boys but our meetings were chaperoned, there were curfews, no "come upstairs for a drink," and a public show of affection could result in arrest!

I studied poetry, we had art classes in the Prado, and of course, I took normal liberal arts college classes - normal, except that they were all in Spanish. I had taken Spanish previously, but I found that real-life conversations had nothing to do with what I had learned in high school. I was suddenly thrown into the deep end, where everything I had known, everything I was, no longer mattered. I had cool parents who had done exceptional things, and I was part of that. But being in this whole new world was like shedding a skin. Here, Frank Lloyd Wright was irrelevant. In a way I felt reborn.

I missed my family but this adventure was so exciting! Taking part in festivals and cultural events, eating twelve grapes at midnight on New Year's Eve, traveling around Spain on a bus, there were new cities to visit with history that went back as far as I could imagine. In Valencia I discovered las Fallas, a fiery celebration of spring. In Jerez I discovered fine sherry and shortly thereafter, also discovered hangovers. It was a heady six months away, and by the time I returned home to Woodpile Lake, it really wasn't home anymore.

I never had the desire to move back to Woodpile Lake. In later years I realized that there had been a feeling of isolation, and what I lacked was a connection to neighbors, to community. In spite of the guests coming and going it wasn't enough for me. And everything my parents had built, all the links they had made, it was all theirs; I had my own life to create. My sister Ty soon went on her own adult path as well and when the cottage was complete, Mother and D were empty nesters, but with two nests.

A few years later in 1976, while I had moved from Minneapolis to Arcola, the parents had already spent a year living in both the studio and the newly-completed cottage (which Mother was beginning to consider her just-right-sized playhouse). She loved them both but this "musical houses" was becoming hard to manage. The solution would be to have a caretaker or a trusted renter to live in the studio, while they took up full time residence in the cottage. The problem was, who would that person be? The answer came from some close friends.

Elisabeth ("Peter") and Rolf were old friends of our family who had loaned the parents money to finish the studio in 1957, and Peter was a star painting pupil of Mother's. Their son was a young law school student who needed a place to live, and he knew the Lovness' dilemma.

Above left, my "front door" with friends in Spain. It was a far cry from the Wright life I had known, but I loved it.

Above, I never went back to Woodpile Lake to live after that but visited often. This photo is just before Jim moved into the studio. The landscaping was a bit "natural" at the time.

In 1979 as Artist-in-Residence at the Historic Courthouse in Stillwater, I had something my mother never did: a real painting studio. The courthouse also had gallery rooms and I was in charge of organizing shows for other potters, sculptors and painters.

After he talked with his parents about the idea of moving in, Mother and Peter huddled and it was decided: her son and his friend Jim Seidl, also a law school student, would reside in and take care of the two-bedroom studio. They were to pay $300 a month, with restrictions and quite a few responsibilities, as Jim recalled in a letter to Ty and me years later:

My first image of Virginia was on a Saturday morning, when I visited the studio and cottage for the first time. She walked up to us in sunglasses, wearing a stunning Issey Miyake robe, with Nacho, the macaw perched on her shoulder. I was smitten, for life.

It was my most amazing adventure living and playing with Virginia and Don, and all the artistic people who came through. We had to keep the house in "show" condition, but I didn't mind that at all. We had the opportunity to meet Mrs. Wright, her granddaughter Eve—who I was honored to escort around town—and Svetlana Peters - who was also very beautiful, interesting, engaging, curious, and quite magically drew me in with her stories. I learned much about architecture from Wes Peters during his many visits when he stayed in the studio with me, and was continuously mesmerized by his brilliance.

David Byrne, of Talking Heads fame, once stayed at the studio - his wife Bonny Lutz was designing costumes at the Guthrie for a show. A friend told me they were looking for a weekend place and Virginia said, "Of course." I remember them walking into the place totally in awe. While there, David wrote part of his great album "Naked". Years later, he recalled his and Bonny's memorable weekend visit in 1987, how much they enjoyed their dinner with Virginia and Don, their stories of Mr. Wright, and how dazzled Bonny and he were when Virginia brought them down into the vault and showed them her jewelry, art, clothing, shoes, and furs.

As a studio resident, Jim's responsibilities included animal feeding of the margay wild cat, macaw, dogs, birds, owl and ET the squirrel. In the morning he would wake up and go to the cottage to take care of all the animals. The parrot got to know him and would say, 'Hello Jim' every morning. He would feed the baby squirrel with an eye dropper, and clean up around the parrot every morning and evening.

With someone to keep the houses clean and the menagerie managed, Mother and D were able to travel more, sometimes in a motorhome. On the occasion of one return from a trip, the result of D's many years of exposure to strong chemicals became obvious: over time he had lost his sense of smell. Jim remembered a few examples:

One time the power went out and everything in the tool room freezer thawed and started to rot. When Don returned I told him, 'We have to do something, the smell is terrible'. He didn't think it was a problem, as he didn't smell anything. Virginia then came over and verified that something indeed had to be done.

Another time, the water started backing up in the shower and I told Don about it. When I came home one day the septic guy was there, they had been searching and searching and finally found the septic tank. He had dug around the tank and opened the top for pumping. There was Don, lying prone over the edge looking down, chin resting in his large hands, unfazed by the smell. I walked over and as I reached the

D photographed Mother and Jim Seidl at the cottage, drinking wine from flamingo glasses. The three became good friends and like so many others who had spent time in the houses, Jim was soon smitten with Frank Lloyd Wright. A few years later he would have his own Wright-inspired home, designed by David Uppgren and based on plans my parents gave him.

edge he looked up at me and asked with an enormous smile and laugh, "See any of yours in there?"

Aside from paying rent, the two young men were expected to put in some time on maintenance. In addition to keeping the place clean, they were charged with applying creosote each year, using a rag, improvised face-masks, and frequent jumps into the lake to cool off. And the cleaning part could be a challenge. In the early 1980s Canada geese had become much more common and with the lake close by, our front yard was an attractive place for the geese to sun. They had a habit of walking across the patio, leaving droppings all over. Jim told the tale:

Don and I tried every conceivable remedy to get rid of them, from piled lawn furniture, to wire and rope fences, to spraying them routinely with the garden hose. Nothing worked. Until the day I came home to discover they had once again penetrated our barrier. In frustration I ran at them, yelling madly, flailing my arms, only to slip on their calling cards and slide for about 10 feet face down in my new Armani business suit. As they sat and quacked at me from their triumphant perch in one of my lawn chairs.

Something had to be done, and like any other problem, D had his own way of dealing with it. He walked around the back of the house early one Sunday morning in his underwear, shotgun in hand. A sudden blast outside Jim's window. Jim, startled out of sleep, catapults from

The cottage was small, but was perfect for the two of them (and a few animals). The diminutive space saw a rotating stock of Oriental pottery and statuary, some of it huge, (like these Kamakura figures) as my parents' collection expanded after trips to Hong Kong Thailand and Cambodia. In 1997, the cushions became beige, a concession to sun fading.

bed in one leaping bound. Another bird bites the dust. And D's laughter begins the day.

Jim lived in the studio for about eleven years, having admirably fulfilled Mother and D's need for a responsible person who could vacate when a special guest was in town. It was a win-win for all parties, and when my father died in 2001 Jim wrote:

Over the years, Don introduced me to the finer things in life, like cigars, scotch and jazz. Oh, how I cherish those nights smoking, drinking, laughing and listening. Those were truly the best-of-times and I miss them greatly.

And oh how we laughed. Virginia knew the stories well and a few of them will remain our forever secret, but over the past few days, amidst the tears, I've thought about those stories, including Hoot the owl, the frozen mice, and Don's careful instructions on mice-thawing and owl-feeding. He taught me more about owls and mice than you will ever know, but by so doing he also taught me how to overcome one of my fears. To this day, I reason, if I can feed an owl a frozen mouse, I can do just about anything.

The Curator

In 1977 Robert Jacobsen began a job as curator of the Asian Art department at the Minneapolis Institute of Arts. On his second week at the job he got a call from D, who explained he'd like to have Bob look at some Japanese things; temple bells, Buddhas. They met at the museum and Bob noted that in art, my father seemed to have "a sense of what matters, a spark of recognition." Although D and Mother were self-taught about Oriental art, Bob soon recognized their knowledge and enthusiasm. As someone who acquires art for a living, Bob knew about collectors. "Frank Lloyd Wright was the number one US dealer in Japanese prints during the period from about 1915-1920," he said. "In Japan he would buy groups of hundreds; he had a big sideline as a dealer." And just as Wright loved his art, so did my parents. Bob described them:

Collecting art comes from a need to do something with (the house). They didn't have their ego wrapped up in the items they collected. Many collectors think, mine's more expensive, mine's a world record, that guy's got junk, I've got great stuff, etc. When you get into the millions of dollars at auctions, museums don't want to be known as buyers - but these guys do. So many people who came to the Lovness houses didn't know a Japanese statue from a Korean one. It wasn't about projecting their wealth, it was about living with the stuff. They had a genuine love for it.

When he was first invited to the cottage Bob says, "I couldn't believe my eyes." They became good friends and Bob visited often. Some of his education had been in architecture, and inspired by what he had seen at Woodpile Lake, he designed a house for his parents in a Wright style, using D's counsel and his connection with Cardinal Glass for windows. Bob loved the cottage, describing it as "a muscular thing; it's little but it has such presence." He had many stories to tell:

Teddy the Bouvier looked like a teddy bear but he was definitely not a lap dog.

The first time in the cottage, I saw this fabulous overhang and said "God, how did you do that?" Don explained that was the original design but Wes had talked with him about pushing that thing a good six feet out further. I said, "Yes, but how do you support all that?" and he told me I was the first person that had asked about it. "Do you do that with an I-beam?"

"Yeah, or a (wooden) box beam," he explained.

They were party animals, in a way. The "kids" would get away from the control and restrictions at Taliesin and party at Woodpile Lake. There was always a vibrancy at those parties. Patricia and I would walk to the car afterwards and say, "God, are we boring!" You can't compete with that energy. At Taliesin Don and Virginia would be invited along with groups of tourists because they would answer questions. If the weather was fine, they would take a corner out of the sun and talk for hours. It was a generosity thing.

Above left, the Lovness collection contributed many pieces to exhibitions at the MIA, usually under the name "Anonymous". Bob discusses a piece with Mother in a back room at the museum.

Above right, the Jacobsens, and their wedding at Woodpile Lake, one of many weddings Mother and D hosted for friends.

Left, the lake house Bob designed for his parents, with help and inspiration from D. It was one of several homes that would come to be because of my parents' influence.

A lot of professors or other professionals that could talk for an hour or two just aren't going to do it. But they took it on at a level that was always understandable, there was always a joke somewhere in there. It was special.

And Virginia's fur coats! During a party or tour at the cottage, the women would all disappear, leaving the men by themselves. About 20 minutes later they would reappear, each of them decked out in a different outrageous fur coat.

We were going to parties there and Patricia and I were often the last ones to leave. In 1982 on a visit with just the four of us I told them we were going to get married. Don asked what were we, Christian or agnostic or what? We told them we're really not religious, we'd probably just have a service at a Unitarian church or something. They stopped, looked at each other and said, "No, no, you're going to get married here at the house. It'll be a July wedding so that's perfect, we have the bells." Virginia ran out and came back with a robe for Patricia, a Japanese Uchikake, red and white with gold thread. And just like that it was decided.

It was a small list of people we would invite. We were expected 20 and there were 150 in attendance. There was a blue-eyed monk from California who officiated, and several nuns in black robes and shaved heads. We went through the whole ceremony with bells, took three steps, etc. We were down to the cake round, people were mixing it up, talking with one another and Teddy came out and bit one of the Buddhist nuns.

Travel can be exhausting—and Mother looked it—but she was always smartly dressed, event to visit ruins.

Jim Seidl was there and worried that Teddy might be a problem, as he was a jumper. D just said, "No, Teddy's fine, he doesn't need to be chained up." It was just at that point that Teddy made a direct line for his target, the Buddhist nun, and jumped on her causing some ugly gashes. Thankfully, there was no serious injury.

Bob oversaw a show at the Institute in 1990 featuring many of the parents' pieces, entitled, "The Lively Art of the Han", depicting in pottery how life was conducted in China 2000 years ago. He joined my parents on at least one of their buying trips to Hong Kong, where they had established connections with dealers in Chinese antiquities. For several years in the '90s they would spend some of the winter months in Hong Kong and Bangkok where they got to know the vendors who could find the good stuff. They also got to know the best places to stay for cheap. Mother always laughed when she told about negotiating the price of their long-term hotel room down to $20. They loved the food and D enjoyed trying new menu items like snake and crickets. They made friends among the dealers and their families, often celebrating birthdays and holidays with them.

Cambodia and Thailand were side trip destinations, with visits to Angkor Wat and the Bridge on the River Kwai, and friends from home—including Taliesin people—would sometimes join them on their Oriental excursions. For them, finding art was a hobby, a treasure hunt, but the pace of buying, along with the prices paid, ticked up a notch or two after they met the Pizza Tiger from Michigan.

Above, Mother and Bob Jacobsen at a Hong Kong antiques store. Right, Ty and I joined the parents and a local friend in the winter of 1994. Below, D poses in Hong Kong with a painted warrior figure. He and Mother became experts at judging what was authentic and what was fake.

Dick Carney and Mother at Angkor Wat in Cambodia. Tom Casey and Effi Casey from Taliesin were along as well. David Glickman, son of Taliesin's early structural engineer Mendel Glickman, helped make arrangements for inexpensive places to stay during the trip.

Collecting with Tom Monaghan

Following Mr. Wright's passion for Asian art and Japanese prints, Mother and D set out to collect ancient Chinese bronzes, Tang dynasty ceramic horses, Hokusai and Hiroshige Japanese prints, Ming dynasty porcelains and wooden carved furniture. They found many new friends and collectors through this passion, and like all other aspects of their life, they jumped into this one with both feet and amassed quite a collection! Their friend Robert Poor was a professor at the University of Minnesota Art history department for 45 years and specialized in Ancient Chinese Bronzes. D amassed books on everything Chinese and had a mind for memorization and could tell you the years of every dynasty, the special characteristics of different types of collectibles and often which museum collections housed them. Mother had more of the artist's eye and was able to spot a real find easily, although she was fooled on occasion. Her knowledge wasn't scholarly but intuitive. The combination of their unique talents helped them collect beautiful pieces to accent the architecture, similar to what you would see at Taliesin.

In the 1980s Mother and D were invited to a symposium at the University of Michigan in Ann Arbor. It was being hosted by Tom Monaghan, an enthusiastic collector of Wright's work: buildings, documents, furniture and artifacts. Tom had enrolled at the U of Michigan to study architecture in 1959, and bought a small pizza parlor to help pay for school. That business turned into Domino's Pizza and he left school, but never left behind his interest in architecture, and Frank Lloyd Wright. Tom was later the owner of the Detroit Tigers baseball team, and amassed a sizeable collection of classic cars and Wright items.

At the symposium Mother and D were to take part in a discussion about Wright and relate their experiences as homeowners. This meeting led to a friendship between my parents and Tom, who was excited to visit Woodpile Lake, where he stayed in a Wright home for the first time. For several years, a working partnership with my parents allowed his collection of Oriental art to expand, complementing his Wright items. D arranged for Tom to buy pieces from the Little house, including the entire bedroom, and important items from other Wright houses as well. Tom also bought some items directly from my parents: the first gate that Mr. Wright had designed, some of the Hollyhock chairs from the cottage, other furniture and things they had collected over the years. D recalled Tom's interest in the gate in a Taliesin interview:

The original design was eight feet wide; (Wright) was designing things when cars were very narrow, and horse-and-buggies. So we made the gate larger, and it really wrecked the design of the gate. By enlarging the thing it made it more of a rectangle than a square. We did a really crappy job of building the gate, too. We didn't have a good welder - we built it out of pipe.

And so when Monaghan was up that time he wanted to buy the gate. That was the best news. I said, "Take it away!" I don't even know how much we got for it, it wasn't much, but it was enough to build another gate.

Domino's Pizza
International

Prairie House, Domino's Farms
30 Frank Lloyd Wright Dr., P.O. Box 997
Ann Arbor, Michigan 48106-0997
313-665-5500
313-995-4310-FAX

Virginia Lovness
International Consultant

Mother and D had official roles as buyers for Tom Monaghan. Below, Mother speaking at one of the many seminars she and D attended.

From top left, one of the panels Mother and D took part in, talking about their Wright experiences. They loved riding on Tom's plane. Mother convinced everyone who visited, male or female, to try on her coats. Sotheby's catalog for their June, 2014 sale carried this photo of D's original gate, bought by Tom Monaghan in about 1989. It was sold at that 2014 auction for $17,500.00. A Martin House purple martin house replica was a gift from Tom.

Growing Up Wright **251**

At Christmas 1986 Ty and Pat look over a Lego brochure, one of the many gifts our son Dana got that year, as an only grandchild.

Tom owned a large parcel on Drummond Island, on Lake Huron near the Canadian border where he built a conference center on 2000 acres. He also hired Taliesin Associated Architects to adapt some of Wright's unbuilt designs, but that collaboration did not bear fruit. David Uppgren had finished his architecture studies and on D's recommendation, went to work for Tom on buildings at the island and later, at Prairie School-inspired Domino's Farms corporate office park in Ann Arbor. There, "The National Center for the Study of Frank Lloyd Wright at Domino's Farms" was established. Another project was Ave Maria University, founded by Tom in 1998 in Ypsilanti, Michigan but moved to Florida in 2003 where the entire campus was built from scratch. Personal building projects and collecting went forward for years until 1998, when he sold most of the pizza company to an investment firm.

Mother and D enjoyed Tom's company, and he would visit often. They especially enjoyed flying on his private jet, and became advisors on his museum board, and special consultants as buyers for his oriental art collection. Tom was hands-on helping with the sprites, and had a special gift made for the parents: a wooden replica of the Martin house (Buffalo, New York, 1905) purple martin bird houses. On their visits to Stillwater, Mother would of course press Tom and his wife Marge to try on her furs and hats. Their close relationship with Tom faded somewhat when he began to focus his attention on building a Catholic university in Florida and advancing the causes of the church.

Ty returns home

Ty didn't feel exactly the same way as I did about living at Woodpile Lake. She and her husband Pat were married in 1986 and moved to a condo in White Bear Lake. (That town is some kind of portal or rite of passage for the Lovnesses, I guess!) They were invited to move to the studio soon thereafter, and stayed for ten years. Pat was a farm boy who knew his way around equipment, and even though he was an executive at Harvest States Cooperative he enjoyed helping D with all the chores around the place. Pat even had a partnership with neighbor Art Welander to farm 40 acres nearby. My sister was extremely responsible in keeping the house orderly, and they made improvements like a rebuilt kitchen divider, cabinets and appliances. In spite of D's disapproval of the cost, they had natural gas hooked up to the studio, and later, D acquiesced and extended it to the cottage as well. The gardens got a big upgrade under Ty's discerning eye, and when guests would stay, our old bedroom was still available.

Pat remembers mixing drinks at the cottage for Wes Peters, Jack Howe, Aaron Green and others one night. He still shakes his head thinking about those conversations: "We should have recorded it all." They would make airport runs to pick up art that was shipped from Hong Kong, and watch over the cottage when Mother and D were traveling. Having Ty and Pat holding down the fort was a blessing for the parents, and a pleasant place for them to live for a decade. In 1996 they moved to a home just two miles away where Ty spends much of her time tending her lovely gardens when they are not traveling.

Rolling cross country

When D was winding down from actively working at Judd Ringer Corporation in the '80s, he and Mother decided to see the USA and bought a Dodge motorhome that she called, "My cute little bug." A few years later they upgraded to a used GMC motorhome. They drove to Canada and west, visiting the national parks in Canada and the western US. D was behind the wheel while mother manned the CB radio, chatting up big rig drivers with the handle "Calico Cat". Truckers loved hearing her voice and of course, she reveled in the attention. They enjoyed their self-contained freedom and years later, Mother was intent on re-living those days when she bought a used RV at age 89. That vehicle came to an unhappy end, but like everything else in her life, she was not about to give up the things she loved without a fight.

What she loved to do is travel, and the RV gave Mother and D a home-away-from-home to use as a base. They flew from time to time (and particularly enjoyed riding on the Domino's Pizza jet) but driving vacations were a long-standing tradition for these two. They visited Arizona, serving breakfast to Taliesin friends in the small dining area. They went to the West Coast, Mother keeping a detailed diary of the stops they made and the things they saw. The only real drawback was limited closet space for her clothing, but other than that, they had the time and enjoyed life on the road.

The RV became notorious for causing a crisis with the driveway gate at Woodpile Lake. D clipped a corner of the gate with the vehicle, which was a full eight feet wide, taking out part of the stonework. The original gate had a narrow opening and a new, wider one had just been finished, with Pat and D working on it together. It was more than a little frustrating to D that a repair was needed so soon. He was more careful afterwards.

One road trip took them to Drummond Island (via ferry) where they saw some of Tom Monaghan's Wright-inspired buildings going up there.

The Chicago girls

Frank Lloyd Wright was 46 in 1913 when he received a commission from developers to design a "concert garden" in Chicago. Concerts, beer and food were three traditions brought to America by German immigrants who were a large part of Chicago's population. Work began with Wright drawing plans with his son John at his side (two of his boys became architects), developer E. C. Waller raising money and recruiting investors and soon, an army of union construction workers erecting what Brendan Gill called a "fantasy on a prodigious scale" and a "masterpiece of joyous pagan fancy." Brick and textured concrete blocks were complemented by heavily stylized sculptures of young maidens, holding sheaves of barley (representing the elements of beer) and assorted geometric shapes. With just a few male examples, these mostly female "sprites" were scattered around the 600 x 600-foot complex, indoors and out. Their expressions varied but most were smiling and exhibited a grace and warmth that was—if you stop to consider it—quite a feat to convey in the medium used: angular cast concrete. Some formed the base for light "totems" which illuminated the large central seating, dining and concert area. While Wright took complete credit for these lovely statues, most were sculpted by Alphonso Iannelli and some were likely his designs.

Coming to America from Italy as a boy in 1898, Iannelli studied under Gutzon Borglum (who later carved Mount Rushmore) and beginning a career as an artist in 1910, designed posters for vaudeville acts at a Los Angeles theater. John Wright met him there and in 1914 invited him to work on the Midway Gardens. Afterwards, he continued in a design career that brought much acclaim, with statuary and interiors in several important buildings, industrial design pieces and a well-regarded studio in Chicago.

He never worked with Wright again, however, having been denied credit for creating the sprites. It is said that after becoming successful Ianelli was embarrassed of the crassly commercial early posters he had created, even attempting to have any remaining copies destroyed. Thankfully, he was unsuccessful and my parents later acquired a set.

The Midway Gardens enjoyed two years of success and large crowds, but the First World War, which also began in 1914, brought anti-German sentiment and less reason to feel the exuberance that the project represented. It was sold to a brewery in 1916 (after the original organization went bankrupt) and sold yet again in 1921 after prohibition was passed. It was demolished in 1929 and many of the sprites (or "spindles' as they were called originally) were scattered to the winds, more or less forgotten for decades.

Over the years some sprites had found their way to Taliesin and one was on display near the entrance road in the 1970s. David Uppgren recalls:

Don saw the big one that was on the bridge at Taliesin. It was pushed off by some kids and broken, lying in the ditch. Don probably said to Mrs. Wright, "Why don't you let me take that and I'll fix it for you and bring it back?" We took the green Dodge power wagon to Taliesin and picked two of them up, and

Two of D's sprites at Woodpile Lake. Of the sprites at the Biltmore in Phoenix, in 1987 Taliesin Associated Architects gave copies of the sprites to the Arizona Biltmore "in gratitude for a financial donation that Rostland Arizona Inc, the Biltmore's owner, made to Taliesin." The molds were made by a local sculpture and mold-maker George Kerish. The Foundation later made the sprite sculptures a licensed product.

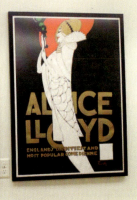

Mother and D found a set of prints of Ianelli's designs from around the time he was working on the Midway Gardens sprites. It's easy to see his style throughout the prints and sculptures.

Midway Gardens on Chicago's south side covered an entire block with both indoor and outdoor drinking and dining areas. A bandstand featured performances by some of the best orchestras of the time. D reproduced four versions of the sprites along with the planter bowls.

Above,1980s production at Woodpile Lake. The molds were heavy duty, as the figurines weighed several hundred pounds. Work took place outdoors in the woods behind the cottage.

Even the forms used to make the sprite molds were interesting pieces of art. The "beer mugs" for the light totem sprites were intricate wooden sculptures.

Below, One of the painted Taliesin West sprites.

Right, three versions of sprites along the driveway wall near the studio. D also reproduced the hemispherical urns from the midway gardens.

brought them back (to Stillwater). We repaired that one and made a mold. That original one is now out in Taliesin West, painted some goofy colors. We reproduced the sprites using wooden forms to make silicone molds. The big ones were made in multiple pieces then bolted together. Those big ones were poured vertically, with scaffolding. We would take the buckets of concrete, lift them up and dump them in. Then the mold was vibrated.

This was heavy work and required a crew. A chemist friend from 3M helped, as did David, Pat Kluempke and anyone else who was available. Tom Monaghan pitched in when he visited. There were a lot chemicals involved, to create the different kinds of molds, to modify the concrete mixture, mold release to keep the pieces from sticking, sealing agents. etc. This, of course, was all right up D's alley.

Dozens of sprites were produced and many of them found their way into collector's hands. Some of them were purchased by Horst Rechelbacher and displayed above his Aveda / Intelligent Nutrients building in Minneapolis. D's creations have been seen by thousands of people and have helped renew interest in these wonderful figures and the fascinating story of their origin at the Midway Gardens.

The influencers

It's impossible to say how many people who met my parents and saw the homes, or even photos in a book, were moved to discover more about Frank Lloyd Wright. Some were happy to simply chalk up another Wright house on their "seen it" list, and others may have given some serious thought to what they wanted in their next home. A number of visitors to the houses

Casting sprites was a backyard industry that took some hard work. From top left, anyone stumbling on this sight would have wondered what was going on. D inspects a cement maiden before freeing her from her cocoon. Empty mold halves await another pour. A vertical mold is carefully lowered to horizontal. Tom and David lift a mold away from a casting.

Jim Seidl (left) and David Uppgren experienced the homes on Woodpile Lake up close and became devotees of the style, as client and designer.

Below, David (left) oversees erecting the garden sprite.

were inspired to become architects, like David Uppgren. Still others weren't inclined to spend a career at the drafting table, but the idea of having a Wright-inspired house became pretty important in their lives.

In 1978 David Uppgren, on D's recommendation, was hired to design a home for Roger O'Shaughnessy, who owned Cardinal Glass. The company had built custom insulated glass for the studio and cottage, spending months perfecting sealing techniques for the mitered windows. It was David's first commission, and he helped build it. 30 years later, after working independently and for Tom Monaghan over many years, as a kind of bookend to his career he designed a home for Jim Seidl.

Jim had lived in the studio for about eleven years, and during that time got to know David Uppgren well, as a friend and admired architect. Over the course of their friendship, Jim was able to advise my parents in many areas, as a lawyer, legal researcher, and businessman. After D died in 2001, Jim's counsel was important in helping Mother maintain the property and later, to deal with potential buyers, some of whom had unusually creative acquisition ideas. He was a great help to her over the years and as a way of repaying him, she agreed to let Jim build a home using the Wright plans for "Cottage C", the Maginel cottage. David would be the one to make it a reality.

Jim and his business partner owned a lot on a lovely lake north of Stillwater. It was a challenging property, however, with a steep slope, and the Cottage C plans were drawn for a relatively flat lot. David worked on ideas using the original drawings as is but it was clear to him it might not work - not only because of topography, but for what the clients were seeking. As David told it:

The approach was, we want to build this house but we need more space to make it practical. The first design variation took the house, as is, with a wing behind it. It had a really awkward hallway to draw it together. The original design was a single bedroom, single bath, kitchen, living room and that's it. But they wanted more space and a garage. I said, "Guys, you either build the original building or take the design as a starting point."

With Virginia's permission to modify the design, something unique and stunning is indeed what they gratefully received. "A true work of Wright- and Uppgren-inspired art," in Jim's praiseful words.

The house is two stories with full-height south windows and mitered glass overlooking the lake below, lovely stonework, the distinctive angular "Maginel" roof and even a garage - separate but perfectly complementing the house. One of D's tall light totem sprites was a gift and graces a rock garden pool overlooking a patio. Inside, the two-story living room connects to an open kitchen and up a stairway are two bedrooms. The home is an impressive tribute to Wright's ideas and a recognition of Don and Virginia's influence and imagination.

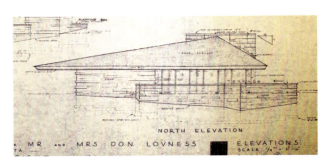

A striking variation on a theme, David Uppgren says, "It's a superbly well built house – a testament to the craft and skill of the contractor David Wallin." A plaque reads "With thanks to Don and Virginia Lovness, whose generosity and love of architecture made Bear Run possible."

NORTH ELEVATION

MR and MRS DON LOVNESS   ELEVATIONS
                          SCALE ⅛"=1'-0"

Mother the clothes horse

On one of their trips to Tokyo many years ago, Ty brought back a gift for Mother: an Issey Miyake coat. To say it was well received is an understatement; it was the beginning of a large collection of Miyake pieces as he became Mother's favorite designer. She went to a show in New York and bought some things of his things right off the runway. And although much of what she acquired came from used sources, Dayton's Oval Room would call her when they got a new Miyake item in. Mother would try things on while D sat stoically in a chair. It was one of the rare times they bought retail.

My mother always had a very dramatic, daring sense of style. Never one to miss a trend, she loved the look of the '50s with circle skirts in harlequin patterns and nipped in waists. Her long dark hair was often worn in a high pony tail and she kept her bangs short, like the style of the era. She was thin and petite so clothes looked great on her and she could definitely carry off the dramatic look. Dark eyes with plenty of liner and bright red lipstick were like a uniform for her. She wore high heels in part to bridge the height difference between her and my father. The 1960s gave her a chance to really have some fun with different looks. The Mexican influence, and bright Pucci prints, bold stripes, ethnic outfits from all countries, feather boas, large dramatic hats, bright psychedelic colors and cut-out dresses.

As she grew older and more sophisticated she found many Japanese designers whose work she liked. She and my father would visit the Issey Miyake boutique in New York and Hong Kong where she found outlandish outfits like one bright orange creation with a bee keeper's hat in matching orange. I remember cringing a bit when she still wore the Miyake tatoo body suit to a recital dinner when she was into her early 70s.

It seems that she always had a crazy wide brimmed hat of some sort to round out any outfit. Hats suited her and really completed the sensational look she created. People would constantly stop her on the street and in stores to comment on her outfit. Always ready to be the center of attention, she attracted all kinds of different friends.

Her jewelry was as bold and exciting as the rest of her outfits. Much of the jewelry was real gold, silver, ruby and pearl but she appreciated costume jewelry with the styles of every decade. The key to the jewelry was it had to match and had to stand out above and beyond the already wild clothing. Two Iranian heavy cuff bracelets that looked like gauntlets were her constant companions and everyone joked that she was "pumping jewelry" since they weighed a lot. Rings on every finger on her manicured red nails filled in the rest of the theatrical costume. She was never a wallflower!

For her, finding interesting clothes was the exciting part. The hunt was the whole point, it's why she loved the Goodwill, auctions and consignment shops; you never knew what would turn up. How boring it was to buy a retail dress off the rack when you could explore, discover and be delighted with an unexpected bargain find. Her jewelry, shoes and accessories were varied and unusual as well, but there was one constant in her wardrobe, one universal accessory: a warm smile.

She was a fashionista all her life, reveling in unusual outfits and outrageous jewelry. Even at 90 years old she would fill a cart at the Goodwill, one of her favorite places to shop.

On a studio tour once, Paul Ringstrom remembered, "...the dress that Virginia was wearing that looked like two pleated banana leafs, and thinking she was the only person I knew who could have pulled that look off."

Right, Issey Miyake's origami-look clothes were her favorites, but she had an endless array of outfits that she loved to wear at Easter at Taliesin West.

Show and tell

There was an event in 2017 that brought an important part of Mother's life to a successful full circle; that summer she had the biggest gallery show of her life. She had not actively worked as an artist for decades—she and D had been busy with a few other things—and aside from a few small watercolors displayed on a tabletop in her apartment, there wasn't much to show how prolific she had been in her younger days.

She was in a senior apartment building, living independently with her companion, and on one of our regular visits, Gordie and I helped her clean and organize the bedroom. Under the bed we found some plastic tubs, filled with watercolors, drawings, prints, charcoal sketches and paintings. It was a cornucopia of art spanning decades, and as we looked through it she reminisced about each piece. I remembered seeing many of them, years before, but some of them pre-dated me and others were a surprise. These tubs had been moved several times since she had sold the houses a few years before, but we were unaware of them and their contents. Over the next few days Gordie and I talked about what would happen to all these pieces. Were they dumpster material? We certainly didn't need any more art in our home, as the walls were full. How could we preserve her artistic legacy, we wondered.

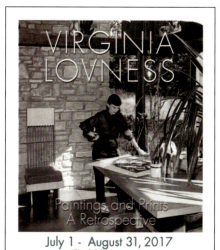

Over a few weeks we formulated a plan: an artist should do what an artist does: have a show. I was connected to several arts organizations around the area, and I went to see the gallery director at the Stillwater Library, a lovely 1910 Carnegie building that had been updated with a new section, a large patio and a long, wide connecting hallway that served as a gallery. Shows of all types of media ran for two months each, and director Sue Hedin was excited to present Mother's pieces. We tentatively called it "92 at 92" (the number of paintings and her age) and it went on the calendar for July and August, 2017.

Choosing pieces was a challenge, as there were so many. Mother had kept drawings she made in high school, the ones that had won scholarships for her, and a little of everything she'd done since. There were watercolors, of course, but also block prints, drawings, oils, and a surprise while we were preparing the show. In disassembling the studio, Ted Muntz had discovered that some the masonite panels covering the top of the light valances were in fact Mother's paintings. Some had holes cut for electical boxes. It was during her non-objective period apparently, and she was using seriously bright colors. When we asked her about it she just laughed.

The next step was daunting: how to frame scores of art pieces, all different shapes and sizes. Faced with a stiff bill for professional matting and framing, we simply did what we'd been doing for years. The local Goodwill store was a regular stop for the three of us girls (where Mother would happily fill a cart if we didn't monitor her), and we nearly cleaned out their framed art stock. We did the same at a few other Goodwills until we had a hundred or so, in various sizes, styles and colors. The next step was matching each piece of art we'd chosen for the show to a properly sized and colored frame, cutting mattes that would work. Gordie and I had an assembly line over several tables in the basement, and after a week, we were ready, although some of the frames showed their "scratch 'n dent" heritage. We made signs for the show explaining: "Virginia Lovness' creativity flowed through her paints and pencils, just as it did through the rough rock she chiseled to build a home and studio. As a seamstress and sculptor she employed bargain materials and often used found objects, always on the hunt for something she could transform from ordinary to extraordinary.

"She is a lifetime bazaar browser and junque aficionado, and we honor that spirit by using only Goodwill picture frames to showcase her art. Please excuse any imperfections and consider each frame as having a new life to a higher calling."

Ty and I created descriptive text and set prices for each piece. We hung the show, completely filling the wall space, along with with several small items in glass cases. Visitors during regular library hours enjoyed the work, and a few of them were sold. An opening was scheduled for a Thursday evening, and the gallery was packed with friends. She was beaming all evening, in spite of the fact that no champagne was at hand (alcohol was not allowed in the library). She told us it was the most exciting thing that had ever happened to her. That may have been a stretch, but it was clear that the accolades she heard from so many people—friends, architects and strangers alike—had her on a cloud and she was thoroughly enjoying every minute. We had created a large display that explained her history with D and the houses, and that probably caused a few people to look closer at the art, but I have to think her work stood on its own merits - most of the pieces in the show sold that night, an astonishing outcome, according to the gallery director.

We didn't know at the time, but it was a final tribute to an artist, a woman who had taken to heart Wright's dictum, "Make your life beautiful wherever you go." She had done just that - in her art, in her style and in the homes she built by hand.

The Lovness girls at the opening. Mother held court from an easy chair to scores of admirers. Below, just one of several library display walls.

A few of the friends and library patrons at the opening.

12

Passing the torch

When my father died of a heart attack in May of 2001 there was an expected period of shock and mourning. Ty and I, along with our husbands, did our best to console and support Mother. There were also many friends who stepped in to help. There was no traditional funeral; the plan was to have him cremated, and a few days after he died we went to the funeral home to sign papers. Mother, shaped by a lifetime of deal-making, asked if she could put it on her credit card so she could get some airline miles.

We held a memorial service where several dozen friends mingled at the studio. There was no program or speech, just a chance for those who lived in the area and knew and appreciated D to pay their respects to Mother. And of course, there was champagne. D's ashes were intended to be scattered around the property and on the edge of Woodpile Lake, but he ended up residing in a closet at the cottage for several years. He finally got to commune again with nature in about 2014 when Mother, Ty and I scattered his ashes on the shoreline.

At the time, adding to our burden of loss, in spite of many indications that his health was less than optimal, D had made few arrangements or any contingency plan for Mother to carry on without him. He was a hands-on guy who had amassed a huge stockpile of tools and equipment, from hammers to tractors. He had done most of the maintenance around the property himself and without him, Mother's only option was to hire people to help. She now had no need for a TIG welder or a zero-turn mower, so one of the first orders of business was to hire an auction company to liquidate all the equipment. Just organizing the removal of a pole-barn full of mechanical stuff was daunting, but there were other things needing attention. An old trailer with sacks of red oxide powder from the original floor proved to be an incredible mess to remove. When Ty's husband Pat hauled D's stash of old chemicals to the county hazardous waste site, several employees there gathered around, asking incredulously, "Where did you *get* this stuff?" Over the next few years many of their Oriental art objects, prints and even Mother's jewelry were sent off to auction houses. She recognized that being alone now, the acquisitions they had made over many years were not so important.

Some things that stayed were her fur coats and many of her more outrageous articles of clothing. And there were a few new items: one of the first things she did that summer was to install a mirrored disco ball in the middle of the cottage. It's hard to imagine a more incongruous item in that space, but I think her true self was coming out, unrestrained by D.

Even with a circle of friends, there was naturally some loneliness, and within two years she had succumbed to the advances of a man who was a friend of my father. It evolved into a live-together, travel together arrangement and they began to spend winters in Florida, and much of the summer in northern Wisconsin. She enjoyed the moving around and trips they would take, but the Woodpile Lake property began to suffer in her absence. Now almost 50 years old, the studio was showing its age, and regular maintenance like bleeding the old pressure tank for the well sometimes went undone. The cottage roof's cedar shingles were rotting in places where a huge oak shaded it. In 2004 the studio in-floor heating system failed when salt from the water softener got into the floor through cracks and corroded the pipes from the outside. David Uppgren oversaw a repair where the area near the furnace was dug up and piping replaced. But in a tribute to D's original work, the pipe that had not been affected was still black and shiny, you could read the painted words on the pipes. A new modern boiler and water heater were installed and the heating system filled with antifreeze.

Mother tried to replicate the arrangement she had had with Jim Seidl, but the studio renters she found, even the ones who were architecture students, were not very responsible or self-sufficient. Loaning the cottage for a weekend to a friend resulted in a water leak and a complaint that the toilet was backing up. Roto-rooter found a cracked sewer pipe, inconveniently located directly under one of the huge boulders near the front door. Someone had pushed the refrigerator back and broken the icemaker water line. The well needed a new submersible pump. It was just one thing after another.

What to do? Clearly, managing the property was getting out of hand. She and D had considered putting the houses on the National Register of Historic Places, and now that he was gone she discussed an arrangement where the Washington County Historical Society would use the property as their headquarters. It was deemed unsuitable for parking and location, however. The Minnesota Historical Society and the University of Minnesota were unwilling to take on the upkeep expenses, and the logistics of conducting tours was a problem.

In 2007 she signed a real estate sales agreement to market the property. The lovely brochures and inclusion in high-end real estate ads were impressive but brought few interested parties. As happens with many properties, the company and agent changed after a year on the market. Kimberly Falker was a Stillwater agent for Sotheby's who took on the listing in 2008 and put a lot of work into the sales effort. While Mother was away in Florida that winter there were two break-ins at the studio, and poor Kimberly was the one the police called. Mother's companion had put up "no trespassing" signs and a fake camera on a tree, thinking it would be a deterrent. His judgement in this area was on par with his driving skill, as he wrecked her motorhome on the way back from Florida that year. His ability to maintain anything at the houses was also next to useless but Mother depended on him. Ty and I were alarmed.

Max

Things looked up when Max Weinberg, a Wright enthusiast, got in touch and was shown the property while Mother was away. Max was a musician, the drummer in Bruce Springsteen's E Street Band, and the bandleader on a late-night talk show. In March of 2008 he wrote to Mother, complimenting her on building "a home - and a work of art for the ages." He explained that he had, as a child, built with Froebel blocks, and with an older cousin had explored the Guggenheim (then under construction) when he was seven years old. "My mother," he wrote, "still remembers my coming home and telling her it was like walking inside a seashell!" At 15 he excitedly explored a John Rattenbury home being built near his home in Maplewood, New Jersey. Ten years later, as a member of the E Street Band, he played at the Gammage Auditorium in Phoenix, writing, "Performing there was a double thrill for me!"

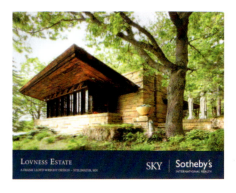

LOVNESS ESTATE
A FRANK LLOYD WRIGHT DESIGN · STILLWATER, MN
SKY | Sotheby's
INTERNATIONAL REALTY

It looked great on paper, but the "Lovness Estate" turned out to be a tough sell at 3.75 million.

Mother and D had spent some time looking toward the future, thinking about the houses as a museum, as an architectural appendage to some institution, as an interpretive center, an office for a historical society and other uses. Their ideas never got any traction, however. The property was too small, too isolated, too restricted by codes, required too much upkeep or a hundred other reasons that prevented any organization from seriously considering taking over.

Private buyers, it became clear after a few years of marketing, were not stepping up to the plate either. Other Wright homes, and in particular, Usonians, came and went on the market with widely varying results. There really were no comps or precedent for the "Lovness Estate".

Max went on, with more compliments for Mother: "All of the homes Mr. Wright designed have a backstory, but to me, yours is the most personal and moving." He continued, "I was astonished as I sat in the main room of the studio." In describing his ideas for purchasing the Lovness houses, he emphasized that he and his wife desired to live in an *original* Wright house. The problem was, Mothers' original houses were in the wrong place. His plan involved dismantling and moving each of the houses from Woodpile Lake; the cottage to his property in New Jersey as a "repose" for him and his wife, now empty nesters, and the studio to Los Angeles, where he would be working on the Tonight Show. Max assured her that both buildings would be rebuilt without any changes, including furniture.

It was as much a love letter as a real estate proposal, and Mother was smitten. Max visited several times—once bringing his mover to inspect— and over a period of a year, proposals were presented and contracts drawn, involving the structures, the property and associated furniture, art and original documents. In November, Max began production of a documentary film featuring Mother and by January, a near-final agreement for the sale was in place, stipulating that Mother could live out her remaining years in the cottage after the studio was moved. Now at age 84, it was likely she wouldn't have many more years of independent living there. Jim Seidl was in her corner helping with appraisals, contracts and long-distance negotiations while she was in Florida.

Pushback to the plan came from other Wright enthusiasts and organizations like the Frank Lloyd Wright Building Conservancy, who felt moving the houses would be a sacrilege. Mother's response to one letter was succinct: "Life creates situations in which we must all compromise to some extent," she wrote, and added, "I am open to ideas and encourage you or any other interested party to contact my real estate agent Kimberly Falker with a plan to purchase and conserve the site." Touché!

In the spring of 2009 Bruce Springsteen was in St. Paul and Mother went to the concert, with a limo ride to the event, a back-stage pass, and a meeting with the band. I remember thinking, here I am in bed at 10:00 and my 85-year-old mother is out rockin' the town! Max was always very kind to Mother, treating her with respect, always aware of her devotion to what she and D had created. He was fascinated with her story and loved the houses but in the end, in spite of the enthusiasm shown, and after many drafts, a final agreement was never reached. Max's relationship with the Conan O'Brien Tonight Show in L.A. was changing, and Mother had serious second thoughts about the houses being moved. It was back to square one.

For a few years there were no more serious offers and Mother resigned herself to living out her years in the cottage.

Mother got to be a rock groupie, at least for one night in 2009 courtesy of Max Weinberg.

Ted and Debi

Dubuque, Iowa has a beautiful public space on a high bluff overlooking the Mississippi, appropriately named Eagle Point Park, established in 1909. During the depression the park was given a federal WPA grant for construction of new buildings. The City's new park superintendant was Alfred Caldwell, a landscape architect who admired Wright's work. He designed and had built several structures and gardens emulating Wright's style in the 1930s, and in the 1950s and '60s these made a deep impression on a young man named Ted Muntz who lived nearby.

In 1994, Ted and his wife Debi had just built a new home for their family in the northwest suburbs of Minneapolis. To mark the occasion, and knowing her husband's interest in Wright, Debi gave him a copy of Carla Lind's new book *The Wright Style*. In it, four pages of Norman McGrath photos accompanied text in which Lind described the Lovness studio: "Together, architect and clients created a home with the richness and serenity of a temple." Like Eagle Point Park, it made an impression on Ted. For her part, Debi was also a Wright fan, having lived in Pennsylvania and toured Fallingwater there.

"We had a few Wright touches in our house," Ted recalled, "but I didn't know about the Lovness houses. Paging through the book I thought it just looked like a beautiful place, peaceful and wild." That sentiment remained dormant but strong for 13 years until Ted and Debi heard that the Lovness estate was on the market in 2007. They contacted the agent and viewed the property that spring, as they recall:

Alfred Caldwell was enamored of Wright's Prairie School homes and built several buildings in that style at Eagle Point Park with funds from Roosevelt's Works Progress Adminstration.

Mother loved to show off her wild furs and hats. On one visit, Max got to try on her star-spangled mink and Kimberly wore a dyed patchwork fur in the cottage basement. Max was sincere and patient in explaining his plan to Mother, but in the end, she couldn't accept that the buildings would not be on Woodpile Lake, the site Mr. Wright had approved in 1955.

Debi: I didn't see the vision he saw, I just thought, oh, he's losing his mind. We can't do this. I couldn't fathom living here. We didn't even talk about restoring anything.

Ted: It was just a curiosity thing. I really wanted to see it. We didn't pursue anything with the realtor, but I kept thinking about it. And then the great recession hit and I had to spend time with my businesses. We didn't get that back on track until about three years later.

Ted owned Fab Pipe, Inc., a company that fabricated and distributed large iron pipes for water systems, and he was a partner in Metalfit, a Mexican firm that produced industrial iron fittings. By 2011, with the businesses stable, he was considering retirement, encouraged by Debi - who knew he was a workaholic. After setting up the company so that a new owner could easily step in, it was sold within a year. No longer needing to live near the business, they began to look for a new home in the St. Coix Valley, a place they had visited for years on weekends.

In January of 2012 Ted wrote Mother a letter, which was forwarded to Florida, asking if the houses had been sold. A few weeks later, she called and explained that she was pretty much resigned to staying in the cottage, but invited them to come visit in May, on her return to Minnesota. Of that meeting and subsequent discussions, the Muntzes have vivid recollections:

Ted: The first time we met her we had champagne, of course, and we got along really well. She wanted to know what our intentions were; she had not liked the previous idea of moving the houses. Talking to her as much as we did, it became clear she had her whole life invested in this, and she was not really ready to go. I knew I had to explain our vision in detail, and furthermore, she had to like whoever would buy the property. We had more meetings, went out to dinner, even visited her the following winter in Florida.

When I first saw it in 2007 I was not thinking of a purchase, I just wanted to see it. But the place started working on me, and we took a couple of years to think about it.

Debi: And she took a couple of years to decide if we were the right people! The first time I met her I thought, wow! And you could tell, this was all her; Don just went along for the ride. Every time she came into the studio she ran her hand along the seam of a stone on the fireplace; one of the joints she had laid and tuckpointed so many years before.

Ted: She was particularly proud of the big stone on the bottom of the mantel. (The one she replaced against Don's objection and while he was at work in 1956.) When we began to talk about a purchase, we told her that we didn't have a real timeline and we could make whatever accommodations were needed so she could stay on for a while.

After many months, with details about price worked out, the inclusion of pieces of art, original plans and most importantly, an arrangement for Mother to remain in the cottage for a year, the sale went through in September, 2013. Ted and Debi began to make weekly 50 mile runs to the studio, bringing a few belongings each trip.

Overcoming deferred maintenance problems like a non-functioning cooktop, they got acquainted with their new home over long weekends and started making plans for the next steps.

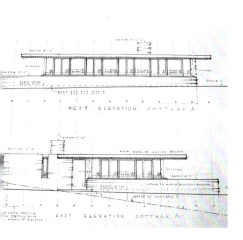

Cottage A was a simple, flat-roofed cabin. It seemed a perfect starting point for Ted's needs.

That winter they got to know Mother better, celebrating Christmas and her birthday in January together. By May, however, the back-and-forth was becoming burdensome. While Ted and Debi originally planned to remain in St. Michael and have the restoration work finished before they moved to Woodpile Lake, they instead moved in that spring and devised a schedule for renovating both houses - and building a third structure. That additional building would be an adaptation of the 1958 Wright plan for "Cottage A" that had laid dormant for so many years.

The enormity of rebuilding both the studio and the cottage was daunting, but adding a new building to the mix would seem over the top. Ted explained the decision and the schedule they devised:

We went into this with our eyes wide open. I knew it would be a total renovation. We were fortunate to find Kelly Davis for the job. When we first saw the property in 2007, we had told the agent, "Well, we don't know if we want to buy something or build, but this was something we had to see." She said if you do decide to build, and you like this kind of architecture, you should get in touch with a local architect named Kelly Davis.

In February, 2014, Ted did just that. He had already determined that more space than the two small houses would be needed, for family, guest visits and storage. And like Virginia 60 years before, he wanted a separate work area. He had a consulting LLC, served on industry boards and technical committees, and needed an office. And there was one other consideration: "I just wanted to realize a Wright design," he says.

Ted contacted Kelly to confer:

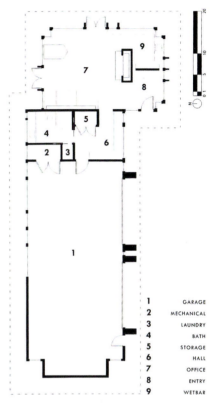

1	GARAGE
2	MECHANICAL
3	LAUNDRY
4	BATH
5	STORAGE
6	HALL
7	OFFICE
8	ENTRY
9	WETBAR

The tiny Cottage A (7,8,9 above) was just a starting point for the "office".

Left, in 2014 the studio was showing signs of age on the outside, but many of the real issues were hidden inside.

I already had the plans for Cottage A, so when Kelly and I got together I showed him the drawings and said, "Why don't we see if we can incorporate elements of this basic design into something that's functional for me as an office. I still have my fingers in a few things, with a lot of paperwork, and I need a place that's not there (the studio)." And we needed a garage, because we live in Minnesota. In the design we came up with, the east end is cottage A, then we added a storage area and a bathroom behind, then a garage area to that. In the fall of 2014 work began.

The office has a bathroom (above) but no kitchen or bedroom, owing to zoning restrictions. A "wet bar" with a small refrigerator and sink behind the fireplace fills the need for refreshments and snacks while working.

Kelly was joined in the project by another architect at SALA. Tim Old and I went to high school together and he had been a friend of our family ever since. Like Kelly, Tim knew well and appreciated the homes and had worked in the Wright style. They had collaborated on projects for years and made a good team. The new "office" was the first project underway, preceeded by removal of D's old corrugated metal shed and a cleanup of the "Love Canal' area behind it. Perfectly nestled into the hill, the new structure is unobtrusive and looks out on to the peaceful pond and rolling hills beyond. This long-ignored part of the property had been home to my father's beehives and hence, we were used to staying away from it. The wonderful site plan for the new garage structure allowed the beauty of this section of land to come alive! It was the first step in a two-year-plus process that next saw the cottage updated, then a full restoration of the studio.

Stonework on the "office" resembles the cottage, using cut Kasota limestone from Mankato, Minnesota, with strong horizontal elements and protruding pieces. Although the garage doors are front and center by necessity, the piers of stone extending on either side prevent them from being obtrusive, and their design, with a strong vertical rib and tiny windows, doesn't shout "garage door".

A low wall as you approach the building, and another at the entrance are welcoming elements and help the structure blend into the slight changes in grade. More low walls on the "backside" help delineate a concrete patio that extends in a sawtooth pattern to the north and east. Inside and outside, the floors are exposed aggregate concrete.

While the original Cottage A design called for seven-foot ceilings throughout, "That might have been deadly," Kelly notes. Ceiling heights vary from 7' 2" to 8'. It's a lovely small house and although city zoning does not allow a third residence on the property (it does not have a kitchen or bedroom), each time I visit I tell Ted with a smile, "I can move in any time."

Kelly Davis and Tim Old were on-site regularly, but building from scratch is easier than re-building existing structures, and the next phase—updating the cottage—was just a warmup for the main event, the challenging task of bringing the studio into the 21st century. All of this was complicated further by people living on the property during construction. Kelly recalls the situation:

While the office was under design, Ted and Debi sold their suburban house and made the full-time move to Woodpile Lake during the summer of 2014. Virginia was still living in the cottage at the time,

With a gestation period of almost sixty years, cottage A came to life as "the office" in 2015. It blends nicely with the studio, a few hundred feet away. Furniture inside reflects what is used in both other buildings.

The cottage bathroom was tastefully modernized with a new smaller toilet and a new vanity (note the square hole "pulls" that mirror the Little house cabinet doors in the adjoining bedroom. The old tub was replaced (not seen behind the door at right). The door at left is access to the stairway leading to the loft.

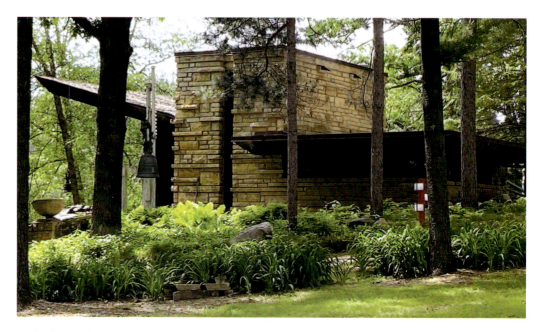

and what I believe to be a serendipitous result of this arrangement began to evolve. There were frequent get-togethers, often over late-afternoon glasses of champagne, and Virginia would share the history of building the two houses and the wealth of stories about Mr. and Mrs. Wright and the lore of the Taliesin Fellowship with Ted and Debi. A lasting bond of friendship was formed; one that would continue until Virginia's death in early 2018.

By late summer, 2015, the office was nearing completion and Virginia had moved to nearby Mahtomedi (ironically, just a mile from the home on White Bear Lake she and Don had planned to remodel in 1955). In 2016 cosmetic improvements to the kitchen and bath of the cottage were made, as it would serve as home to Ted and Debi while the studio was under construction.

The cottage was the easier by far of the two existing buildings to renovate. It was almost twenty years newer than the studio, and Mother and D had much more experience and knowledge about construction when they built it. There were just two serious issues: the roof and some chimney rock work. New cedar shingles were a pretty straightforward solution, but parts of the chimney had suffered water damage and the cap was leaking. Advanced Masonry Restoration replaced about 30 stones and tuckpointed the entire chimney. In addition to "weathered' tuckpointing, the large protruding stones' edges were shaved by 1/16 inch around the outside to allow water to flow more freely. A new copper cap and bottom skirt were installed.

Inside, like many home buyers, the Muntzes wanted a new kitchen and bath. Both were small spaces so care had to be taken to maximize efficiency. Since this was more of an update than a full-blown restoration, they worked with a designer to renew the two spaces, using the same basic cabinet heights and dimensions. In the kitchen, a new built-in refrigerator with

The cottage loft is accessed via a stairway from the bathroom door (opposite). It got new upholstery and a new, custom-made skylight panel by Josie Geiger. Before this 2020 photo I had not been up there in years. It needed a new roof, both cedar shingles and flat membrane with gravel. The chimney got tuckpointed with a new copper cap and skirt. The kitchen was remodeled with new countertops and built-ins.

The low wall of the carport and loggia was rebuilt with new capstones but the lanterns D built were retained. These were replicas of the pieces outside the Little house. D had made replacements for the Stevensons in the 1960s, and also made a few for the studio.

He also replicated the living room sconces from the Little house. These are currently awaiting a new use.

cabinet-front doors is very attractive, and new cabinets, stove, countertops, backsplash and lighting all work together nicely.

Ted and his son sledgehammered the old tub and installed a new one with a modern surround, and put in a new vanity and toilet. The main room of the house was not changed, but in thoroughly scrubbing the limestone floors, he noticed water pooling in one area. Some jacking and bracing in the basement was needed.

The studio gets some attention

Kelly Davis and Tim Old had been working on all the details for renovating the studio. The cottage was nearing completion, and since the masons were already on site, they were tasked with rebuilding the studio chimney as well. In this effort it became clear that Mother and D had made some key mistakes in that first year of building, 1956. Even though water leaks over the years had been minor and confined to the south end of the fireplace, workers found some serious deterioration of the stone work, mostly because the original masons (my parents) had laid some stones with their bedding planes (the natural sedimentary layers) vertical. Those rock shapes were interesting but they would absorb water over time and spall. Mother's tuckpointing with a brake adjustment tool had resulted in flat seams that did not shed water easily. Worst of all was that the center of the chimney was filled with rubble. It's sad to think that Ty and I spent all that time with our little buckets collecting rocks for "backfill" when it should have been concrete blocks behind the stones instead.

After photographing the stone sizes and patterns, the masons rebuilt the core with block backing, insulation, then laid new stones with a Grace flexible membrane for flashing at the base with a weep system to drain water. Weathered joints were used (as on the cottage as well), where the bottom of the mortar seam angles out to the edge of the lower stone, helping shed water. Later, a copper cap and skirt was installed by the roofers, completing the job. The chimney was ready for another half century, or more. But then there was the rest of the house. Kelly gave an overview:

As the Muntzes prepared for their move to the cottage in spring, 2016, drawings for the studio had been completed and work commenced in early June. More appropriately deemed reconstruction as opposed to remodeling, the scope of the work was significant. Windows, doors, cabinetry, millwork and interior partitions were removed and scheduled for replacement. Concrete floors were taken out in order to facilitate the addition of air-conditioning and update heating and plumbing systems. For a time, stripped to its essence, the building once again took on the appearance of a fantastic stone ruin.

To allow construction to continue through the winter of 2016, the entire structure was tented and, during those frigid months, I often wondered if Ted and Debi had any inkling of what they had gotten themselves into when they purchased the property two years earlier. But by mid-April, 2017, construction was substantially complete and by July the studio was ready once again for its new occupants. A Herculean effort had been accomplished.

The studio chimney was repaired first, taking advantage of the masons who were already on site for the cottage repairs.

Below, in the summer of 2016 the studio interior was gutted to the walls, then the floor came out in pieces.

The floor and old heating pipe came out in cut sections, then trenches were dug for the AC and forced air heating PVC pipes.

Below, the color layer of the original floor concrete can be seen.

Ted and Debi had spent over a year in the studio, and although that wasn't their original plan, it turned out to be extremely beneficial. "The advantage of living here for a year helped us figure out how we wanted it to flow when we were done," Debi said. Over that time they had adjusted their lifestyle to the house with two small bedrooms. Now it was time to adjust the house somewhat to their lifestyle. They moved to the freshly-updated cottage and the studio project began, with Braden Construction's men moving equipment onto the site.

The furniture came out first, then the built-ins in every room. When everything from wall to wall was gone, the floor was cut in sections and hauled outside onto a pile. What was left of the original heating pipe was removed and trenches dug for 10 inch PVC pipe to carry the air conditioning flow. It would double as an auxiliary forced air heating system, for times when the house needed to be warmed quickly. Insulated water and drain pipes, and electrical and communication wiring were laid on the graded surface. A layer of rigid foam insulation was covered with flexible pex tubing for in-floor heat. It was a far cry from the bending, cutting and welding that was necessary to make the wrought iron pipe work that hot summer of 1957.

Adding lights and upgrading to modern electrical standards meant taking apart some walls for new conduit and switches. Notes and photos were made in each case to replicate the stone work as closely to original as possible.

After the framing went up in August, poly film covered the structure and work began on the roof by removing the diagonal decking. At left, roof framing was exposed and in several places additional supports were added to aging, and in some cases, sagging structural members. Foam insulation was blown into the cavities. Copper cap and flashing was added to the chimney after the gravel roof was applied.

Copper trim includes roof drains. Below, PEX tubing provides underfloor heat in zones, and all new water and waste lines were installed to serve the kitchen and master bathroom. New electrical switches near the front door required some masonry R & R.

Under the big top

In August it was warm, but looking ahead to winter, late that month a huge enclosure was built of 2x4s and 2x6s, covered with polyethylene. It would be weather protection from rain while the roof was rebuilt, and also allow construction to proceed during cold weather. It was one of those decisions that seems reasonable, and there probably was no other way to do it, but about that winter, Ted just shakes his head when remembering a $3600 heating bill for a single month. The show must go on!

Work on the roof that fall involved removing the gravel and membrane, then all the diagonal roof boards (standard construction method in the days before plywood was readily available). The fascia was removed and LVL lumber used to brace some areas.. The steel "flitch plates" were removed and modern bracing installed, especially over my old bedroom, where some sag had taken place. There, the vertical window framing had the job of holding up the roof, and it was only just up to the task. Unobtrusive steel reinforcements were added. Diagonal 18-foot long steel beams replaced shorter originals. As Ted describes it, "More lumber, more steel." Plywood decking supports the new membrane and gravel roof, with copper edge trim. The flat roof had been essentially that—flat—for all these years, so slightly beveled rigid foam was placed between the plywood and membrane to ease water runoff.

New cedar fascia was installed, with less grain showing than the original pine, and finished with a paint/stain that approximated the color of creosote. This would solve the long-standing problem of the water-soluble creosote leaving a brown sheen on the glass when it rained or during window washing.

New LED ceiling fixtures in the kitchen and bedrooms complemented the original square lights, and small recessed LED lighting elements were installed in the living room ceiling,

All new electrical wiring was installed, plus new plumbing and HVAC systems. The "tent" allowed concrete and masonry work to progress into winter, including an extension of the patio. By the time the poly frame was removed in the spring, the house was ready for final interior work.

then foam insulation followed. Most windows were replaced with Argon-filled, inch-thick insulated glass. The casements in the bedrooms are from Marvin. The large doors and fixed windows on the west side facing the lake were refinished and received the same kind of energy-efficient glass. The mitered corner windows were also replaced but remained single pane as the experimental pieces from Cardinal Glass, made specifically for the studio in the 1990s were failing. No mitered glass product currently on the market would preserve the aesthetic, so Ted used 1/2" thick glass in the corners. Regular condensation clean-up is the price, but he continues to look for an insulated glass source. The front door was replaced with a single-light unit - a breath of fresh air to me, after living with a solid panel door when growing up.

Opposite, the patio has been extended in front, and in the entrance driveway area as well. A walkway, steps and stylish railing now connect the studio and cottage. This page, our old bedroom is now a comfortable lounge and our bathroom is open and inviting. The distinctive Kohler "Neoangle" tub ($308 in 1957) was refinished and retained. Below, Mr. Wright had told my parents to buy comfortable Danish furniture in 1957; maybe he was right after all.

The kitchen, or "workspace' as Wright called it, got a significant makeover. The aisle was widened and a curved cut-out on the east counter makes movement through the space so much easier. All new cabinetry is topped by light stone counters and backsplash, with two sinks. Refrigerator and freezer are built-in with cabinet doors, with the refrigerator door sections in the old spot, but below counter level. A happy result is that the divider facing the dining area no longer needs to be tall enough to hide a standard refrigerator, and is lower by a foot, opening up the space considerably. "I wrestled with that," Kelly says, but it makes the space much more user-friendly, he also points out. A new double oven is in the same spot as the old one in the side of the fireplace, but with an extended lower opening.

The kitchen divider is lower than the original and is open on the left side, allowing a glimpse of the lake from the area by the sink. The refrigerator and freezer are now part of the lower cabinet, adding counter space to the small work area. Built-ins and replicas of the original furniture in the house were made with rift-sawn oak.

My parents' bathroom, adjacent to the kitchen, was expanded slightly, stealing a foot of space at the entrance to their bedroom. An inspired idea was to open a spot between upper kitchen cabinets nearby. Kelly Davis notes that a significant change was made in that small master bath, where the toilet was re-aligned to make the space more efficient. In Ty's and my old bathroom the diagonal tub was refinished and the rest of the space updated for a much airier and attractive space.

The floor is color-impregnated concrete, as the original, with a coating of Silane-Siloxane sealer to increase its water resistance. The four-foot grid seams are, as Kelly puts it, "more strongly articulated" than the originals, but it is attractive overall.

All of the original built-in furniture was removed and replaced with new, sometimes modified pieces, like the couches and desk in what had been our girls' bedroom. Ted had a good working relationship with Braden Construction and notes:

We were so blessed to have contractors and workers who were really into it. Many of them had never seen this kind of architecture before and they gave it their all. Very little of the cabinetry that was "built-in" originally had been fitted to the rock, and the carpenter who was recreating it gave up his vacation to

Above, the passage through the kitchen is now much easier to navigate, with the curved counter. A Japanese screen covers the electrical service breaker panel. Part of the all-new built-ins is a headboard for the master bedroom, which my parents never had.

Left, landscape architect Jason Aune brought connection and continuity among the three structures. This wall includes concrete panels made by my father, based on Midway Garden designs. Behind the wall is a fenced vegetable garden. The low wall behind the studio hides vents, hoses and A/C components.

finish the job. He was using multiple laser levels to get everything square; he must have had 20 of them going with their red beams. It looked like one of those bank heist movies.

The built-ins weren't the only originals replaced. Looking for comfort, the Muntzes chose to retire the "regal" dining chairs Wright had designed, and the well-worn original tables and other chairs as well. Interior designer Talla Skogmo found comfortable lounge chairs and a sofa in a light color that wasn't at odds with the wood and stone, additions that will make the space more livable for the family, who plan to be here for a long time.

The house in its new form is different, but at its core, it's the same design with thoughtful

and sensitive updates. If anything, the "new" studio is even more breathtaking than the one that has awed visitors for 60 years, and will certainly do so for 60 more. I am so pleased that my mother got to see the studio and the cottage—the homes that she and my father had devoted most of their lives to—brought back to life, in a literal sense. It was a perfect ending and a new beginning. Kelly Davis recalled the day Mother saw the finished result:

Completing the circle that had begun more than fifty years earlier, the last time I saw Virginia was the day the studio was professionally photographed in November of 2017. As she now approached her ninety-third birthday, Ted and Debi were thoughtful to invite her to make a visit during the photo shoot, and then the three of them would go off to dinner. When Lonnie and Gordon dropped her off late in the afternoon, the house was alive and humming with activity; equipment and lights and baffles and people were everywhere. The moment Virginia walked in the door however, it all stopped; immediately, and as it should. Although there were hints of frailty and she now walked carefully, she looked incredibly beautiful in her white coat with a fur collar and all the requisite jewelry. Her presence and irrepressible spirit remained undiminished. Then, seated with a glass of champagne in hand and, as she had countless times before, Virginia once again began to charm her audience as she held court in the magnificent stone home she and Don had built.

Standing behind Mother during her last visit in November 2017, from left: architect Kelly Davis, Debi Muntz, Ted Muntz, architect Tim Old, interior designers Jennifer Zirkelbach and Talla Skogmo.

All images in this book are from the Lovness archives with the exception of those noted here:

Image credits

We gratefully acknowledge assistance from Ted and Debi Muntz, who provided access to original plans, and photos of the restoration.